INTERNATIONAL FINANCIAL STATEMENT ANALYSIS WORKBOOK

T0305519

CFA Institute is the premier association for investment professionals around the world, with more than 150,000 CFA charterholders worldwide in 165+ countries and regions. Since 1963 the organization has developed and administered the renowned Chartered Financial Analyst® Program. With a rich history of leading the investment profession, CFA Institute has set the highest standards in ethics, education, and professional excellence within the global investmentcommunity and is the foremost authority on investment profession conduct and practice. Each book in the CFA Institute Investment Series is geared toward industry practitioners along with graduate-level finance students and covers the most important topics in the industry. The authors of these cutting-edge books are themselves industry professionals and academics and bring their wealth of knowledge and expertise to this series.

INTERNATIONAL FINANCIAL STATEMENT ANALYSIS WORKBOOK

Fourth Edition

Thomas R. Robinson, CFA

Elaine Henry, CFA

Michael A. Broihahn, CFA

WILEY

CONTENTS

PART I

LEARNING OBJECTIVES, SUMMARY OVERVIEW, AND PROBLEMS

CHAPTER 1

INTRODUCTION TO FINANCIAL STATEMENT ANALYSIS

LEARNING OUTCOMES

After completing this chapter, you will be able to do the following:

- describe the roles of financial reporting and financial statement analysis;
- describe the roles of the statement of financial position, statement of comprehensive income, statement of changes in equity, and statement of cash flows in evaluating a company's performance and financial position;
- describe the importance of financial statement notes and supplementary information—including disclosures of accounting policies, methods, and estimates—and management's commentary;
- describe the objective of audits of financial statements, the types of audit reports, and the importance of effective internal controls;
- identify and describe information sources that analysts use in financial statement analysis besides annual financial statements and supplementary information;
- describe the steps in the financial statement analysis framework.

SUMMARY OVERVIEW

The information presented in financial and other reports, including the financial statements, notes, and management's commentary, helps the financial analyst to assess a company's performance and financial position. An analyst may be called on to perform a financial analysis for a variety of reasons, including the valuation of equity securities, the assessment of credit risk, the performance of due diligence on an acquisition, and the evaluation of a subsidiary's performance relative to other business units. Major considerations in both equity analysis and credit analysis are evaluating a company's financial position, its ability to generate profits and cash flow, and its potential to generate future growth in profits and cash flow.

This chapter has presented an overview of financial statement analysis. Among the major points covered are the following:

- The primary purpose of financial reports is to provide information and data about a company's financial position and performance, including profitability and cash flows. The information presented in the reports —including the financial statements and notes and management's commentary or management's discussion and analysis—allows the financial analyst to assess a company's financial position and performance and trends in that performance.
- The primary financial statements are the statement of financial position (i.e., the balance sheet), the statement of comprehensive income (or two statements consisting of an income statement and a statement of comprehensive income), the statement of changes in equity, and the statement of cash flows.
- The balance sheet discloses what resources a company controls (assets) and what it owes (liabilities) at a specific point in time. Owners' equity represents the net assets of the company; it is the owners' residual interest in, or residual claim on, the company's assets after deducting its liabilities. The relationship among the three parts of the balance sheet (assets, liabilities, and owners' equity) may be shown in equation form as follows: Assets = Liabilities + Owners' equity.
- The income statement presents information on the financial results of a company's business activities over a period of time. The income statement communicates how much revenue and other income the company generated during a period and what expenses, including losses, it incurred in connection with generating that revenue and other income. The basic equation underlying the income statement is Revenue + Other income – Expenses = Net income.
- The statement of comprehensive income includes all items that change owners' equity except transactions with owners. Some of these items are included as part of net income, and some are reported as other comprehensive income (OCI).
- The statement of changes in equity provides information about increases or decreases in the various components of owners' equity.
- Although the income statement and balance sheet provide measures of a company's success, cash and cash flow are also vital to a company's long-term success. Disclosing the sources and uses of cash helps creditors, investors, and other statement users evaluate the company's liquidity, solvency, and financial flexibility.
- The notes (also referred to as footnotes) that accompany the financial statements are an integral part of those statements and provide information that is essential to understanding the statements. Analysts should evaluate note disclosures regarding the use of alternative accounting methods, estimates, and assumptions.
- In addition to the financial statements, a company provides other sources of information that are useful to the financial analyst. As part of his or her analysis, the financial analyst should read and assess this additional information, particularly that presented in the management commentary (also called management report[ing], operating and financial review, and management's discussion and analysis [MD&A]).
- A publicly traded company must have an independent audit performed on its annual financial statements. The auditor's report expresses an opinion on the financial statements and

provides some assurance about whether the financial statements fairly present a company's financial position, performance, and cash flows. In addition, for US publicly traded companies, auditors must also express an opinion on the company's internal control systems.

• Information on the economy, industry, and peer companies is useful in putting the company's financial performance and position in perspective and in assessing the company's future. In most cases, information from sources apart from the company are crucial to an analyst's effectiveness.

• The financial statement analysis framework provides steps that can be followed in any financial statement analysis project. These steps are:
  • articulate the purpose and context of the analysis;
  • collect input data;
  • process data;
  • analyze/interpret the processed data;
  • develop and communicate conclusions and recommendations; and
  • follow up.

PROBLEMS

1. Providing information about the performance and financial position of companies so that users can make economic decisions *best* describes the role of:
   A. auditing.
   B. financial reporting.
   C. financial statement analysis.

2. Which of the following *best* describes the role of financial statement analysis?
   A. To provide information about a company's performance.
   B. To provide information about a company's changes in financial position.
   C. To form expectations about a company's future performance and financial position.

3. The role of financial statement analysis is *best* described as:
   A. providing information useful for making investment decisions.
   B. evaluating a company for the purpose of making economic decisions.
   C. using financial reports prepared by analysts to make economic decisions.

4. A company's financial position would *best* be evaluated using the:
   A. balance sheet.
   B. income statement.
   C. statement of cash flows.

5. A company's profitability for a period would *best* be evaluated using the:
   A. balance sheet.
   B. income statement.
   C. statement of cash flows.

6. The financial statement that presents a shareholder's residual claim on assets is the:
   A. balance sheet.
   B. income statement.
   C. cash flow statement.

7. A company's profitability over a period of time is *best* evaluated using the:
   A. balance sheet.
   B. income statement.
   C. cash flow statement.

8. The income statement is *best* used to evaluate a company's:
   A. financial position.
   B. sources of cash flow.
   C. financial results from business activities.

9. Accounting policies, methods, and estimates used in preparing financial statements are *most likely* to be found in the:
   A. auditor's report.
   B. management commentary.
   C. notes to the financial statements.

10. Information about management and director compensation are *least likely* to be found in the:
    A. auditor's report.
    B. proxy statement.
    C. notes to the financial statements.

11. Information about a company's objectives, strategies, and significant risks are *most likely* to be found in the:
    A. auditor's report.
    B. management commentary.
    C. notes to the financial statements.

12. Which of the following *best* describes why the notes that accompany the financial statements are required? The notes:
    A. permit flexibility in statement preparation.
    B. standardize financial reporting across companies.
    C. provide information necessary to understand the financial statements.

13. What type of audit opinion is preferred when analyzing financial statements?
    A. Qualified.
    B. Adverse.
    C. Unqualified.

14. An auditor determines that a company's financial statements are prepared in accordance with applicable accounting standards except with respect to inventory reporting. This exception is *most likely* to result in an audit opinion that is:
    A. adverse.
    B. qualified.
    C. unqualified.

15. An independent audit report is *most likely* to provide:
    A. absolute assurance about the accuracy of the financial statements.
    B. reasonable assurance that the financial statements are fairly presented.
    C. a qualified opinion with respect to the transparency of the financial statements.

16. Interim financial reports released by a company are *most likely* to be:
    A. monthly.
    B. unaudited.
    C. unqualified.

17. Which of the following sources of information used by analysts is found outside a company's annual report?
    A. Auditor's report.
    B. Peer company analysis.
    C. Management's discussion and analysis.

18. Ratios are an input into which step in the financial statement analysis framework?
    A. Process data.
    B. Collect input data.
    C. Analyze/interpret the processed data.

19. Which phase in the financial statement analysis framework is *most likely* to involve producing updated reports and recommendations?
    A. Follow-up.
    B. Analyze/interpret the processed data.
    C. Develop and communicate conclusions and recommendations.

CHAPTER 2

FINANCIAL REPORTING
STANDARDS

LEARNING OUTCOMES

After completing this chapter, you will be able to do the following:

- describe the objective of financial reporting and the importance of financial reporting standards in security analysis and valuation;
- describe the roles of financial reporting standard-setting bodies and regulatory authorities in establishing and enforcing reporting standards;
- describe the International Accounting Standards Board's conceptual framework, including qualitative characteristics of financial reports, constraints on financial reports, and required reporting elements;
- describe general requirements for financial statements under International Financial Reporting Standards (IFRS);
- describe implications for financial analysis of alternative financial reporting systems and the importance of monitoring developments in financial reporting standards.

SUMMARY OVERVIEW

An awareness of financial reporting and underlying financial reporting standards can assist in security valuation and other financial analysis. This chapter describes the conceptual objectives of financial reporting standards, the parties involved in standard-setting processes, and the implication for analysts in monitoring developments in reporting standards.

Some key points of the chapter are summarized below:

- The objective of financial reporting is to provide financial information about the reporting entity that is useful to existing and potential investors, lenders, and other creditors in making decisions about providing resources to the entity.
- Financial reporting requires policy choices and estimates. These choices and estimates require judgment, which can vary from one preparer to the next. Accordingly, standards are needed to ensure increased consistency in these judgments.

- Private-sector standard-setting bodies and regulatory authorities play significant but different roles in the standard-setting process. In general, standard-setting bodies make the rules, and regulatory authorities enforce the rules. However, regulators typically retain legal authority to establish financial reporting standards in their jurisdiction.
- The IFRS framework sets forth the concepts that underlie the preparation and presentation of financial statements for external users.
- The objective of fair presentation of useful information is the center of the IASB's *Conceptual Framework*. The qualitative characteristics of useful information include fundamental and enhancing characteristics. Information must exhibit the fundamental characteristics of relevance and faithful representation to be useful. The enhancing characteristics identified are comparability, verifiability, timeliness, and understandability.
- *IFRS Financial Statements*: IAS No. 1 prescribes that a complete set of financial statements includes a statement of financial position (balance sheet), a statement of comprehensive income (either two statements—one for net income and one for comprehensive income—or a single statement combining both net income and comprehensive income), a statement of changes in equity, a cash flow statement, and notes. The notes include a summary of significant accounting policies and other explanatory information.
- Financial statements need to reflect certain basic features: fair presentation, going concern, accrual basis, materiality and aggregation, and no offsetting.
- Financial statements must be prepared at least annually, must include comparative information from the previous period, and must be consistent.
- Financial statements must follow certain presentation requirements including a classified statement of financial position (balance sheet) and minimum information on both the face of the financial statements and in the notes.
- A significant number of the world's listed companies report under either IFRS or US GAAP.
- In many cases, a user of financial statements will lack the information necessary to make specific adjustments required to achieve comparability between companies that use IFRS and companies that use US GAAP. Instead, an analyst must maintain general caution in interpreting comparative financial measures produced under different accounting standards and monitor significant developments in financial reporting standards.
- Analysts can remain aware of ongoing developments in financial reporting by monitoring new products or types of transactions; actions of standard setters, regulators, and other groups; and company disclosures regarding critical accounting policies and estimates.

PROBLEMS

1. Which of the following is *most likely* not an objective of financial statements?
   A. To provide information about the performance of an entity.
   B. To provide information about the financial position of an entity.
   C. To provide information about the users of an entity's financial statements.

2. International financial reporting standards are currently developed by which entity?
   A. The IFRS Foundation.
   B. The International Accounting Standards Board.
   C. The International Organization of Securities Commissions.

3. US generally accepted accounting principles are currently developed by which entity?
   A. The Securities and Exchange Commission.
   B. The Financial Accounting Standards Board.
   C. The Public Company Accounting Oversight Board.

4. A core objective of the International Organization of Securities Commissions is to:
   A. eliminate systemic risk.
   B. protect users of financial statements.
   C. ensure that markets are fair, efficient, and transparent.

5. According to the *Conceptual Framework for Financial Reporting*, which of the following is *not* an enhancing qualitative characteristic of information in financial statements?
   A. Accuracy.
   B. Timeliness.
   C. Comparability.

6. Which of the following is *not* a constraint on the financial statements according to the *Conceptual Framework*?
   A. Understandability.
   B. Benefit versus cost.
   C. Balancing of qualitative characteristics.

7. The assumption that an entity will continue to operate for the foreseeable future is called:
   A. accrual basis.
   B. comparability.
   C. going concern.

8. The assumption that the effects of transactions and other events are recognized when they occur, not when the cash flows occur, is called:
   A. relevance.
   B. accrual basis.
   C. going concern.

9. Neutrality of information in the financial statements most closely contributes to which qualitative characteristic?
   A. Relevance.
   B. Understandability.
   C. Faithful representation.

10. Valuing assets at the amount of cash or equivalents paid or the fair value of the consideration given to acquire them at the time of acquisition most closely describes which measurement of financial statement elements?
    A. Current cost.
    B. Historical cost.
    C. Realizable value.

11. The valuation technique under which assets are recorded at the amount that would be received in an orderly disposal is:
    A. current cost.
    B. present value.
    C. realizable value.

12. Which of the following is *not* a required financial statement according to IAS No. 1?
    A. Statement of financial position.
    B. Statement of changes in income.
    C. Statement of comprehensive income.

13. Which of the following elements of financial statements is *most* closely related to measurement of performance?
    A. Assets.
    B. Expenses.
    C. Liabilities.

14. Which of the following elements of financial statements is *most* closely related to measurement of financial position?
    A. Equity.
    B. Income.
    C. Expenses.

15. Which of the following disclosures regarding new accounting standards provides the *most* meaningful information to an analyst?
    A. The impact of adoption is discussed.
    B. The standard will have no material impact.
    C. Management is still evaluating the impact.

CHAPTER 3

UNDERSTANDING INCOME STATEMENTS

LEARNING OUTCOMES

After completing this chapter, you will be able to do the following:

- describe the components of the income statement and alternative presentation formats of that statement;
- Describe general principles of revenue recognition and accounting standards for revenue recognition;
- calculate revenue given information that might influence the choice of revenue recognition method;
- describe general principles of expense recognition, specific expense recognition applications, and implications of expense recognition choices for financial analysis;
- describe the financial reporting treatment and analysis of non-recurring items (including discontinued operations, unusual or infrequent items) and changes in accounting policies;
- distinguish between the operating and non-operating components of the income statement;
- describe how earnings per share is calculated and calculate and interpret a company's earnings per share (both basic and diluted earnings per share) for both simple and complex capital structures;
- distinguish between dilutive and antidilutive securities and describe the implications of each for the earnings per share calculation;
- convert income statements to common-size income statements;
- evaluate a company's financial performance using common-size income statements and financial ratios based on the income statement;
- describe, calculate, and interpret comprehensive income;
- describe other comprehensive income and identify major types of items included in it.

SUMMARY OVERVIEW

This chapter has presented the elements of income statement analysis. The income statement presents information on the financial results of a company's business activities over a period of time; it communicates how much revenue the company generated during a period and what costs it incurred in connection with generating that revenue. A company's net income and its components (e.g., gross margin, operating earnings, and pretax earnings) are critical inputs into both the equity and credit analysis processes. Equity analysts are interested in earnings because equity markets often reward relatively high- or low-earnings growth companies with above-average or below-average valuations, respectively. Fixed-income analysts examine the components of income statements, past and projected, for information on companies' abilities to make promised payments on their debt over the course of the business cycle. Corporate financial announcements frequently emphasize income statements more than the other financial statements.

Key points to this chapter include the following:

- The income statement presents revenue, expenses, and net income.
- The components of the income statement include: revenue; cost of sales; sales, general, and administrative expenses; other operating expenses; non-operating income and expenses; gains and losses; non-recurring items; net income; and EPS.
- An income statement that presents a subtotal for gross profit (revenue minus cost of goods sold) is said to be presented in a multi-step format. One that does not present this subtotal is said to be presented in a single-step format.
- Revenue is recognized in the period it is earned, which may or may not be in the same period as the related cash collection. Recognition of revenue when earned is a fundamental principal of accrual accounting.
- An analyst should identify differences in companies' revenue recognition methods and adjust reported revenue where possible to facilitate comparability. Where the available information does not permit adjustment, an analyst can characterize the revenue recognition as more or less conservative and thus qualitatively assess how differences in policies might affect financial ratios and judgments about profitability.
- As of the beginning of 2018, revenue recognition standards have converged. The core principle of the converged standards is that revenue should be recognized to "depict the transfer of promised goods or services to customers in an amount that reflects the consideration to which the entity expects to be entitled in an exchange for those goods or services."
- To achieve the core principle, the standard describes the application of five steps in recognizing revenue. The standard also specifies the treatment of some related contract costs and disclosure requirements.
- The general principles of expense recognition include a process to match expenses either to revenue (such as, cost of goods sold) or to the time period in which the expenditure occurs (period costs such as administrative salaries) or to the time period of expected benefits of the expenditures (such as depreciation).
- In expense recognition, choice of method (i.e., depreciation method and inventory cost method), as well as estimates (i.e., uncollectible accounts, warranty expenses, assets' useful life, and salvage value) affect a company's reported income. An analyst should identify

differences in companies' expense recognition methods and adjust reported financial statements where possible to facilitate comparability. Where the available information does not permit adjustment, an analyst can characterize the policies and estimates as more or less conservative and thus qualitatively assess how differences in policies might affect financial ratios and judgments about companies' performance.

- To assess a company's future earnings, it is helpful to separate those prior years' items of income and expense that are likely to continue in the future from those items that are less likely to continue.

- Under IFRS, a company should present additional line items, headings, and subtotals beyond those specified when such presentation is relevant to an understanding of the entity's financial performance. Some items from prior years clearly are not expected to continue in future periods and are separately disclosed on a company's income statement. Under US GAAP, unusual and/or infrequently occurring items, which are material, are presented separately within income from continuing operations.

- Non-operating items are reported separately from operating items on the income statement. Under both IFRS and US GAAP, the income statement reports separately the effect of the disposal of a component operation as a "discontinued" operation.

- Basic EPS is the amount of income available to common shareholders divided by the weighted average number of common shares outstanding over a period. The amount of income available to common shareholders is the amount of net income remaining after preferred dividends (if any) have been paid.

- If a company has a simple capital structure (i.e., one with no potentially dilutive securities), then its basic EPS is equal to its diluted EPS. If, however, a company has dilutive securities, its diluted EPS is lower than its basic EPS.

- Diluted EPS is calculated using the if-converted method for convertible securities and the treasury stock method for options.

- Common-size analysis of the income statement involves stating each line item on the income statement as a percentage of sales. Common-size statements facilitate comparison across time periods and across companies of different sizes.

- Two income-statement-based indicators of profitability are net profit margin and gross profit margin.

- Comprehensive income includes *both* net income and other revenue and expense items that are excluded from the net income calculation.

PROBLEMS

1. Expenses on the income statement may be grouped by:
   A. nature, but not by function.
   B. function, but not by nature.
   C. either function or nature.

2. An example of an expense classification by function is:
   A. tax expense.
   B. interest expense.
   C. cost of goods sold.

3. Denali Limited, a manufacturing company, had the following income statement information:

Revenue	$4,000,000
Cost of goods sold	$3,000,000
Other operating expenses	$500,000
Interest expense	$100,000
Tax expense	$120,000

Denali's gross profit is equal to:
A. $280,000.
B. $500,000.
C. $1,000,000.

4. Under IFRS, income includes increases in economic benefits from:
A. increases in liabilities not related to owners' contributions.
B. enhancements of assets not related to owners' contributions.
C. increases in owners' equity related to owners' contributions.

5. Fairplay had the following information related to the sale of its products during 2009, which was its first year of business:

Revenue	$1,000,000
Returns of goods sold	$100,000
Cash collected	$800,000
Cost of goods sold	$700,000

Under the accrual basis of accounting, how much net revenue would be reported on Fairplay's 2009 income statement?
A. $200,000.
B. $900,000.
C. $1,000,000.

6. Apex Consignment sells items over the internet for individuals on a consignment basis. Apex receives the items from the owner, lists them for sale on the internet, and receives a 25 percent commission for any items sold. Apex collects the full amount from the buyer and pays the net amount after commission to the owner. Unsold items are returned to the owner after 90 days. During 2009, Apex had the following information:
• Total sales price of items sold during 2009 on consignment was €2,000,000.
• Total commissions retained by Apex during 2009 for these items was €500,000.
How much revenue should Apex report on its 2009 income statement?
A. €500,000.
B. €2,000,000.
C. €1,500,000.

7. A company previously expensed the incremental costs of obtaining a contract. All else being equal, adopting the May 2014 IASB and FASB converged accounting standards on revenue recognition makes the company's profitability initially appear:
A. lower.
B. unchanged.
C. higher.

8. During 2009, Accent Toys Plc., which began business in October of that year, purchased 10,000 units of a toy at a cost of £10 per unit in October. The toy sold well in October. In anticipation of heavy December sales, Accent purchased 5,000 additional units in November at a cost of £11 per unit. During 2009, Accent sold 12,000 units at a price of £15 per unit. Under the first in, first out (FIFO) method, what is Accent's cost of goods sold for 2009?
   A. £120,000.
   B. £122,000.
   C. £124,000.

9. Using the same information as in Question 8, what would Accent's cost of goods sold be under the weighted average cost method?
   A. £120,000.
   B. £122,000.
   C. £124,000.

10. Which inventory method is least likely to be used under IFRS?
    A. First in, first out (FIFO).
    B. Last in, first out (LIFO).
    C. Weighted average.

11. At the beginning of 2009, Glass Manufacturing purchased a new machine for its assembly line at a cost of $600,000. The machine has an estimated useful life of 10 years and estimated residual value of $50,000. Under the straight-line method, how much depreciation would Glass take in 2010 for financial reporting purposes?
    A. $55,000.
    B. $60,000.
    C. $65,000.

12. Using the same information as in Question 16, how much depreciation would Glass take in 2009 for financial reporting purposes under the double-declining balance method?
    A. $60,000.
    B. $110,000.
    C. $120,000.

13. Which combination of depreciation methods and useful lives is most conservative in the year a depreciable asset is acquired?
    A. Straight-line depreciation with a short useful life.
    B. Declining balance depreciation with a long useful life.
    C. Declining balance depreciation with a short useful life.

14. Under IFRS, a loss from the destruction of property in a fire would most likely be classified as:
    A. continuing operations.
    B. discontinued operations.
    C. other comprehensive income.

15. A company chooses to change an accounting policy. This change requires that, if practical, the company restate its financial statements for:
    A. all prior periods.
    B. current and future periods.
    C. prior periods shown in a report.

16. For 2009, Flamingo Products had net income of $1,000,000. At 1 January 2009, there were 1,000,000 shares outstanding. On 1 July 2009, the company issued 100,000 new shares for $20 per share. The company paid $200,000 in dividends to common shareholders. What is Flamingo's basic earnings per share for 2009?
    A. $0.80.
    B. $0.91.
    C. $0.95.

17. For its fiscal year-end, Calvan Water Corporation (CWC) reported net income of $12 million and a weighted average of 2,000,000 common shares outstanding. The company paid $800,000 in preferred dividends and had 100,000 options outstanding with an average exercise price of $20. CWC's market price over the year averaged $25 per share. CWC's diluted EPS is *closest* to:
    A. $5.33.
    B. $5.54.
    C. $5.94.

18. A company with no debt or convertible securities issued publicly traded common stock three times during the current fiscal year. Under both IFRS and US GAAP, the company's:
    A. basic EPS equals its diluted EPS.
    B. capital structure is considered complex at year-end.
    C. basic EPS is calculated by using a simple average number of shares outstanding.

19. Laurelli Builders (LB) reported the following financial data for year-end December 31:

Common shares outstanding, January 1	2,020,000
Common shares issued as stock dividend, June 1	380,000
Warrants outstanding, January 1	500,000
Net income	$3,350,000
Preferred stock dividends paid	$430,000
Common stock dividends paid	$240,000

Which statement about the calculation of LB's EPS is *most* accurate?
    A. LB's basic EPS is $1.12.
    B. LB's diluted EPS is equal to or less than its basic EPS.
    C. The weighted average number of shares outstanding is 2,210,000.

20. Cell Services Inc. (CSI) had 1,000,000 average shares outstanding during all of 2009. During 2009, CSI also had 10,000 options outstanding with exercise prices of $10 each. The average stock price of CSI during 2009 was $15. For purposes of computing diluted earnings per share, how many shares would be used in the denominator?
    A. 1,003,333.
    B. 1,006,667.
    C. 1,010,000.

21. For its fiscal year-end, Sublyme Corporation reported net income of $200 million and a weighted average of 50,000,000 common shares outstanding. There are 2,000,000 convertible preferred shares outstanding that paid an annual dividend of $5. Each

preferred share is convertible into two shares of the common stock. The diluted EPS is *closest to*:
  A. $3.52.
  B. $3.65.
  C. $3.70.

22. When calculating diluted EPS, which of the following securities in the capital structure increases the weighted average number of common shares outstanding without affecting net income available to common shareholders?
  A. Stock options.
  B. Convertible debt that is dilutive.
  C. Convertible preferred stock that is dilutive.

23. Which statement is *most* accurate? A common-size income statement:
  A. restates each line item of the income statement as a percentage of net income.
  B. allows an analyst to conduct cross-sectional analysis by removing the effect of company size.
  C. standardizes each line item of the income statement but fails to help an analyst identify differences in companies' strategies.

24. Selected year-end financial statement data for Workhard are shown below.

	$ millions
Beginning shareholders' equity	475
Ending shareholders' equity	493
Unrealized gain on available-for-sale securities	5
Unrealized loss on derivatives accounted for as hedges	–3
Foreign currency translation gain on consolidation	2
Dividends paid	1
Net income	15

Workhard's comprehensive income for the year:
  A. is $18 million.
  B. is increased by the derivatives accounted for as hedges.
  C. includes $4 million in other comprehensive income.

25. When preparing an income statement, which of the following items would *most likely* be classified as other comprehensive income?
  A. A foreign currency translation adjustment.
  B. An unrealized gain on a security held for trading purposes.
  C. A realized gain on a derivative contract not accounted for as a hedge.

CHAPTER 4

UNDERSTANDING BALANCE SHEETS

LEARNING OUTCOMES

After completing this chapter, you will be able to do the following:

- describe the elements of the balance sheet: assets, liabilities, and equity;
- describe uses and limitations of the balance sheet in financial analysis;
- describe alternative formats of balance sheet presentation;
- distinguish between current and non-current assets and current and non-current liabilities;
- describe different types of assets and liabilities and the measurement bases of each;
- describe the components of shareholders' equity;
- convert balance sheets to common-size balance sheets and interpret common-size balance sheets;
- calculate and interpret liquidity and solvency ratios.

SUMMARY OVERVIEW

The balance sheet (also referred to as the statement of financial position) discloses what an entity owns (assets) and what it owes (liabilities) at a specific point in time. Equity is the owners' residual interest in the assets of a company, net of its liabilities. The amount of equity is increased by income earned during the year, or by the issuance of new equity. The amount of equity is decreased by losses, by dividend payments, or by share repurchases.

An understanding of the balance sheet enables an analyst to evaluate the liquidity, solvency, and overall financial position of a company.

- The balance sheet distinguishes between current and non-current assets, and between current and non-current liabilities unless a presentation based on liquidity provides more relevant and reliable information.
- The concept of liquidity relates to a company's ability to pay for its near-term operating needs. With respect to a company overall, liquidity refers to the availability of cash to pay

those near-term needs. With respect to a particular asset or liability, liquidity refers to its "nearness to cash."

- Some assets and liabilities are measured on the basis of fair value, and some are measured at historical cost. Notes to financial statements provide information that is helpful in assessing the comparability of measurement bases across companies.

- Assets expected to be liquidated or used up within one year or one operating cycle of the business, whichever is greater, are classified as current assets. Assets not expected to be liquidated or used up within one year or one operating cycle of the business, whichever is greater, are classified as non-current assets.

- Liabilities expected to be settled or paid within one year or one operating cycle of the business, whichever is greater, are classified as current liabilities. Liabilities not expected to be settled or paid within one year or one operating cycle of the business, whichever is greater, are classified as non-current liabilities.

- Trade receivables, also referred to as accounts receivable, are amounts owed to a company by its customers for products and services already delivered. Receivables are reported net of the allowance for doubtful accounts.

- Inventories are physical products that will eventually be sold to the company's customers, either in their current form (finished goods) or as inputs into a process to manufacture a final product (raw materials and work-in-process). Inventories are reported at the lower of cost or net realizable value. If the net realizable value of a company's inventory falls below its carrying amount, the company must write down the value of the inventory and record an expense.

- Inventory cost is based on specific identification or estimated using the first-in, first-out or weighted average cost methods. Some accounting standards (including US GAAP but not IFRS) also allow last-in, first-out as an additional inventory valuation method.

- Accounts payable, also called trade payables, are amounts that a business owes its vendors for purchases of goods and services.

- Deferred revenue (also known as unearned revenue) arises when a company receives payment in advance of delivery of the goods and services associated with the payment received.

- Property, plant, and equipment (PPE) are tangible assets that are used in company operations and expected to be used over more than one fiscal period. Examples of tangible assets include land, buildings, equipment, machinery, furniture, and natural resources such as mineral and petroleum resources.

- IFRS provide companies with the choice to report PPE using either a historical cost model or a revaluation model. US GAAP permit only the historical cost model for reporting PPE.

- Depreciation is the process of recognizing the cost of a long-lived asset over its useful life. (Land is not depreciated.)

- Under IFRS, property used to earn rental income or capital appreciation is considered to be an investment property. IFRS provide companies with the choice to report an investment property using either a historical cost model or a fair value model.

- Intangible assets refer to identifiable non-monetary assets without physical substance. Examples include patents, licenses, and trademarks. For each intangible asset, a company assesses whether the useful life is finite or indefinite.

- An intangible asset with a finite useful life is amortized on a systematic basis over the best estimate of its useful life, with the amortization method and useful-life estimate reviewed at least annually. Impairment principles for an intangible asset with a finite useful life are the same as for PPE.

- An intangible asset with an indefinite useful life is not amortized. Instead, it is tested for impairment at least annually.
- For internally generated intangible assets, IFRS require that costs incurred during the research phase must be expensed. Costs incurred in the development stage can be capitalized as intangible assets if certain criteria are met, including technological feasibility, the ability to use or sell the resulting asset, and the ability to complete the project.
- The most common intangible asset that is not a separately identifiable asset is goodwill, which arises in business combinations. Goodwill is not amortized; instead it is tested for impairment at least annually.
- Financial instruments are contracts that give rise to both a financial asset of one entity and a financial liability or equity instrument of another entity. In general, there are two basic alternative ways that financial instruments are measured: fair value or amortized cost. For financial instruments measured at fair value, there are two basic alternatives in how net changes in fair value are recognized: as profit or loss on the income statement, or as other comprehensive income (loss), which bypasses the income statement.
- Typical long-term financial liabilities include loans (i.e., borrowings from banks) and notes or bonds payable (i.e., fixed-income securities issued to investors). Liabilities such as bonds issued by a company are usually reported at amortized cost on the balance sheet.
- Deferred tax liabilities arise from temporary timing differences between a company's income as reported for tax purposes and income as reported for financial statement purposes.
- Six potential components that comprise the owners' equity section of the balance sheet include: contributed capital, preferred shares, treasury shares, retained earnings, accumulated other comprehensive income, and non-controlling interest.
- The statement of changes in equity reflects information about the increases or decreases in each component of a company's equity over a period.
- Vertical common-size analysis of the balance sheet involves stating each balance sheet item as a percentage of total assets.
- Balance sheet ratios include liquidity ratios (measuring the company's ability to meet its short-term obligations) and solvency ratios (measuring the company's ability to meet long-term and other obligations).

PROBLEMS

1. Resources controlled by a company as a result of past events are:
   A. equity.
   B. assets.
   C. liabilities.

2. Equity equals:
   A. Assets − Liabilities.
   B. Liabilities − Assets.
   C. Assets + Liabilities.

3. Distinguishing between current and non-current items on the balance sheet and presenting a subtotal for current assets and liabilities is referred to as:
   A. a classified balance sheet.
   B. an unclassified balance sheet.
   C. a liquidity-based balance sheet.

4. Shareholders' equity reported on the balance sheet is *most likely* to differ from the market value of shareholders' equity because:
   A. historical cost basis is used for all assets and liabilities.
   B. some factors that affect the generation of future cash flows are excluded.
   C. shareholders' equity reported on the balance sheet is updated continuously.

5. The information provided by a balance sheet item is limited because of uncertainty regarding:
   A. measurement of its cost or value with reliability.
   B. the change in current value following the end of the reporting period.
   C. the probability that any future economic benefit will flow to or from the entity.

6. Which of the following is *most likely* classified as a current liability?
   A. Payment received for a product due to be delivered at least one year after the balance sheet date.
   B. Payments for merchandise due at least one year after the balance sheet date but still within a normal operating cycle.
   C. Payment on debt due in six months for which the company has the unconditional right to defer settlement for at least one year after the balance sheet date.

7. The *most likely* company to use a liquidity-based balance sheet presentation is a:
   A. bank.
   B. computer manufacturer holding inventories.
   C. software company with trade receivables and payables.

8. All of the following are current assets *except*:
   A. cash.
   B. goodwill.
   C. inventories.

9. The *most* likely costs included in both the cost of inventory and property, plant, and equipment are:
   A. selling costs.
   B. storage costs.
   C. delivery costs.

10. Debt due within one year is considered:
    A. current.
    B. preferred.
    C. convertible.

11. Money received from customers for products to be delivered in the future is recorded as:
    A. revenue and an asset.
    B. an asset and a liability.
    C. revenue and a liability.

12. An example of a contra asset account is:
    A. depreciation expense.
    B. sales returns and allowances.
    C. allowance for doubtful accounts.

13. The carrying value of inventories reflects:
    A. their historical cost.
    B. their current value.
    C. the lower of historical cost or net realizable value.

14. When a company pays its rent in advance, its balance sheet will reflect a reduction in:
    A. assets and liabilities.
    B. assets and shareholders' equity.
    C. one category of assets and an increase in another.

15. Accrued expenses (accrued liabilities) are:
    A. expenses that have been paid.
    B. created when another liability is reduced.
    C. expenses that have been reported on the income statement but not yet paid.

16. The initial measurement of goodwill is *most likely* affected by:
    A. an acquisition's purchase price.
    B. the acquired company's book value.
    C. the fair value of the acquirer's assets and liabilities.

17. Defining total asset turnover as revenue divided by average total assets, all else equal, impairment write-downs of long-lived assets owned by a company will *most likely* result in an increase for that company in:
    A. the debt-to-equity ratio but not the total asset turnover.
    B. the total asset turnover but not the debt-to-equity ratio.
    C. both the debt-to-equity ratio and the total asset turnover.

18. A company has total liabilities of £35 million and total stockholders' equity of £55 million. Total liabilities are represented on a vertical common-size balance sheet by a percentage *closest* to:
    A. 35%.
    B. 39%.
    C. 64%.

19. For financial assets classified as trading securities, how are unrealized gains and losses reflected in shareholders' equity?
    A. They are not recognized.
    B. They flow through income into retained earnings.
    C. They are a component of accumulated other comprehensive income.

20. For financial assets classified as available for sale, how are unrealized gains and losses reflected in shareholders' equity?
    A. They are not recognized.
    B. They flow through retained earnings.
    C. They are a component of accumulated other comprehensive income.

21. For financial assets classified as held to maturity, how are unrealized gains and losses reflected in shareholders' equity?
    A. They are not recognized.
    B. They flow through retained earnings.
    C. They are a component of accumulated other comprehensive income.

22. The non-controlling (minority) interest in consolidated subsidiaries is presented on the balance sheet:
    A. as a long-term liability.
    B. separately, but as a part of shareholders' equity.
    C. as a mezzanine item between liabilities and shareholders' equity.

23. The item "retained earnings" is a component of:
    A. assets.
    B. liabilities.
    C. shareholders' equity.

24. When a company buys shares of its own stock to be held in treasury, it records a reduction in:
    A. both assets and liabilities.
    B. both assets and shareholders' equity.
    C. assets and an increase in shareholders' equity.

25. Which of the following would an analyst *most likely* be able to determine from a common-size analysis of a company's balance sheet over several periods?
    A. An increase or decrease in sales.
    B. An increase or decrease in financial leverage.
    C. A more efficient or less efficient use of assets.

26. An investor concerned whether a company can meet its near-term obligations is *most likely* to calculate the:
    A. current ratio.
    B. return on total capital.
    C. financial leverage ratio.

27. The most stringent test of a company's liquidity is its:
    A. cash ratio.
    B. quick ratio.
    C. current ratio.

28. An investor worried about a company's long-term solvency would *most likely* examine its:
    A. current ratio.
    B. return on equity.
    C. debt-to-equity ratio.

29. Using the information presented in Exhibit 4, the quick ratio for SAP Group at 31 December 2017 is *closest* to:
    A. 1.00.
    B. 1.07.
    C. 1.17.

30. Using the information presented in Exhibit 14, the financial leverage ratio for SAP Group at December 31, 2017 is *closest* to:
    A. 1.50.
    B. 1.66.
    C. 2.00.

Questions 31 through 34 refer to Exhibit 1.

EXHIBIT 1   Common-Size Balance Sheets for Company A, Company B, and Sector Average

	Company A	Company B	Sector Average
ASSETS			
Current assets			
Cash and cash equivalents	5	5	7
Marketable securities	5	0	2
Accounts receivable, net	5	15	12
Inventories	15	20	16
Prepaid expenses	5	15	11
Total current assets	35	55	48
Property, plant, and equipment, net	40	35	37
Goodwill	25	0	8
Other assets	0	10	7
Total assets	100	100	100
LIABILITIES AND SHAREHOLDERS' EQUITY			
Current liabilities			
Accounts payable	10	10	10
Short-term debt	25	10	15
Accrued expenses	0	5	3
Total current liabilities	35	25	28
Long-term debt	45	20	28
Other non-current liabilities	0	10	7
Total liabilities	80	55	63
Total shareholders' equity	20	45	37
Total liabilities and shareholders' equity	100	100	100

31. Based on Exhibit 1, which statement is *most likely* correct?
    A. Company A has below-average liquidity risk.
    B. Company B has above-average solvency risk.
    C. Company A has made one or more acquisitions.

32. The quick ratio for Company A is *closest* to:
    A. 0.43.
    B. 0.57.
    C. 1.00.

33. Based on Exhibit 1, the financial leverage ratio for Company B is *closest* to:
    A. 0.55.
    B. 1.22.
    C. 2.22.

34. Based on Exhibit 1, which ratio indicates lower liquidity risk for Company A compared with Company B?
    A. Cash ratio.
    B. Quick ratio.
    C. Current ratio.

CHAPTER 5

UNDERSTANDING CASH FLOW STATEMENTS

LEARNING OUTCOMES

After completing this chapter, you will be able to do the following:

- compare cash flows from operating, investing, and financing activities and classify cash flow items as relating to one of those three categories given a description of the items;
- describe how non-cash investing and financing activities are reported;
- contrast cash flow statements prepared under International Financial Reporting Standards (IFRS) and US generally accepted accounting principles (US GAAP);
- distinguish between the direct and indirect methods of presenting cash from operating activities and describe arguments in favor of each method;
- describe how the cash flow statement is linked to the income statement and the balance sheet;
- describe the steps in the preparation of direct and indirect cash flow statements, including how cash flows can be computed using income statement and balance sheet data;
- convert cash flows from the indirect to the direct method;
- analyze and interpret both reported and common-size cash flow statements;
- calculate and interpret free cash flow to the firm, free cash flow to equity, and performance and coverage cash flow ratios.

SUMMARY OVERVIEW

The cash flow statement provides important information about a company's cash receipts and cash payments during an accounting period as well as information about a company's operating, investing, and financing activities. Although the income statement provides a measure of a company's success, cash and cash flow are also vital to a company's long-term success. Information on the sources and uses of cash helps creditors, investors, and other statement users evaluate the company's liquidity, solvency, and financial flexibility. Key concepts are as follows:

- Cash flow activities are classified into three categories: operating activities, investing activities, and financing activities. Significant non-cash transaction activities (if present) are reported by using a supplemental disclosure note to the cash flow statement.
- Cash flow statements under IFRS and US GAAP are similar; however, IFRS provide companies with more choices in classifying some cash flow items as operating, investing, or financing activities.
- Companies can use either the direct or the indirect method for reporting their operating cash flow:
  - The direct method discloses operating cash inflows by source (e.g., cash received from customers, cash received from investment income) and operating cash outflows by use (e.g., cash paid to suppliers, cash paid for interest) in the operating activities section of the cash flow statement.
  - The indirect method reconciles net income to operating cash flow by adjusting net income for all non-cash items and the net changes in the operating working capital accounts.
- The cash flow statement is linked to a company's income statement and comparative balance sheets and to data on those statements.
- Although the indirect method is most commonly used by companies, an analyst can generally convert it to an approximation of the direct format by following a simple three-step process.
- An evaluation of a cash flow statement should involve an assessment of the sources and uses of cash and the main drivers of cash flow within each category of activities.
- The analyst can use common-size statement analysis for the cash flow statement. Two approaches to developing the common-size statements are the total cash inflows/total cash outflows method and the percentage of net revenues method.
- The cash flow statement can be used to determine free cash flow to the firm (FCFF) and free cash flow to equity (FCFE).
- The cash flow statement may also be used in financial ratios that measure a company's profitability, performance, and financial strength.

PROBLEMS

1. The three major classifications of activities in a cash flow statement are:
   A. inflows, outflows, and net flows.
   B. operating, investing, and financing.
   C. revenues, expenses, and net income.

2. The sale of a building for cash would be classified as what type of activity on the cash flow statement?
   A. Operating.
   B. Investing.
   C. Financing.

3. Under which section of a manufacturing company's cash flow statement are the following activities reported?
   Item 1: Purchases of securities held for trading
   Item 2: Sales of securities considered cash equivalents

    A. Both items are investing activities.

    B. Both items are operating activities.

    C. Only Item 1 is an investing activity.

4. Which of the following is an example of a financing activity on the cash flow statement under US GAAP?

    A. Payment of interest.

    B. Receipt of dividends.

    C. Payment of dividends.

5. A conversion of a face value $1 million convertible bond for $1 million of common stock would most likely be:

    A. reported as a $1 million investing cash inflow and outflow.

    B. reported as a $1 million financing cash outflow and inflow.

    C. reported as supplementary information to the cash flow statement.

6. A company recently engaged in a non-cash transaction that significantly affected its property, plant, and equipment. The transaction is:

    A. reported under the investing section of the cash flow statement.

    B. reported differently in cash flow from operations under the direct and indirect methods.

    C. disclosed as a separate note or in a supplementary schedule to the cash flow statement.

7. Interest paid is classified as an operating cash flow under:

    A. US GAAP but may be classified as either operating or investing cash flows under IFRS.

    B. IFRS but may be classified as either operating or investing cash flows under US GAAP.

    C. US GAAP but may be classified as either operating or financing cash flows under IFRS.

8. Cash flows from taxes on income must be separately disclosed under:

    A. IFRS only.

    B. US GAAP only.

    C. both IFRS and US GAAP.

9. Which of the following components of the cash flow statement may be prepared under the indirect method under both IFRS and US GAAP?

    A. Operating.

    B. Investing.

    C. Financing.

10. Which of the following is *most likely* to appear in the operating section of a cash flow statement under the indirect method?

    A. Net income.

    B. Cash paid to suppliers.

    C. Cash received from customers.

11. A benefit of using the direct method rather than the indirect method when reporting operating cash flows is that the direct method:

    A. mirrors a forecasting approach.

    B. is easier and less costly.

    C. provides specific information on the sources of operating cash flows.

12. Mabel Corporation (MC) reported accounts receivable of $66 million at the end of its second fiscal quarter. MC had revenues of $72 million for its third fiscal quarter and reported accounts receivable of $55 million at the end of its third fiscal quarter. Based on this information, the amount of cash MC collected from customers during the third fiscal quarter is:
    A. $61 million.
    B. $72 million.
    C. $83 million.

13. When computing net cash flow from operating activities using the indirect method, an addition to net income is *most likely* to occur when there is a:
    A. gain on the sale of an asset.
    B. loss on the retirement of debt.
    C. decrease in a deferred tax liability.

14. Red Road Company, a consulting company, reported total revenues of $100 million, total expenses of $80 million, and net income of $20 million in the most recent year. If accounts receivable increased by $10 million, how much cash did the company receive from customers?
    A. $90 million.
    B. $100 million.
    C. $110 million.

15. In 2018, a company using US GAAP made cash payments of $6 million for salaries, $2 million for interest expense, and $4 million for income taxes. Additional information for the company is provided in the table:

($ millions)	2017	2018
Revenue	42	37
Cost of goods sold	18	16
Inventory	36	40
Accounts receivable	22	19
Accounts payable	14	12

Based only on the information given, the company's operating cash flow for 2018 is *closest to*:
    A. $6 million.
    B. $10 million.
    C. $14 million.

16. Green Glory Corp., a garden supply wholesaler, reported cost of goods sold for the year of $80 million. Total assets increased by $55 million, including an increase of $5 million in inventory. Total liabilities increased by $45 million, including an increase of $2 million in accounts payable. The cash paid by the company to its suppliers is most likely *closest* to:
    A. $73 million.
    B. $77 million.
    C. $83 million.

17. Purple Fleur S.A., a retailer of floral products, reported cost of goods sold for the year of $75 million. Total assets increased by $55 million, but inventory declined by $6 million. Total liabilities increased by $45 million, and accounts payable increased by $2 million. The cash paid by the company to its suppliers is most likely *closest* to:
    A. $67 million.
    B. $79 million.
    C. $83 million.

18. White Flag, a women's clothing manufacturer, reported salaries expense of $20 million. The beginning balance of salaries payable was $3 million, and the ending balance of salaries payable was $1 million. How much cash did the company pay in salaries?
    A. $18 million.
    B. $21 million.
    C. $22 million.

19. An analyst gathered the following information from a company's 2018 financial statements (in $ millions):

Year ended December 31	2017	2018
Net sales	245.8	254.6
Cost of goods sold	168.3	175.9
Accounts receivable	73.2	68.3
Inventory	39.0	47.8
Accounts payable	20.3	22.9

Based only on the information above, the company's 2018 statement of cash flows in the direct format would include amounts (in $ millions) for cash received from customers and cash paid to suppliers, respectively, that are *closest* to:

	Cash Received from Customers	Cash Paid to Suppliers
A.	249.7	169.7
B.	259.5	174.5
C.	259.5	182.1

20. Golden Cumulus Corp., a commodities trading company, reported interest expense of $19 million and taxes of $6 million. Interest payable increased by $3 million, and taxes payable decreased by $4 million over the period. How much cash did the company pay for interest and taxes?
    A. $22 million for interest and $10 million for taxes.
    B. $16 million for interest and $2 million for taxes.
    C. $16 million for interest and $10 million for taxes.

21. An analyst gathered the following information from a company's 2018 financial statements (in $ millions):

Balances as of Year Ended December 31	2017	2018
Retained earnings	120	145
Accounts receivable	38	43
Inventory	45	48
Accounts payable	36	29

In 2018, the company declared and paid cash dividends of $10 million and recorded depreciation expense in the amount of $25 million. The company considers dividends paid a financing activity. The company's 2018 cash flow from operations (in $ millions) was *closest* to
A. 25.
B. 45.
C. 75.

22. Silverago Incorporated, an international metals company, reported a loss on the sale of equipment of $2 million in 2018. In addition, the company's income statement shows depreciation expense of $8 million, and the cash flow statement shows capital expenditure of $10 million, all of which was for the purchase of new equipment. Using the following information from the comparative balance sheets, how much cash did the company receive from the equipment sale?

Balance Sheet Item	12/31/2017	12/31/2018	Change
Equipment	$100 million	$105 million	$5 million
Accumulated depreciation—equipment	$40 million	$46 million	$6 million

A. $1 million.
B. $2 million.
C. $3 million.

23. Jaderong Plinkett Stores reported net income of $25 million. The company has no outstanding debt. Using the following information from the comparative balance sheets (in millions), what should the company report in the financing section of the statement of cash flows in 2018?

Balance Sheet Item	12/31/2017	12/31/2018	Change
Common stock	$100	$102	$ 2
Additional paid-in capital common stock	$100	$140	$40
Retained earnings	$100	$115	$15
Total stockholders' equity	$300	$357	$57

A. Issuance of common stock of $42 million; dividends paid of $10 million.
B. Issuance of common stock of $38 million; dividends paid of $10 million.
C. Issuance of common stock of $42 million; dividends paid of $40 million.

24. Based on the following information for Star Inc., what are the total net adjustments that the company would make to net income in order to derive operating cash flow?

Income Statement Item		Year Ended 12/31/2018	
Net income		$20 million	
Depreciation		$ 2 million	
Balance Sheet Item	12/31/2017	12/31/2018	Change
Accounts receivable	$25 million	$22 million	($3 million)
Inventory	$10 million	$14 million	$4 million
Accounts payable	$ 8 million	$13 million	$5 million

    A. Add $2 million.
    B. Add $6 million.
    C. Subtract $6 million.

25. The first step in cash flow statement analysis should be to:
    A. evaluate consistency of cash flows.
    B. determine operating cash flow drivers.
    C. identify the major sources and uses of cash.

26. Which of the following would be valid conclusions from an analysis of the cash flow statement for Telefónica Group presented in Exhibit 3?
    A. The primary use of cash is financing activities.
    B. The primary source of cash is operating activities.
    C. Telefónica classifies dividends paid as an operating activity.

27. The following information is extracted from Sweetfall Incorporated's financial statements.

Income Statement		Balance Sheet Changes	
Revenue	$56,800	Decrease in accounts receivable	$1,324
Cost of goods sold	27,264	Decrease in inventory	501
Other operating expense	562	Increase in prepaid expense	6
Depreciation expense	2,500	Increase in accounts payable	1,063

The amount of cash Sweetfall Inc. paid to suppliers is:
    A. $25,700.
    B. $26,702.
    C. $27,826.

28. Which is an appropriate method of preparing a common-size cash flow statement?
    A. Show each item of revenue and expense as a percentage of net revenue.
    B. Show each line item on the cash flow statement as a percentage of net revenue.
    C. Show each line item on the cash flow statement as a percentage of total cash outflows.

29. Which of the following is an appropriate method of computing free cash flow to the firm?
    A. Add operating cash flows to capital expenditures and deduct after-tax interest payments.
    B. Add operating cash flows to after-tax interest payments and deduct capital expenditures.
    C. Deduct both after-tax interest payments and capital expenditures from operating cash flows.

30. An analyst has calculated a ratio using as the numerator the sum of operating cash flow, interest, and taxes and as the denominator the amount of interest. What is this ratio, what does it measure, and what does it indicate?
    A. This ratio is an interest coverage ratio, measuring a company's ability to meet its interest obligations and indicating a company's solvency.
    B. This ratio is an effective tax ratio, measuring the amount of a company's operating cash flow used for taxes and indicating a company's efficiency in tax management.
    C. This ratio is an operating profitability ratio, measuring the operating cash flow generated accounting for taxes and interest and indicating a company's liquidity.

CHAPTER 6

FINANCIAL
ANALYSIS TECHNIQUES

LEARNING OUTCOMES

After completing this chapter, you will be able to do the following:

- describe tools and techniques used in financial analysis, including their uses and limitations;
- classify, calculate, and interpret activity, liquidity, solvency, profitability, and valuation ratios;
- describe relationships among ratios and evaluate a company using ratio analysis;
- demonstrate the application of DuPont analysis of return on equity and calculate and interpret effects of changes in its components;
- calculate and interpret ratios used in equity analysis and credit analysis;
- explain the requirements for segment reporting and calculate and interpret segment ratios;
- describe how ratio analysis and other techniques can be used to model and forecast earnings.

SUMMARY OVERVIEW

Financial analysis techniques, including common-size financial statements and ratio analysis, are useful in summarizing financial reporting data and evaluating the performance and financial position of a company. The results of financial analysis techniques provide important inputs into security valuation. Key facets of financial analysis include the following:

- Common-size financial statements and financial ratios remove the effect of size, allowing comparisons of a company with peer companies (cross-sectional analysis) and comparison of a company's results over time (trend or time-series analysis).
- Activity ratios measure the efficiency of a company's operations, such as collection of receivables or management of inventory. Major activity ratios include inventory turnover, days of inventory on hand, receivables turnover, days of sales outstanding, payables turnover, number of days of payables, working capital turnover, fixed asset turnover, and total asset turnover.

- Liquidity ratios measure the ability of a company to meet short-term obligations. Major liquidity ratios include the current ratio, quick ratio, cash ratio, and defensive interval ratio.
- Solvency ratios measure the ability of a company to meet long-term obligations. Major solvency ratios include debt ratios (including the debt-to-assets ratio, debt-to-capital ratio, debt-to-equity ratio, and financial leverage ratio) and coverage ratios (including interest coverage and fixed charge coverage).
- Profitability ratios measure the ability of a company to generate profits from revenue and assets. Major profitability ratios include return on sales ratios (including gross profit margin, operating profit margin, pretax margin, and net profit margin) and return on investment ratios (including operating ROA, ROA, return on total capital, ROE, and return on common equity).
- Ratios can also be combined and evaluated as a group to better understand how they fit together and how efficiency and leverage are tied to profitability.
- ROE can be analyzed as the product of the net profit margin, asset turnover, and financial leverage. This decomposition is sometimes referred to as DuPont analysis.
- Valuation ratios express the relation between the market value of a company or its equity (for example, price per share) and some fundamental financial metric (for example, earnings per share).
- Ratio analysis is useful in the selection and valuation of debt and equity securities, and is a part of the credit rating process.
- Ratios can also be computed for business segments to evaluate how units within a business are performing.
- The results of financial analysis provide valuable inputs into forecasts of future earnings and cash flow.

PROBLEMS

1. Comparison of a company's financial results to other peer companies for the same time period is called:
   A. technical analysis.
   B. time-series analysis.
   C. cross-sectional analysis.

2. In order to assess a company's ability to fulfill its long-term obligations, an analyst would *most likely* examine:
   A. activity ratios.
   B. liquidity ratios.
   C. solvency ratios.

3. Which ratio would a company *most likely* use to measure its ability to meet short-term obligations?
   A. Current ratio.
   B. Payables turnover.
   C. Gross profit margin.

4. Which of the following ratios would be *most* useful in determining a company's ability to cover its lease and interest payments?
   A. ROA.
   B. Total asset turnover.
   C. Fixed charge coverage.

5. An analyst is interested in assessing both the efficiency and liquidity of Spherion PLC. The analyst has collected the following data for Spherion:

	FY3	FY2	FY1
Days of inventory on hand	32	34	40
Days sales outstanding	28	25	23
Number of days of payables	40	35	35

Based on this data, what is the analyst *least likely* to conclude?
   A. Inventory management has contributed to improved liquidity.
   B. Management of payables has contributed to improved liquidity.
   C. Management of receivables has contributed to improved liquidity.

6. An analyst is evaluating the solvency and liquidity of Apex Manufacturing and has collected the following data (in millions of euro):

	FY5 (€)	FY4 (€)	FY3 (€)
Total debt	2,000	1,900	1,750
Total equity	4,000	4,500	5,000

Which of the following would be the analyst's *most likely* conclusion?
   A. The company is becoming increasingly less solvent, as evidenced by the increase in its debt-to-equity ratio from 0.35 to 0.50 from FY3 to FY5.
   B. The company is becoming less liquid, as evidenced by the increase in its debt-to-equity ratio from 0.35 to 0.50 from FY3 to FY5.
   C. The company is becoming increasingly more liquid, as evidenced by the increase in its debt-to-equity ratio from 0.35 to 0.50 from FY3 to FY5.

7. With regard to the data in Problem 6, what would be the *most* reasonable explanation of the financial data?
   A. The decline in the company's equity results from a decline in the market value of this company's common shares.
   B. The €250 increase in the company's debt from FY3 to FY5 indicates that lenders are viewing the company as increasingly creditworthy.
   C. The decline in the company's equity indicates that the company may be incurring losses, paying dividends greater than income, and/or repurchasing shares.

8. An analyst observes a decrease in a company's inventory turnover. Which of the following would *most likely* explain this trend?
   A. The company installed a new inventory management system, allowing more efficient inventory management.
   B. Due to problems with obsolescent inventory last year, the company wrote off a large amount of its inventory at the beginning of the period.
   C. The company installed a new inventory management system but experienced some operational difficulties resulting in duplicate orders being placed with suppliers.

9. Which of the following would *best* explain an increase in receivables turnover?
   A. The company adopted new credit policies last year and began offering credit to customers with weak credit histories.

   B. Due to problems with an error in its old credit scoring system, the company had accumulated a substantial amount of uncollectible accounts and wrote off a large amount of its receivables.
   C. To match the terms offered by its closest competitor, the company adopted new payment terms now requiring net payment within 30 days rather than 15 days, which had been its previous requirement.

10. Brown Corporation had average days of sales outstanding of 19 days in the most recent fiscal year. Brown wants to improve its credit policies and collection practices, and decrease its collection period in the next fiscal year to match the industry average of 15 days. Credit sales in the most recent fiscal year were $300 million, and Brown expects credit sales to increase to $390 million in the next fiscal year. To achieve Brown's goal of decreasing the collection period, the change in the average accounts receivable balance that must occur is *closest* to:
   A. +$0.41 million.
   B. −$0.41 million.
   C. −$1.22 million.

11. An analyst observes the following data for two companies:

	Company A ($)	Company B ($)
Revenue	4,500	6,000
Net income	50	1,000
Current assets	40,000	60,000
Total assets	100,000	700,000
Current liabilities	10,000	50,000
Total debt	60,000	150,000
Shareholders' equity	30,000	500,000

   Which of the following choices *best* describes reasonable conclusions that the analyst might make about the two companies' ability to pay their current and long-term obligations?
   A. Company A's current ratio of 4.0 indicates it is more liquid than Company B, whose current ratio is only 1.2, but Company B is more solvent, as indicated by its lower debt-to-equity ratio.
   B. Company A's current ratio of 0.25 indicates it is less liquid than Company B, whose current ratio is 0.83, and Company A is also less solvent, as indicated by a debt-to-equity ratio of 200 percent compared with Company B's debt-to-equity ratio of only 30 percent.
   C. Company A's current ratio of 4.0 indicates it is more liquid than Company B, whose current ratio is only 1.2, and Company A is also more solvent, as indicated by a debt-to-equity ratio of 200 percent compared with Company B's debt-to-equity ratio of only 30 percent.

The following information relates to Questions 12–15

The data in Exhibit 1 appear in the five-year summary of a major international company. A business combination with another major manufacturer took place in FY13.

EXHIBIT 1

Financial statements	FY10 GBP m	FY11 GBP m	FY12 GBP m	FY13 GBP m	FY14 GBP m
Income statements					
Revenue	4,390	3,624	3,717	8,167	11,366
Profit before interest and taxation (EBIT)	844	700	704	933	1,579
Net interest payable	−80	−54	−98	−163	−188
Taxation	−186	−195	−208	−349	−579
Minorities	−94	−99	−105	−125	−167
Profit for the year	484	352	293	296	645
Balance sheets					
Fixed assets	3,510	3,667	4,758	10,431	11,483
Current asset investments, cash at bank and in hand	316	218	290	561	682
Other current assets	558	514	643	1,258	1,634
Total assets	4,384	4,399	5,691	12,250	13,799
Interest-bearing debt (long term)	−602	−1,053	−1,535	−3,523	−3,707
Other creditors and provisions (current)	−1,223	−1,054	−1,102	−2,377	−3,108
Total liabilities	−1,825	−2,107	−2,637	−5,900	−6,815
Net assets	2,559	2,292	3,054	6,350	6,984
Shareholders' funds	2,161	2,006	2,309	5,572	6,165
Equity minority interests	398	286	745	778	819
Capital employed	2,559	2,292	3,054	6,350	6,984
Cash flow					
Working capital movements	−53	5	71	85	107
Net cash inflow from operating activities	864	859	975	1,568	2,292

12. The company's total assets at year-end FY9 were GBP 3,500 million. Which of the following choices *best* describes reasonable conclusions an analyst might make about the company's efficiency?

    A. Comparing FY14 with FY10, the company's efficiency improved, as indicated by a total asset turnover ratio of 0.86 compared with 0.64.

    B. Comparing FY14 with FY10, the company's efficiency deteriorated, as indicated by its current ratio.

    C. Comparing FY14 with FY10, the company's efficiency deteriorated due to asset growth faster than turnover revenue growth.

13. Which of the following choices *best* describes reasonable conclusions an analyst might make about the company's solvency?
    A. Comparing FY14 with FY10, the company's solvency improved, as indicated by an increase in its debt-to-assets ratio from 0.14 to 0.27.
    B. Comparing FY14 with FY10, the company's solvency deteriorated, as indicated by a decrease in interest coverage from 10.6 to 8.4.
    C. Comparing FY14 with FY10, the company's solvency improved, as indicated by the growth in its profits to GBP 645 million.

14. Which of the following choices *best* describes reasonable conclusions an analyst might make about the company's liquidity?
    A. Comparing FY14 with FY10, the company's liquidity improved, as indicated by an increase in its debt-to-assets ratio from 0.14 to 0.27.
    B. Comparing FY14 with FY10, the company's liquidity deteriorated, as indicated by a decrease in interest coverage from 10.6 to 8.4.
    C. Comparing FY14 with FY10, the company's liquidity improved, as indicated by an increase in its current ratio from 0.71 to 0.75.

15. Which of the following choices *best* describes reasonable conclusions an analyst might make about the company's profitability?
    A. Comparing FY14 with FY10, the company's profitability improved, as indicated by an increase in its debt-to-assets ratio from 0.14 to 0.27.
    B. Comparing FY14 with FY10, the company's profitability deteriorated, as indicated by a decrease in its net profit margin from 11.0 percent to 5.7 percent.
    C. Comparing FY14 with FY10, the company's profitability improved, as indicated by the growth in its shareholders' equity to GBP 6,165 million.

---

16. Assuming no changes in other variables, which of the following would decrease ROA?
    A. A decrease in the effective tax rate.
    B. A decrease in interest expense.
    C. An increase in average assets.

17. An analyst compiles the following data for a company:

	FY13	FY14	FY15
ROE	19.8%	20.0%	22.0%
Return on total assets	8.1%	8.0%	7.9%
Total asset turnover	2.0	2.0	2.1

Based only on the information above, the *most* appropriate conclusion is that, over the period FY13 to FY15, the company's:
A. net profit margin and financial leverage have decreased.
B. net profit margin and financial leverage have increased.
C. net profit margin has decreased, but its financial leverage has increased.

18. A decomposition of ROE for Integra SA is as follows:

	FY12	FY11
ROE	18.90%	18.90%
Tax burden	0.70	0.75
Interest burden	0.90	0.90
EBIT margin	10.00%	10.00%
Asset turnover	1.50	1.40
Leverage	2.00	2.00

Which of the following choices *best* describes reasonable conclusions an analyst might make based on this ROE decomposition?
A. Profitability and the liquidity position both improved in FY12.
B. The higher average tax rate in FY12 offset the improvement in profitability, leaving ROE unchanged.
C. The higher average tax rate in FY12 offset the improvement in efficiency, leaving ROE unchanged.

19. A decomposition of ROE for Company A and Company B is as follows:

	Company A		Company B	
	FY15	FY14	FY15	FY14
ROE	26.46%	18.90%	26.33%	18.90%
Tax burden	0.7	0.75	0.75	0.75
Interest burden	0.9	0.9	0.9	0.9
EBIT margin	7.00%	10.00%	13.00%	10.00%
Asset turnover	1.5	1.4	1.5	1.4
Leverage	4	2	2	2

An analyst is *most likely* to conclude that:
A. Company A's ROE is higher than Company B's in FY15, and one explanation consistent with the data is that Company A may have purchased new, more efficient equipment.
B. Company A's ROE is higher than Company B's in FY15, and one explanation consistent with the data is that Company A has made a strategic shift to a product mix with higher profit margins.
C. the difference between the two companies' ROE in FY15 is very small and Company A's ROE remains similar to Company B's ROE mainly due to Company A increasing its financial leverage.

20. What does the P/E ratio measure?
A. The "multiple" that the stock market places on a company's EPS.
B. The relationship between dividends and market prices.
C. The earnings for one common share of stock.

21. A creditor *most likely* would consider a decrease in which of the following ratios to be positive news?
    A. Interest coverage (times interest earned).
    B. Debt-to-total assets.
    C. Return on assets.
22. When developing forecasts, analysts should *most likely*:
    A. develop possibilities relying exclusively on the results of financial analysis.
    B. use the results of financial analysis, analysis of other information, and judgment.
    C. aim to develop extremely precise forecasts using the results of financial analysis.

CHAPTER 7

INVENTORIES

LEARNING OUTCOMES

After completing this chapter, you will be able to do the following:

- distinguish between costs included in inventories and costs recognized as expenses in the period in which they are incurred;
- describe different inventory valuation methods (cost formulas);
- calculate and compare cost of sales, gross profit, and ending inventory using different inventory valuation methods and using perpetual and periodic inventory systems;
- calculate and explain how inflation and deflation of inventory costs affect the financial statements and ratios of companies that use different inventory valuation methods;
- explain LIFO reserve and LIFO liquidation, and their effects on financial statements and ratios;
- explain LIFO reserve and LIFO liquidation, and their effects on financial statements and ratios;
- convert a company's reported financial statements from LIFO to FIFO for purposes of comparison;
- describe implications of valuing inventory at net realizable value for financial statements and ratios;
- describe the measurement of inventory at the lower of cost and net realizable value;
- describe the financial statement presentation of and disclosures relating to inventories;
- explain issues that analysts should consider when examining a company's inventory disclosures and other sources of information;
- calculate and compare ratios of companies, including companies that use different inventory methods;
- analyze and compare the financial statements of companies, including companies that use different inventory methods.

SUMMARY OVERVIEW

The choice of inventory valuation method (cost formula or cost flow assumption) can have a potentially significant impact on inventory carrying amounts and cost of sales. These in turn impact other financial statement items, such as current assets, total assets, gross profit, and net income. The financial statements and accompanying notes provide important information about a company's inventory accounting policies that the analyst needs to correctly assess financial performance and compare it with that of other companies. Key concepts in this chapter are as follows:

- Inventories are a major factor in the analysis of merchandising and manufacturing companies. Such companies generate their sales and profits through inventory transactions on a regular basis. An important consideration in determining profits for these companies is measuring the cost of sales when inventories are sold.
- The total cost of inventories comprises all costs of purchase, costs of conversion, and other costs incurred in bringing the inventories to their present location and condition. Storage costs of finished inventory and abnormal costs due to waste are typically treated as expenses in the period in which they occurred.
- The allowable inventory valuation methods implicitly involve different assumptions about cost flows. The choice of inventory valuation method determines how the cost of goods available for sale during the period is allocated between inventory and cost of sales.
- IFRS allow three inventory valuation methods (cost formulas): first-in, first-out (FIFO); weighted average cost; and specific identification. The specific identification method is used for inventories of items that are not ordinarily interchangeable and for goods or services produced and segregated for specific projects. US GAAP allow the three methods above plus the last-in, first-out (LIFO) method. The LIFO method is widely used in the United States for both tax and financial reporting purposes because of potential income tax savings.
- The choice of inventory method affects the financial statements and any financial ratios that are based on them. As a consequence, the analyst must carefully consider inventory valuation method differences when evaluating a company's performance over time or in comparison to industry data or industry competitors.
- A company must use the same cost formula for all inventories having a similar nature and use to the entity.
- The inventory accounting system (perpetual or periodic) may result in different values for cost of sales and ending inventory when the weighted average cost or LIFO inventory valuation method is used.
- Under US GAAP, companies that use the LIFO method must disclose in their financial notes the amount of the LIFO reserve or the amount that would have been reported in inventory if the FIFO method had been used. This information can be used to adjust reported LIFO inventory and cost of goods sold balances to the FIFO method for comparison purposes.
- LIFO liquidation occurs when the number of units in ending inventory declines from the number of units that were present at the beginning of the year. If inventory unit costs have generally risen from year to year, this will produce an inventory-related increase in gross profits.
- Consistency of inventory costing is required under both IFRS and US GAAP. If a company changes an accounting policy, the change must be justifiable and applied retrospectively to the financial statements. An exception to the retrospective restatement is when a company reporting under US GAAP changes to the LIFO method.

- Under IFRS, inventories are measured at the lower of cost and net realizable value. Net realizable value is the estimated selling price in the ordinary course of business less the estimated costs necessary to make the sale. Under US GAAP, inventories are measured at the lower of cost, market value, or net realizable value depending upon the inventory method used. Market value is defined as current replacement cost subject to an upper limit of net realizable value and a lower limit of net realizable value less a normal profit margin. Reversals of previous write-downs are permissible under IFRS but not under US GAAP.
- Reversals of inventory write-downs may occur under IFRS but are not allowed under US GAAP.
- Changes in the carrying amounts within inventory classifications (such as raw materials, work-in-process, and finished goods) may provide signals about a company's future sales and profits. Relevant information with respect to inventory management and future sales may be found in the Management Discussion and Analysis or similar items within the annual or quarterly reports, industry news and publications, and industry economic data.
- The inventory turnover ratio, number of days of inventory ratio, and gross profit margin ratio are useful in evaluating the management of a company's inventory.
- Inventory management may have a substantial impact on a company's activity, profitability, liquidity, and solvency ratios. It is critical for the analyst to be aware of industry trends and management's intentions.
- Financial statement disclosures provide information regarding the accounting policies adopted in measuring inventories, the principal uncertainties regarding the use of estimates related to inventories, and details of the inventory carrying amounts and costs. This information can greatly assist analysts in their evaluation of a company's inventory management.

PROBLEMS

1. Inventory cost is *least likely* to include:
   A. production-related storage costs.
   B. costs incurred as a result of normal waste of materials.
   C. transportation costs of shipping inventory to customers.

2. Mustard Seed PLC adheres to IFRS. It recently purchased inventory for €100 million and spent €5 million for storage prior to selling the goods. The amount it charged to inventory expense (€ millions) was *closest* to:
   A. €95.
   B. €100.
   C. €105.

3. Carrying inventory at a value above its historical cost would *most likely* be permitted if:
   A. the inventory was held by a producer of agricultural products.
   B. financial statements were prepared using US GAAP.
   C. the change resulted from a reversal of a previous write-down.

The following information relates to Questions 4 and 5.

A retail company is comparing different approaches to valuing inventory. The company has one product that it sells for $50.

EXHIBIT 1   Units Purchased and Sold (first quarter)

Date	Units Purchased	Purchase Price	Units Sold	Selling Price	Inventory Units on Hand
Jan 2	1,000	$20.00			1,000
Jan 17			500	$50.00	500
Feb 16	1,000	$18.00			1,500
Mar 3			1,200	$50.00	300
Mar 13	1,000	$17.00			1,300
Mar 23			500	$50.00	800
End of quarter totals:	3,000	$55,000	2,200	$110,000	

EXHIBIT 2   Comparison of Inventory Methods and Models

End of Quarter Valuations

March 31	Perpetual LIFO	Periodic LIFO	Perpetual FIFO
Sales	$110,000	$110,000	$110,000
Ending inventory		$16,000	$13,600
Cost of goods sold		$39,000	$41,400
Gross profit		$71,000	$68,600
Inventory turnover ratio	279%		

Note: LIFO is last in, first out and FIFO is first in, first out.

4. What is the value of ending inventory for the first quarter if the company uses a perpetual LIFO inventory valuation method?
   A. $14,500.
   B. $15,000.
   C. $16,000.

5. Which inventory accounting method results in the lowest inventory turnover ratio for the first quarter?
   A. Periodic LIFO.
   B. Perpetual LIFO.
   C. Perpetual FIFO.

---

6. During periods of rising inventory unit costs, a company using the FIFO method rather than the LIFO method will report a lower:
   A. current ratio.
   B. inventory turnover.
   C. gross profit margin.

7. LIFO reserve is *most likely* to increase when inventory unit:
   A. costs are increasing.
   B. costs are decreasing.
   C. levels are decreasing.

8. If inventory unit costs are increasing from period-to-period, a LIFO liquidation is *most likely* to result in an increase in:
   A. gross profit.
   B. LIFO reserve.
   C. inventory carrying amounts.

9. A company using the LIFO method reports the following in £:

	2018	2017
Cost of goods sold (COGS)	50,800	48,500
Ending inventories	10,550	10,000
LIFO reserve	4,320	2,600

   Cost of goods sold for 2018 under the FIFO method is *closest* to:
   A. £48,530.
   B. £49,080.
   C. £52,520.

10. Eric's Used Book Store prepares its financial statements in accordance with IFRS. Inventory was purchased for £1 million and later marked down to £550,000. One of the books, however, was later discovered to be a rare collectible item, and the inventory is now worth an estimated £3 million. The inventory is *most likely* reported on the balance sheet at:
    A. £550,000.
    B. £1,000,000.
    C. £3,000,000.

11. Fernando's Pasta purchased inventory and later wrote it down. The current net realizable value is higher than the value when written down. Fernando's inventory balance will *most likely* be:
    A. higher if it complies with IFRS.
    B. higher if it complies with US GAAP.
    C. the same under US GAAP and IFRS.

12. A write down of the value of inventory to its net realizable value will have a positive effect on the:
    A. balance sheet.
    B. income statement.
    C. inventory turnover ratio.

For Questions 13–24, assume the companies use a periodic inventory system.

13. Cinnamon Corp. started business in 2017 and uses the weighted average cost method. During 2017, it purchased 45,000 units of inventory at €10 each and sold 40,000 units

for €20 each. In 2018, it purchased another 50,000 units at €11 each and sold 45,000 units for €22 each. Its 2018 cost of sales (€ thousands) was *closest* to:
   A. €490.
   B. €491.
   C. €495.

14. Zimt AG started business in 2017 and uses the FIFO method. During 2017, it purchased 45,000 units of inventory at €10 each and sold 40,000 units for €20 each. In 2018, it purchased another 50,000 units at €11 each and sold 45,000 units for €22 each. Its 2018 ending inventory balance (€ thousands) was *closest* to:
   A. €105.
   B. €109.
   C. €110.

15. Zimt AG uses the FIFO method, and Nutmeg Inc. uses the LIFO method. Compared to the cost of replacing the inventory, during periods of rising prices, the cost of sales reported by:
   A. Zimt is too low.
   B. Nutmeg is too low.
   C. Nutmeg is too high.

16. Zimt AG uses the FIFO method, and Nutmeg Inc. uses the LIFO method. Compared to the cost of replacing the inventory, during periods of rising prices the ending inventory balance reported by:
   A. Zimt is too high.
   B. Nutmeg is too low.
   C. Nutmeg is too high.

17. Like many technology companies, TechnoTools operates in an environment of declining prices. Its reported profits will tend to be *highest* if it accounts for inventory using the:
   A. FIFO method.
   B. LIFO method.
   C. weighted average cost method.

18. Compared to using the weighted average cost method to account for inventory, during a period in which prices are generally rising, the current ratio of a company using the FIFO method would *most likely* be:
   A. lower.
   B. higher.
   C. dependent upon the interaction with accounts payable.

19. Zimt AG wrote down the value of its inventory in 2017 and reversed the write-down in 2018. Compared to the ratios that would have been calculated if the write-down had never occurred, Zimt's reported 2017:
   A. current ratio was too high.
   B. gross margin was too high.
   C. inventory turnover was too high.

20. Zimt AG wrote down the value of its inventory in 2017 and reversed the write-down in 2018. Compared to the results the company would have reported if the write-down had never occurred, Zimt's reported 2018:
    A. profit was overstated.
    B. cash flow from operations was overstated.
    C. year-end inventory balance was overstated.

21. Compared to a company that uses the FIFO method, during periods of rising prices a company that uses the LIFO method will *most likely* appear more:
    A. liquid.
    B. efficient.
    C. profitable.

22. Nutmeg, Inc. uses the LIFO method to account for inventory. During years in which inventory unit costs are generally rising and in which the company purchases more inventory than it sells to customers, its reported gross profit margin will *most likely* be:
    A. lower than it would be if the company used the FIFO method.
    B. higher than it would be if the company used the FIFO method.
    C. about the same as it would be if the company used the FIFO method.

23. Compared to using the FIFO method to account for inventory, during periods of rising prices, a company using the LIFO method is *most likely* to report higher:
    A. net income.
    B. cost of sales.
    C. income taxes.

24. Carey Company adheres to US GAAP, whereas Jonathan Company adheres to IFRS. It is *least likely* that:
    A. Carey has reversed an inventory write-down.
    B. Jonathan has reversed an inventory write-down.
    C. Jonathan and Carey both use the FIFO inventory accounting method.

---

25. Company A adheres to US GAAP, and Company B adheres to IFRS. Which of the following is *most likely* to be disclosed on the financial statements of both companies?
    A. Any material income resulting from the liquidation of LIFO inventory.
    B. The amount of inventories recognized as an expense during the period.
    C. The circumstances that led to the reversal of a write down of inventories.

26. Which of the following *most likely* signals that a manufacturing company expects demand for its product to increase?
    A. Finished goods inventory growth rate higher than the sales growth rate.
    B. Higher unit volumes of work in progress and raw material inventories.
    C. Substantially higher finished goods, with lower raw materials and work-in-process.

27. Compared with a company that uses the FIFO method, during a period of rising unit inventory costs, a company using the LIFO method will *most likely* appear more:
    A. liquid.
    B. efficient.
    C. profitable.

28. In a period of declining inventory unit costs and constant or increasing inventory quantities, which inventory method is *most likely* to result in a higher debt-to-equity ratio?
   A. LIFO.
   B. FIFO.
   C. Weighted average cost.

The following information relates to Questions 29–36

Hans Annan, CFA, a food and beverage analyst, is reviewing Century Chocolate's inventory policies as part of his evaluation of the company. Century Chocolate, based in Switzerland, manufactures chocolate products and purchases and resells other confectionery products to complement its chocolate line. Annan visited Century Chocolate's manufacturing facility last year. He learned that cacao beans, imported from Brazil, represent the most significant raw material and that the work-in-progress inventory consists primarily of three items: roasted cacao beans, a thick paste produced from the beans (called chocolate liquor), and a sweetened mixture that needs to be "conched" to produce chocolate. On the tour, Annan learned that the conching process ranges from a few hours for lower-quality products to six days for the highest-quality chocolates. While there, Annan saw the facility's climate-controlled area where manufactured finished products (cocoa and chocolate) and purchased finished goods are stored prior to shipment to customers. After touring the facility, Annan had a discussion with Century Chocolate's CFO regarding the types of costs that were included in each inventory category.

Annan has asked his assistant, Joanna Kern, to gather some preliminary information regarding Century Chocolate's financial statements and inventories. He also asked Kern to calculate the inventory turnover ratios for Century Chocolate and another chocolate manufacturer for the most recent five years. Annan does not know Century Chocolate's most direct competitor, so he asks Kern to do some research and select the most appropriate company for the ratio comparison.

Kern reports back that Century Chocolate prepares its financial statements in accordance with IFRS. She tells Annan that the policy footnote states that raw materials and purchased finished goods are valued at purchase cost whereas work in progress and manufactured finished goods are valued at production cost. Raw material inventories and purchased finished goods are accounted for using the FIFO (first-in, first-out) method, and the weighted average cost method is used for other inventories. An allowance is established when the net realizable value of any inventory item is lower than the value calculated above.

Kern provides Annan with the selected financial statements and inventory data for Century Chocolate shown in Exhibits 1 through 5. The ratio exhibit Kern prepared compares Century Chocolate's inventory turnover ratios to those of Gordon's Goodies, a US-based company. Annan returns the exhibit and tells Kern to select a different competitor that reports using IFRS rather than US GAAP. During this initial review, Annan asks Kern why she has not indicated whether Century Chocolate uses a perpetual or a periodic inventory system. Kern replies that she learned that Century Chocolate uses a perpetual system but did not include this information in her report because inventory values would be the same under either a perpetual or periodic inventory system. Annan tells Kern she is wrong and directs her to research the matter.

While Kern is revising her analysis, Annan reviews the most recent month's Cocoa Market Review from the International Cocoa Organization. He is drawn to the statement that "the ICCO daily price, averaging prices in both futures markets, reached a 29-year high in US\$ terms and a 23-year high in SDRs terms (the SDR unit comprises a basket of major currencies used in international trade: US\$, euro, pound sterling and yen)." Annan makes a note that he will need to factor the potential continuation of this trend into his analysis.

EXHIBIT 1   Century Chocolate Income Statements (CHF Millions)

For Years Ended December 31	2018	2017
Sales	95,290	93,248
Cost of sales	−41,043	−39,047
Marketing, administration, and other expenses	−35,318	−42,481
Profit before taxes	**18,929**	**11,720**
Taxes	−3,283	−2,962
Profit for the period	**15,646**	**8,758**

EXHIBIT 2   Century Chocolate Balance Sheets (CHF Millions)

December 31	2018	2017
Cash, cash equivalents, and short-term investments	6,190	8,252
Trade receivables and related accounts, net	11,654	12,910
Inventories, net	8,100	7,039
Other current assets	2,709	2,812
Total current assets	**28,653**	**31,013**
Property, plant, and equipment, net	18,291	19,130
Other non-current assets	45,144	49,875
Total assets	**92,088**	**100,018**
Trade and other payables	10,931	12,299
Other current liabilities	17,873	25,265
Total current liabilities	**28,804**	**37,564**
Non-current liabilities	15,672	14,963
Total liabilities	**44,476**	**52,527**
Equity		
Share capital	332	341
Retained earnings and other reserves	47,280	47,150
Total equity	**47,612**	**47,491**
Total liabilities and shareholders' equity	**92,088**	**100,018**

EXHIBIT 3   Century Chocolate Supplementary Footnote Disclosures: Inventories (CHF Millions)

December 31	2018	2017
Raw Materials	2,154	1,585
Work in Progress	1,061	1,027
Finished Goods	5,116	4,665
Total inventories before allowance	8,331	7,277
Allowance for write-downs to net realizable value	−231	−238
Total inventories net of allowance	8,100	7,039

EXHIBIT 4   Century Chocolate Inventory Record for Purchased Lemon Drops

Date		Cartons	Per Unit Amount (CHF)
	Beginning inventory	100	22
Feb. 4, 09	Purchase	40	25
Apr. 3, 09	Sale	50	32
Jul. 23, 09	Purchase	70	30
Aug. 16, 09	Sale	100	32
Sep. 9, 09	Sale	35	32
Nov. 15, 09	Purchase	100	28

EXHIBIT 5   Century Chocolate Net Realizable Value Information for Black Licorice Jelly Beans

	2018	2017
FIFO cost of inventory at December 31 (CHF)	314,890	374,870
Ending inventory at December 31 (Kilograms)	77,750	92,560
Cost per unit (CHF)	4.05	4.05
Net Realizable Value (CHF per Kilograms)	4.20	3.95

29. The costs *least likely* to be included by the CFO as inventory are:
    A. storage costs for the chocolate liquor.
    B. excise taxes paid to the government of Brazil for the cacao beans.
    C. storage costs for chocolate and purchased finished goods awaiting shipment to customers.

30. What is the *most likely* justification for Century Chocolate's choice of inventory valuation method for its purchased finished goods?
    A. It is the preferred method under IFRS.
    B. It allocates the same per unit cost to both cost of sales and inventory.
    C. Ending inventory reflects the cost of goods purchased most recently.

31. In Kern's comparative ratio analysis, the 2018 inventory turnover ratio for Century Chocolate is *closest* to:
    A. 5.07.
    B. 5.42.
    C. 5.55.

32. The *most accurate* statement regarding Annan's reasoning for requiring Kern to select a competitor that reports under IFRS for comparative purposes is that under US GAAP:
    A. fair values are used to value inventory.
    B. the LIFO method is permitted to value inventory.
    C. the specific identification method is permitted to value inventory.

33. Annan's statement regarding the perpetual and periodic inventory systems is most significant when which of the following costing systems is used?
    A. LIFO.
    B. FIFO.
    C. Specific identification.

34. Using the inventory record for purchased lemon drops shown in Exhibit 4, the cost of sales for 2018 will be *closest* to:
    A. CHF 3,550.
    B. CHF 4,550.
    C. CHF 4,850.

35. Ignoring any tax effect, the 2018 net realizable value reassessment for the black licorice jelly beans will *most likely* result in:
    A. an increase in gross profit of CHF 7,775.
    B. an increase in gross profit of CHF 11,670.
    C. no impact on cost of sales because under IFRS, write-downs cannot be reversed.

36. If the trend noted in the ICCO report continues and Century Chocolate plans to maintain constant or increasing inventory quantities, the *most likely* impact on Century Chocolate's financial statements related to its raw materials inventory will be:
    A. a cost of sales that more closely reflects current replacement values.
    B. a higher allocation of the total cost of goods available for sale to cost of sales.
    C. a higher allocation of the total cost of goods available for sale to ending inventory.

The following information relates to Questions 37–42

John Martinson, CFA, is an equity analyst with a large pension fund. His supervisor, Linda Packard, asks him to write a report on Karp Inc. Karp prepares its financial statements in accordance with US GAAP. Packard is particularly interested in the effects of the company's use of the LIFO method to account for its inventory. For this purpose, Martinson collects the financial data presented in Exhibits 1 and 2.

EXHIBIT 1   Balance Sheet Information (US$ Millions)

As of December 31	2018	2017
Cash and cash equivalents	172	157
Accounts receivable	626	458
Inventories	620	539
Other current assets	125	65
Total current assets	1,543	1,219
Property and equipment, net	3,035	2,972
Total assets	4,578	4,191
Total current liabilities	1,495	1,395
Long-term debt	644	604
Total liabilities	2,139	1,999
Common stock and paid in capital	1,652	1,652
Retained earnings	787	540
Total shareholders' equity	2,439	2,192
Total liabilities and shareholders' equity	4,578	4,191

EXHIBIT 2   Income Statement Information (US$ Millions)

For the Year Ended December 31	2018	2017
Sales	4,346	4,161
Cost of goods sold	2,211	2,147
Depreciation and amortization expense	139	119
Selling, general, and administrative expense	1,656	1,637
Interest expense	31	18
Income tax expense	62	48
Net income	247	192

Martinson finds the following information in the notes to the financial statements:

- The LIFO reserves as of December 31, 2018 and 2017 are $155 million and $117 million respectively, and
- The effective income tax rate applicable to Karp for 2018 and earlier periods is 20 percent.

37. If Karp had used FIFO instead of LIFO, the amount of inventory reported as of 31 December 2018 would have been *closest* to:
    A. $465 million.
    B. $658 million.
    C. $775 million.

38. If Karp had used FIFO instead of LIFO, the amount of cost of goods sold reported by Karp for the year ended 31 December 2018 would have been *closest* to:
    A. $2,056 million.
    B. $2,173 million.
    C. $2,249 million.

39. If Karp had used FIFO instead of LIFO, its reported net income for the year ended 31 December 2018 would have been higher by an amount *closest to*:
    A. $30 million.
    B. $38 million.
    C. $155 million.

40. If Karp had used FIFO instead of LIFO, Karp's retained earnings as of 31 December 2018 would have been higher by an amount *closest to*:
    A. $117 million.
    B. $124 million.
    C. $155 million.

41. If Karp had used FIFO instead of LIFO, which of the following ratios computed as of 31 December 2018 would *most likely* have been lower?
    A. Cash ratio.
    B. Current ratio.
    C. Gross profit margin.

42. If Karp had used FIFO instead of LIFO, its debt to equity ratio computed as of 31 December 2018 would have:
    A. increased.
    B. decreased.
    C. remained unchanged.

The following information relates to Questions 43–48

Robert Groff, an equity analyst, is preparing a report on Crux Corp. As part of his report, Groff makes a comparative financial analysis between Crux and its two main competitors, Rolby Corp. and Mikko Inc. Crux and Mikko report under US GAAP, and Rolby reports under IFRS.

Groff gathers information on Crux, Rolby, and Mikko. The relevant financial information he compiles is in Exhibit 1. Some information on the industry is in Exhibit 2.

EXHIBIT 1   Selected Financial Information (US$ Millions)

	Crux	Rolby	Mikko
Inventory valuation method	LIFO	FIFO	LIFO
From the Balance Sheets			
As of December 31, 2018			
Inventory, gross	480	620	510
Valuation allowance	20	25	14
Inventory, net	460	595	496
Total debt	1,122	850	732
Total shareholders' equity	2,543	2,403	2,091
As of December 31, 2017			
Inventory, gross	465	602	401
Valuation allowance	23	15	12
Inventory, net	442	587	389

(continued)

EXHIBIT 1   (Continued)

	Crux	Rolby	Mikko
From the Income Statements			
Year Ended December 31, 2018			
Revenues	4,609	5,442	3,503
Cost of goods sold[a]	3,120	3,782	2,550
Net income	229	327	205
[a]Charges included in cost of goods sold for inventory write-downs*	13	15	15

* This does not match the change in the inventory valuation allowance because the valuation allowance is reduced to reflect the valuation allowance attached to items sold and increased for additional necessary write-downs.

LIFO Reserve			
As of December 31, 2018	55	0	77
As of December 31, 2017	72	0	50
As of December 31, 2016	96	0	43

Tax Rate			
Effective tax rate	30%	30%	30%

EXHIBIT 2   Industry Information

	2018	2017	2016
Raw materials price index	112	105	100
Finished goods price index	114	106	100

To compare the financial performance of the three companies, Groff decides to convert LIFO figures into FIFO figures, and adjust figures to assume no valuation allowance is recognized by any company.

After reading Groff's draft report, his supervisor, Rachel Borghi, asks him the following questions:

Question 1   Which company's gross profit margin would best reflect current costs of the industry?

Question 2   Would Rolby's valuation method show a higher gross profit margin than Crux's under an inflationary, a deflationary, or a stable price scenario?

Question 3   Which group of ratios usually appears more favorable with an inventory write-down?

43. Crux's inventory turnover ratio computed as of December 31, 2018, after the adjustments suggested by Groff, is *closest* to:
    A. 5.67.
    B. 5.83.
    C. 6.13.

44. Rolby's net profit margin for the year ended December 31, 2018, after the adjustments suggested by Groff, is *closest* to:
    A. 6.01%.
    B. 6.20%.
    C. 6.28%.

45. Compared with its unadjusted debt-to-equity ratio, Mikko's debt-to-equity ratio as of December 31, 2018, after the adjustments suggested by Groff, is:
    A. lower.
    B. higher.
    C. the same.

46. The *best* answer to Borghi's Question 1 is:
    A. Crux's.
    B. Rolby's.
    C. Mikko's.

47. The *best* answer to Borghi's Question 2 is:
    A. Stable.
    B. Inflationary.
    C. Deflationary.

48. The *best* answer to Borghi's Question 3 is:
    A. Activity ratios.
    B. Solvency ratios.
    C. Profitability ratios.

The following information relates to Questions 49–55

ZP Corporation is a (hypothetical) multinational corporation headquartered in Japan that trades on numerous stock exchanges. ZP prepares its consolidated financial statements in accordance with US GAAP. Excerpts from ZP's 2018 annual report are shown in Exhibits 1–3.

EXHIBIT 1   Consolidated Balance Sheets (¥ Millions)

December 31	2017	2018
Current Assets		
Cash and cash equivalents	¥542,849	¥814,760
⋮	⋮	⋮
Inventories	608,572	486,465
⋮	⋮	⋮
Total current assets	4,028,742	3,766,309
⋮	⋮	⋮
Total assets	**¥10,819,440**	**¥9,687,346**
⋮	⋮	⋮
Total current liabilities	¥3,980,247	¥3,529,765
⋮	⋮	⋮
Total long-term liabilities	2,663,795	2,624,002
Minority interest in consolidated subsidiaries	218,889	179,843
Total shareholders' equity	3,956,509	3,353,736
Total liabilities and shareholders' equity	**¥10,819,440**	**¥9,687,346**

EXHIBIT 2   Consolidated Statements of Income (¥ Millions)

For the years ended December 31	2016	2017	2018
Net revenues			
Sales of products	¥7,556,699	¥8,273,503	¥6,391,240
Financing operations	425,998	489,577	451,950
	7,982,697	8,763,080	6,843,190
Cost and expenses			
Cost of products sold	6,118,742	6,817,446	5,822,805
Cost of financing operations	290,713	356,005	329,128
Selling, general and administrative	827,005	832,837	844,927
⋮	⋮	⋮	⋮
Operating income (loss)	746,237	756,792	−153,670
⋮	⋮	⋮	⋮
Net income	¥548,011	¥572,626	−¥145,646

EXHIBIT 3   Selected Disclosures in the 2018 Annual Report

Management's Discussion and Analysis of Financial Condition and Results of Operations
Cost reduction efforts were offset by increased prices of raw materials, other production materials and parts. . . . Inventories decreased during fiscal 2009 by ¥122.1 billion, or 20.1%, to ¥486.5 billion. This reflects the impacts of decreased sales volumes and fluctuations in foreign currency translation rates.

Management & Corporate Information
Risk Factors
Industry and Business Risks
The worldwide market for our products is highly competitive. ZP faces intense competition from other manufacturers in the respective markets in which it operates. Competition has intensified due to the worldwide deterioration in economic conditions. In addition, competition is likely to further intensify because of continuing globalization, possibly resulting in industry reorganization. Factors affecting competition include product quality and features, the amount of time required for innovation and development, pricing, reliability, safety, economy in use, customer service, and financing terms. Increased competition may lead to lower unit sales and excess production capacity and excess inventory. This may result in a further downward price pressure.

ZP's ability to adequately respond to the recent rapid changes in the industry and to maintain its competitiveness will be fundamental to its future success in maintaining and expanding its market share in existing and new markets.

Notes to Consolidated Financial Statements
2. Summary of significant accounting policies:
Inventories. Inventories are valued at cost, not in excess of market. Cost is determined on the "average-cost" basis, except for the cost of finished products carried by certain subsidiary

companies, which is determined on a "last-in, first-out" ("LIFO") basis. Inventories valued on the LIFO basis totaled ¥94,578 million and ¥50,037 million at December 31, 2017 and 2018, respectively. Had the "first-in, first-out" basis been used for those companies using the LIFO basis, inventories would have been ¥10,120 million and ¥19,660 million higher than reported at December 31, 2017 and 2018, respectively.

9. Inventories:
Inventories consist of the following:

December 31 (¥ Millions)	2017	2018
Finished goods	¥ 403,856	¥ 291,977
Raw materials	99,869	85,966
Work in process	79,979	83,890
Supplies and other	24,868	24,632
	¥ 608,572	¥ 486,465

49. The MD&A indicated that the prices of raw material, other production materials, and parts increased. Based on the inventory valuation methods described in Note 2, which inventory classification would *least accurately* reflect current prices?
    A. Raw materials.
    B. Finished goods.
    C. Work in process.

50. The 2017 inventory value as reported on the 2018 Annual Report if the company had used the FIFO inventory valuation method instead of the LIFO inventory valuation method for a portion of its inventory would be *closest* to:
    A. ¥104,698 million.
    B. ¥506,125 million.
    C. ¥618,692 million.

51. If ZP had prepared its financial statement in accordance with IFRS, the inventory turnover ratio (using average inventory) for 2018 would be:
    A. lower.
    B. higher.
    C. the same.

52. Inventory levels decreased from 2017 to 2018 for all of the following reasons *except*:
    A. LIFO liquidation.
    B. decreased sales volume.
    C. fluctuations in foreign currency translation rates.

53. Which observation is *most likely* a result of looking only at the information reported in Note 9?
    A. Increased competition has led to lower unit sales.
    B. There have been significant price increases in supplies.
    C. Management expects a further downturn in sales during 2010.

54. Note 2 indicates that, "Inventories valued on the LIFO basis totaled ¥94,578 million and ¥50,037 million at December 31, 2017 and 2018, respectively." Based on this, the LIFO reserve should *most likely*:
    A. increase.
    B. decrease.
    C. remain the same.

55. The Industry and Business Risk excerpt states that, "Increased competition may lead to lower unit sales and excess production capacity and excess inventory. This may result in a further downward price pressure." The downward price pressure could lead to inventory that is valued above current market prices or net realizable value. Any write-downs of inventory are *least likely* to have a significant effect on the inventory valued using:
    A. weighted average cost.
    B. first-in, first-out (FIFO).
    C. last-in, first-out (LIFO).

CHAPTER **8**

LONG-LIVED ASSETS

LEARNING OUTCOMES

After completing this chapter, you will be able to do the following:

- distinguish between costs that are capitalized and costs that are expensed in the period in which they are incurred;
- compare the financial reporting of the following types of intangible assets: purchased, internally developed, acquired in a business combination;
- explain and evaluate how capitalizing versus expensing costs in the period in which they are incurred affects financial statements and ratios;
- describe the different depreciation methods for property, plant, and equipment and calculate depreciation expense;
- describe how the choice of depreciation method and assumptions concerning useful life and residual value affect depreciation expense, financial statements, and ratios;
- describe the different amortization methods for intangible assets with finite lives and calculate amortization expense;
- describe how the choice of amortization method and assumptions concerning useful life and residual value affect amortization expense, financial statements, and ratios;
- describe the revaluation model;
- explain the impairment of property, plant, and equipment and intangible assets;
- explain the derecognition of property, plant, and equipment and intangible assets;
- explain and evaluate how impairment, revaluation, and derecognition of property, plant, and equipment and intangible assets affect financial statements and ratios;
- describe the financial statement presentation of, and disclosures relating to, property, plant, and equipment and intangible assets;
- analyze and interpret financial statement disclosures regarding property, plant, and equipment and intangible assets;
- compare the financial reporting of investment property with that of property, plant, and equipment.

SUMMARY OVERVIEW

Understanding the reporting of long-lived assets at inception requires distinguishing between expenditures that are capitalized (i.e., reported as long-lived assets) and those that are expensed. Once a long-lived asset is recognized, it is reported under the cost model at its historical cost less accumulated depreciation (amortization) and less any impairment or under the revaluation model at its fair value. IFRS permit the use of either the cost model or the revaluation model, whereas US GAAP require the use of the cost model. Most companies reporting under IFRS use the cost model. The choice of different methods to depreciate (amortize) long-lived assets can create challenges for analysts comparing companies.

    Key points include the following:

- Expenditures related to long-lived assets are capitalized as part of the cost of assets if they are expected to provide future benefits, typically beyond one year. Otherwise, expenditures related to long-lived assets are expensed as incurred.
- Although capitalizing expenditures, rather than expensing them, results in higher reported profitability in the initial year, it results in lower profitability in subsequent years; however, if a company continues to purchase similar or increasing amounts of assets each year, the profitability-enhancing effect of capitalization continues.
- Capitalizing an expenditure rather than expensing it results in a greater amount reported as cash from operations because capitalized expenditures are classified as an investing cash outflow rather than an operating cash outflow.
- Companies must capitalize interest costs associated with acquiring or constructing an asset that requires a long period of time to prepare for its intended use.
- Including capitalized interest in the calculation of interest coverage ratios provides a better assessment of a company's solvency.
- IFRS require research costs be expensed but allow all development costs (not only software development costs) to be capitalized under certain conditions. Generally, US accounting standards require that research and development costs be expensed; however, certain costs related to software development are required to be capitalized.
- When one company acquires another company, the transaction is accounted for using the acquisition method of accounting in which the company identified as the acquirer allocates the purchase price to each asset acquired (and each liability assumed) on the basis of its fair value. Under acquisition accounting, if the purchase price of an acquisition exceeds the sum of the amounts that can be allocated to individual identifiable assets and liabilities, the excess is recorded as goodwill.
- The capitalized costs of long-lived tangible assets and of intangible assets with finite useful lives are allocated to expense in subsequent periods over their useful lives. For tangible assets, this process is referred to as depreciation, and for intangible assets, it is referred to as amortization.
- Long-lived tangible assets and intangible assets with finite useful lives are reviewed for impairment whenever changes in events or circumstances indicate that the carrying amount of an asset may not be recoverable.
- Intangible assets with an indefinite useful life are not amortized but are reviewed for impairment annually.
- Impairment disclosures can provide useful information about a company's expected cash flows.
- Methods of calculating depreciation or amortization expense include the straight-line method, in which the cost of an asset is allocated to expense in equal amounts each year over its useful life; accelerated methods, in which the allocation of cost is greater in earlier years; and

the units-of-production method, in which the allocation of cost corresponds to the actual use of an asset in a particular period.

- Estimates required for depreciation and amortization calculations include the useful life of the equipment (or its total lifetime productive capacity) and its expected residual value at the end of that useful life. A longer useful life and higher expected residual value result in a smaller amount of annual depreciation relative to a shorter useful life and lower expected residual value.

- IFRS permit the use of either the cost model or the revaluation model for the valuation and reporting of long-lived assets, but the revaluation model is not allowed under US GAAP.

- Under the revaluation model, carrying amounts are the fair values at the date of revaluation less any subsequent accumulated depreciation or amortization.

- In contrast with depreciation and amortization charges, which serve to allocate the cost of a long-lived asset over its useful life, impairment charges reflect an unexpected decline in the fair value of an asset to an amount lower than its carrying amount.

- IFRS permit impairment losses to be reversed, with the reversal reported in profit. US GAAP do not permit the reversal of impairment losses.

- The gain or loss on the sale of long-lived assets is computed as the sales proceeds minus the carrying amount of the asset at the time of sale.

- Estimates of average age and remaining useful life of a company's assets reflect the relationship between assets accounted for on a historical cost basis and depreciation amounts.

- The average remaining useful life of a company's assets can be estimated as net PPE divided by depreciation expense, although the accounting useful life may not necessarily correspond to the economic useful life.

- Long-lived assets reclassified as held for sale cease to be depreciated or amortized. Long-lived assets to be disposed of other than by a sale (e.g., by abandonment, exchange for another asset, or distribution to owners in a spin-off) are classified as held for use until disposal. Thus, they continue to be depreciated and tested for impairment.

- Investment property is defined as property that is owned (or, in some cases, leased under a finance lease) for the purpose of earning rentals, capital appreciation, or both.

- Under IFRS, companies are allowed to value investment properties using either a cost model or a fair value model. The cost model is identical to the cost model used for property, plant, and equipment, but the fair value model differs from the revaluation model used for property, plant, and equipment. Unlike the revaluation model, under the fair value model, all changes in the fair value of investment property affect net income.

- Under US GAAP, investment properties are generally measured using the cost model.

PROBLEMS

1. JOOVI Inc. has recently purchased and installed a new machine for its manufacturing plant. The company incurred the following costs:

Purchase price	$12,980
Freight and insurance	$1,200
Installation	$700
Testing	$100
Maintenance staff training costs	$500

The total cost of the machine to be shown on JOOVI's balance sheet is *closest* to:

  A. $14,180.
  B. $14,980.
  C. $15,480.

2. Which costs incurred with the purchase of property and equipment are expensed?
  A. Delivery charges.
  B. Installation and testing.
  C. Training required to use the property and equipment.

3. When constructing an asset for sale, directly related borrowing costs are *most likely*:
  A. expensed as incurred.
  B. capitalized as part of inventory.
  C. capitalized as part of property, plant, and equipment.

4. BAURU, S.A., a Brazilian corporation, borrows capital from a local bank to finance the construction of its manufacturing plant. The loan has the following conditions:

Borrowing date	January 1, 2009
Amount borrowed	500 million Brazilian real (BRL)
Annual interest rate	14 percent
Term of the loan	3 years
Payment method	Annual payment of interest only. Principal amortization is due at the end of the loan term.

The construction of the plant takes two years, during which time BAURU earned BRL 10 million by temporarily investing the loan proceeds. Which of the following is the amount of interest related to the plant construction (in BRL million) that can be capitalized in BAURU's balance sheet?
  A. 130.
  B. 140.
  C. 210.

5. After analyzing the financial statements and footnotes of a company that follows IFRS, an analyst identified the following intangible assets:
  • product patent expiring in 40 years;
  • copyright with no expiration date; and
  • goodwill acquired 2 years ago in a business combination.

Which of these assets is an intangible asset with a finite useful life?

	Product Patent	Copyright	Goodwill
A	Yes	Yes	No
B	Yes	No	No
C	No	Yes	Yes

6. Intangible assets with finite useful lives *mostly* differ from intangible assets with infinite useful lives with respect to accounting treatment of:
   A. revaluation.
   B. impairment.
   C. amortization.

7. Costs incurred for intangible assets are generally expensed when they are:
   A. internally developed.
   B. individually acquired.
   C. acquired in a business combination.

8. Under US GAAP, when assets are acquired in a business combination, goodwill *most likely* arises from:
   A. contractual or legal rights.
   B. assets that can be separated from the acquired company.
   C. assets that are neither tangible nor identifiable intangible assets.

9. All else equal, in the fiscal year when long-lived equipment is purchased:
   A. depreciation expense increases.
   B. cash from operations decreases.
   C. net income is reduced by the amount of the purchase.

10. Companies X and Z have the same beginning-of-the-year book value of equity and the same tax rate. The companies have identical transactions throughout the year and report all transactions similarly except for one. Both companies acquire a £300,000 printer with a three-year useful life and a salvage value of £0 on January 1 of the new year. Company X capitalizes the printer and depreciates it on a straight-line basis, and Company Z expenses the printer. The following year-end information is gathered for Company X.

	Company X As of December 31
Ending shareholders' equity	£10,000,000
Tax rate	25%
Dividends	£0.00
Net income	£750,000

Based on the information given, Company Z's return on equity using year-end equity will be *closest* to:
A. 5.4%.
B. 6.1%.
C. 7.5%.

11. A financial analyst is studying the income statement effect of two alternative depreciation methods for a recently acquired piece of equipment. She gathers the following information about the equipment's expected production life and use:

	Year 1	Year 2	Year 3	Year 4	Year 5	Total
Units of production	2,000	2,000	2,000	2,000	2,500	10,500

Compared with the units-of-production method of depreciation, if the company uses the straight-line method to depreciate the equipment, its net income in Year 1 will *most likely* be:
   A. lower.
   B. higher.
   C. the same.

12. A company purchases a piece of equipment for €1,500. The equipment is expected to have a useful life of five years and no residual value. In the first year of use, the units of production are expected to be 15% of the equipment's lifetime production capacity and the equipment is expected to generate €1,500 of revenue and incur €500 of cash expenses.

   The depreciation method yielding the lowest operating profit on the equipment in the first year of use is:
   A. straight line.
   B. units of production.
   C. double-declining balance.

13. Juan Martinez, CFO of VIRMIN, S.A., is selecting the depreciation method to use for a new machine. The machine has an expected useful life of six years. Production is expected to be relatively low initially but to increase over time. The method chosen for tax reporting must be the same as the method used for financial reporting. If Martinez wants to minimize tax payments in the first year of the machine's life, which of the following depreciation methods is Martinez *most likely* to use?
   A. Straight-line method.
   B. Units-of-production method.
   C. Double-declining balance method.

The following information relates to Questions 14–15

Miguel Rodriguez of MARIO S.A., an Uruguayan corporation, is computing the depreciation expense of a piece of manufacturing equipment for the fiscal year ended December 31, 2009. The equipment was acquired on January 1, 2009. Rodriguez gathers the following information (currency in Uruguayan pesos, UYP):

Cost of the equipment	UYP 1,200,000
Estimated residual value	UYP 200,000
Expected useful life	8 years
Total productive capacity	800,000 units
Production in FY 2009	135,000 units
Expected production for the next 7 years	95,000 units each year

14. If MARIO uses the straight-line method, the amount of depreciation expense on MARIO's income statement related to the manufacturing equipment is *closest* to:
   A. 125,000.
   B. 150,000.
   C. 168,750.

15. If MARIO uses the units-of-production method, the amount of depreciation expense (in UYP) on MARIO's income statement related to the manufacturing equipment is *closest* to:
    A. 118,750.
    B. 168,750.
    C. 202,500.

---

16. Which of the following amortization methods is *most likely* to evenly distribute the cost of an intangible asset over its useful life?
    A. Straight-line method.
    B. Units-of-production method.
    C. Double-declining balance method.

17. Which of the following will cause a company to show a lower amount of amortization of intangible assets in the first year after acquisition?
    A. A higher residual value.
    B. A higher amortization rate.
    C. A shorter useful life.

18. A company purchases equipment for $200,000 with a five-year useful life and salvage value of zero. It uses the double-declining balance method of depreciation for two years, then shifts to straight-line depreciation at the beginning of Year 3. Compared with annual depreciation expense under the double-declining balance method, the resulting annual depreciation expense in Year 4 is:
    A. smaller.
    B. the same.
    C. greater.

19. An analyst in the finance department of BOOLDO S.A., a French corporation, is computing the amortization of a customer list, an intangible asset, for the fiscal year ended December 31, 2009. She gathers the following information about the asset:

Acquisition cost	€2,300,000
Acquisition date	January 1, 2008
Expected residual value at time of acquisition	€500,000
The customer list is expected to result in extra sales for three years after acquisition. The present value of these expected extra sales exceeds the cost of the list.	

    If the analyst uses the straight-line method, the amount of accumulated amortization related to the customer list as of December 31, 2009 is *closest* to:
    A. €600,000.
    B. €1,200,000.
    C. €1,533,333.

20. A financial analyst is analyzing the amortization of a product patent acquired by MAKETTI S.p.A., an Italian corporation. He gathers the following information about the patent:

Acquisition cost	€5,800,000
Acquisition date	January 1, 2009
Patent expiration date	December 31, 2015
Total plant capacity of patented product	40,000 units per year
Production of patented product in fiscal year ended December 31, 2009	20,000 units
Expected production of patented product during life of the patent	175,000 units

If the analyst uses the units-of-production method, the amortization expense on the patent for fiscal year 2009 is *closest* to:
A. €414,286.
B. €662,857.
C. €828,571.

21. A company acquires a patent with an expiration date in six years for ¥100 million. The company assumes that the patent will generate economic benefits that will decline over time and decides to amortize the patent using the double-declining balance method. The annual amortization expense in Year 4 is closest to:
A. ¥6.6 million.
B. ¥9.9 million.
C. ¥19.8 million.

22. A company is comparing straight-line and double-declining balance amortization methods for a non-renewable six-year license, acquired for €600,000. The difference between the Year 4 ending net book values using the two methods is *closest to*:
A. €81,400.
B. €118,600.
C. €200,000.

23. MARU S.A. de C.V., a Mexican corporation that follows IFRS, has elected to use the revaluation model for its property, plant, and equipment. One of MARU's machines was purchased for 2,500,000 Mexican pesos (MXN) at the beginning of the fiscal year ended March 31, 2010. As of March 31, 2010, the machine has a fair value of MXN 3,000,000. Should MARU show a profit for the revaluation of the machine?
A. Yes.
B. No, because this revaluation is recorded directly in equity.
C. No, because value increases resulting from revaluation can never be recognized as a profit.

24. An analyst is studying the impairment of the manufacturing equipment of WLP Corp., a UK-based corporation that follows IFRS. He gathers the following information about the equipment:

Fair value	£16,800,000
Costs to sell	£800,000
Value in use	£14,500,000
Net carrying amount	£19,100,000

The amount of the impairment loss on WLP Corp.'s income statement related to its manufacturing equipment is *closest* to:
A. £2,300,000.
B. £3,100,000.
C. £4,600,000.

25. Under IFRS, an impairment loss on a property, plant, and equipment asset is measured as the excess of the carrying amount over the asset's:
A. fair value.
B. recoverable amount.
C. undiscounted expected future cash flows.

26. A financial analyst at BETTO S.A. is analyzing the result of the sale of a vehicle for 85,000 Argentine pesos (ARP) on December 31, 2009. The analyst compiles the following information about the vehicle:

Acquisition cost of the vehicle	ARP 100,000
Acquisition date	January 1, 2007
Estimated residual value at acquisition date	ARP 10,000
Expected useful life	9 years
Depreciation method	Straight-line

The result of the sale of the vehicle is *most likely*:
A. a loss of ARP 15,000.
B. a gain of ARP 15,000.
C. a gain of ARP 18,333.

27. CROCO S.p.A sells an intangible asset with a historical acquisition cost of €12 million and an accumulated depreciation of €2 million and reports a loss on the sale of €3.2 million. Which of the following amounts is *most likely* the sale price of the asset?
A. €6.8 million.
B. €8.8 million.
C. €13.2 million.

28. The impairment of intangible assets with finite lives affects:
A. the balance sheet but not the income statement.
B. the income statement but not the balance sheet.
C. both the balance sheet and the income statement.

29. The gain or loss on a sale of a long-lived asset to which the revaluation model has been applied is *most likely* calculated using sales proceeds less:
A. carrying amount.
B. carrying amount adjusted for impairment.
C. historical cost net of accumulated depreciation.

30. According to IFRS, all of the following pieces of information about property, plant, and equipment must be disclosed in a company's financial statements and footnotes *except for*:
A. useful lives.
B. acquisition dates.
C. amount of disposals.

31. According to IFRS, all of the following pieces of information about intangible assets must be disclosed in a company's financial statements and footnotes *except for*:
    A. fair value.
    B. impairment loss.
    C. amortization rate.

32. Which of the following is a required financial statement disclosure for long-lived intangible assets under US GAAP?
    A. The useful lives of assets.
    B. The reversal of impairment losses.
    C. Estimated amortization expense for the next five fiscal years.

33. Which of the following characteristics is *most likely* to differentiate investment property from property, plant, and equipment?
    A. It is tangible.
    B. It earns rent.
    C. It is long-lived.

34. If a company uses the fair value model to value investment property, changes in the fair value of the asset are *least likely* to affect:
    A. net income.
    B. net operating income.
    C. other comprehensive income.

35. Investment property is *most likely* to:
    A. earn rent.
    B. be held for resale.
    C. be used in the production of goods and services.

36. A company is *most likely* to:
    A. use a fair value model for some investment property and a cost model for other investment property.
    B. change from the fair value model when transactions on comparable properties become less frequent.
    C. change from the fair value model when the company transfers investment property to property, plant, and equipment.

37. Under the revaluation model for property, plant, and equipment and the fair model for investment property:
    A. fair value of the asset must be able to be measured reliably.
    B. net income is affected by all changes in the fair value of the asset.
    C. net income is never affected if the asset increases in value from its carrying amount.

38. Under IFRS, what must be disclosed under the cost model of valuation for investment properties?
    A. Useful lives.
    B. The method for determining fair value.
    C. Reconciliation between beginning and ending carrying amounts of investment property.

The following information relates to Questions 39–42

Melanie Hart, CFA, is a transportation analyst. Hart has been asked to write a research report on Altai Mountain Rail Company (AMRC). Like other companies in the railroad industry, AMRC's operations are capital intensive, with significant investments in such long-lived tangible assets as property, plant, and equipment. In November of 2008, AMRC's board of directors hired a new team to manage the company. In reviewing the company's 2009 annual report, Hart is concerned about some of the accounting choices that the new management has made. These choices differ from those of the previous management and from common industry practice. Hart has highlighted the following statements from the company's annual report:

Statement 1 "In 2009, AMRC spent significant amounts on track replacement and similar improvements. AMRC expensed rather than capitalized a significant proportion of these expenditures."

Statement 2 "AMRC uses the straight-line method of depreciation for both financial and tax reporting purposes to account for plant and equipment."

Statement 3 "In 2009, AMRC recognized an impairment loss of €50 million on a fleet of locomotives. The impairment loss was reported as 'other income' in the income statement and reduced the carrying amount of the assets on the balance sheet."

Exhibits 1 and 2 contain AMRC's 2009 consolidated income statement and balance sheet. AMRC prepares its financial statements in accordance with International Financial Reporting Standards.

EXHIBIT 1   Consolidated Statement of Income

	2009		2008	
For the Years Ended December 31	€ Millions	% Revenues	€ Millions	% Revenues
Operating revenues	2,600	100.0	2,300	100.0
Operating expenses				
Depreciation	(200)	(7.7)	(190)	(8.3)
Other operating expense	(1,590)	(61.1)	(1,515)	(65.9)
Total operating expenses	(1,790)	(68.8)	(1,705)	(74.2)
Operating income	810	31.2	595	25.8
Other income	(50)	(1.9)	—	0.0
Interest expense	(73)	(2.8)	(69)	(3.0)
Income before taxes	687	26.5	526	22.8
Income taxes	(272)	(10.5)	(198)	(8.6)
Net income	415	16	328	14.2

EXHIBIT 2   Consolidated Balance Sheet

As of December 31	2009		2008	
Assets	€ Millions	% Assets	€ Millions	% Assets
Current assets	500	9.4	450	8.5
Property & equipment:				
Land	700	13.1	700	13.2
Plant & equipment	6,000	112.1	5,800	109.4
Total property & equipment	6,700	125.2	6,500	122.6
Accumulated depreciation	(1,850)	(34.6)	(1,650)	(31.1)
Net property & equipment	4,850	90.6	4,850	91.5
Total assets	5,350	100.0	5,300	100.0
Liabilities and Shareholders' Equity				
Current liabilities	480	9.0	430	8.1
Long-term debt	1,030	19.3	1,080	20.4
Other long-term provisions and liabilities	1,240	23.1	1,440	27.2
Total liabilities	2,750	51.4	2,950	55.7
Shareholders' equity				
Common stock and paid-in-surplus	760	14.2	760	14.3
Retained earnings	1,888	35.5	1,600	30.2
Other comprehensive losses	(48)	(0.9)	(10)	(0.2)
Total shareholders' equity	2,600	48.6	2,350	44.3
Total liabilities & shareholders' equity	5,350	100.0	5,300	100.0

39. With respect to Statement 1, which of the following is the *most likely* effect of management's decision to expense rather than capitalize these expenditures?
   A. 2009 net profit margin is higher than if the expenditures had been capitalized.
   B. 2009 total asset turnover is lower than if the expenditures had been capitalized.
   C. Future profit growth will be higher than if the expenditures had been capitalized.

40. With respect to Statement 2, what would be the *most likely* effect in 2010 if AMRC were to switch to an accelerated depreciation method for both financial and tax reporting?
   A. Net profit margin would increase.
   B. Total asset turnover would decrease.
   C. Cash flow from operating activities would increase.

41. With respect to Statement 3, what is the *most likely* effect of the impairment loss?
   A. Net income in years prior to 2009 was likely understated.
   B. Net profit margins in years after 2009 will likely exceed the 2009 net profit margin.
   C. Cash flow from operating activities in 2009 was likely lower due to the impairment loss.

42. Based on Exhibits 1 and 2, the *best estimate* of the average remaining useful life of the company's plant and equipment at the end of 2009 is:
   A. 20.75 years.
   B. 24.25 years.
   C. 30.00 years.

The following information relates to Questions 43–48

Brian Jordan is interviewing for a junior equity analyst position at Orion Investment Advisors. As part of the interview process, Mary Benn, Orion's Director of Research, provides Jordan with information about two hypothetical companies, Alpha and Beta, and asks him to comment on the information on their financial statements and ratios. Both companies prepare their financial statements in accordance with International Financial Reporting Standards (IFRS) and are identical in all respects except for their accounting choices.

Jordan is told that at the beginning of the current fiscal year, both companies purchased a major new computer system and began building new manufacturing plants for their own use. Alpha capitalized, and Beta expensed the cost of the computer system; Alpha capitalized and Beta expensed the interest costs associated with the construction of the manufacturing plants.

Benn asks Jordan, "What was the impact of these decisions on each company's current fiscal year financial statements and ratios?"

Jordan responds, "Alpha's decision to capitalize the cost of its new computer system instead of expensing it results in lower net income, lower total assets, and higher cash flow from operating activities in the current fiscal year. Alpha's decision to capitalize its interest costs instead of expensing them results in a lower fixed asset turnover ratio and a higher interest coverage ratio."

Jordan is told that Alpha uses the straight-line depreciation method and Beta uses an accelerated depreciation method; both companies estimate the same useful lives for long-lived assets. Many companies in their industry use the units-of-production method.

Benn asks Jordan, "What are the financial statement implications of each depreciation method, and how do you determine a company's need to reinvest in its productive capacity?"

Jordan replies, "All other things being equal, the straight-line depreciation method results in the least variability of net profit margin over time, while an accelerated depreciation method results in a declining trend in net profit margin over time. The units-of-production can result in a net profit margin trend that is quite variable. I use a three-step approach to estimate a company's need to reinvest in its productive capacity. First, I estimate the average age of the assets by dividing net property, plant, and equipment by annual depreciation expense. Second, I estimate the average remaining useful life of the assets by dividing accumulated depreciation by depreciation expense. Third, I add the estimates of the average remaining useful life and the average age of the assets in order to determine the total useful life."

Jordan is told that at the end of the current fiscal year, Alpha revalued a manufacturing plant; this increased its reported carrying amount by 15 percent. There was no previous downward revaluation of the plant. Beta recorded an impairment loss on a manufacturing plant; this reduced its carrying by 10 percent.

Benn asks Jordan "What was the impact of these decisions on each company's current fiscal year financial ratios?"

Jordan responds, "Beta's impairment loss increases its debt to total assets and fixed asset turnover ratios, and lowers its cash flow from operating activities. Alpha's revaluation increases its debt to capital and return on assets ratios, and reduces its return on equity."

At the end of the interview, Benn thanks Jordan for his time and states that a hiring decision will be made shortly.

43. Jordan's response about the financial statement impact of Alpha's decision to capitalize the cost of its new computer system is most likely *correct* with respect to:
    A. lower net income.
    B. lower total assets.
    C. higher cash flow from operating activities.

44. Jordan's response about the ratio impact of Alpha's decision to capitalize interest costs is most likely *correct* with respect to the:
    A. interest coverage ratio.
    B. fixed asset turnover ratio.
    C. interest coverage and fixed asset turnover ratios.

45. Jordan's response about the impact of the different depreciation methods on net profit margin is most likely *incorrect* with respect to:
    A. accelerated depreciation.
    B. straight-line depreciation.
    C. units-of-production depreciation.

46. Jordan's response about his approach to estimating a company's need to reinvest in its productive capacity is most likely *correct* regarding:
    A. estimating the average age of the asset base.
    B. estimating the total useful life of the asset base.
    C. estimating the average remaining useful life of the asset base.

47. Jordan's response about the effect of Beta's impairment loss is most likely *incorrect* with respect to the impact on its:
    A. debt to total assets.
    B. fixed asset turnover.
    C. cash flow from operating activities.

48. Jordan's response about the effect of Alpha's revaluation is most likely *correct* with respect to the impact on its:
    A. return on equity.
    B. return on assets.
    C. debt to capital ratio.

CHAPTER 9

INCOME TAXES

LEARNING OUTCOMES

After completing this chapter, you will be able to do the following:

- describe the differences between accounting profit and taxable income, and define key terms, including deferred tax assets, deferred tax liabilities, valuation allowance, taxes payable, and income tax expense;
- explain how deferred tax liabilities and assets are created and the factors that determine how a company's deferred tax liabilities and assets should be treated for the purposes of financial analysis;
- calculate the tax base of a company's assets and liabilities;
- calculate income tax expense, income taxes payable, deferred tax assets, and deferred tax liabilities, and calculate and interpret the adjustment to the financial statements related to a change in the income tax rate;
- evaluate the effect of tax rate changes on a company's financial statements and ratios;
- distinguish between temporary and permanent differences in pre-tax accounting income and taxable income;
- describe the valuation allowance for deferred tax assets—when it is required and what effect it has on financial statements;
- explain recognition and measurement of current and deferred tax items;
- analyze disclosures relating to deferred tax items and the effective tax rate reconciliation, and explain how information included in these disclosures affects a company's financial statements and financial ratios;
- identify the key provisions of and differences between income tax accounting under International Financial Reporting Standards (IFRS) and US generally accepted accounting principles (GAAP).

SUMMARY OVERVIEW

Income taxes are a significant category of expense for profitable companies. Analyzing income tax expenses is often difficult for the analyst because there are many permanent and temporary timing differences between the accounting that is used for income tax reporting and the accounting that is used for financial reporting on company financial statements. The financial statements and notes to the financial statements of a company provide important information that the analyst needs to assess financial performance and to compare a company's financial performance with other companies. Key concepts in this chapter are as follows:

- Differences between the recognition of revenue and expenses for tax and accounting purposes may result in taxable income differing from accounting profit. The discrepancy is a result of different treatments of certain income and expenditure items.
- The tax base of an asset is the amount that will be deductible for tax purposes as an expense in the calculation of taxable income as the company expenses the tax basis of the asset. If the economic benefit will not be taxable, the tax base of the asset will be equal to the carrying amount of the asset.
- The tax base of a liability is the carrying amount of the liability less any amounts that will be deductible for tax purposes in the future. With respect to revenue received in advance, the tax base of such a liability is the carrying amount less any amount of the revenue that will not be taxable in the future.
- Temporary differences arise from recognition of differences in the tax base and carrying amount of assets and liabilities. The creation of a deferred tax asset or liability as a result of a temporary difference will only be allowed if the difference reverses itself at some future date and to the extent that it is expected that the balance sheet item will create future economic benefits for the company.
- Permanent differences result in a difference in tax and financial reporting of revenue (expenses) that will not be reversed at some future date. Because it will not be reversed at a future date, these differences do not constitute temporary differences and do not give rise to a deferred tax asset or liability.
- Current taxes payable or recoverable are based on the applicable tax rates on the balance sheet date of an entity; in contrast, deferred taxes should be measured at the tax rate that is expected to apply when the asset is realized or the liability settled.
- All unrecognized deferred tax assets and liabilities must be reassessed on the appropriate balance sheet date and measured against their probable future economic benefit.
- Deferred tax assets must be assessed for their prospective recoverability. If it is probable that they will not be recovered at all or partly, the carrying amount should be reduced. Under US GAAP, this is done through the use of a valuation allowance.

PROBLEMS

1. Using the straight-line method of depreciation for reporting purposes and accelerated depreciation for tax purposes would *most likely* result in a:
   A. valuation allowance.
   B. deferred tax asset.
   C. temporary difference.

2. In early 2018 Sanborn Company must pay the tax authority €37,000 on the income it earned in 2017. This amount was recorded on the company's December 31, 2017 financial statements as:
   A. taxes payable.
   B. income tax expense.
   C. a deferred tax liability.

3. Income tax expense reported on a company's income statement equals taxes payable, plus the net increase in:
    A. deferred tax assets and deferred tax liabilities.
    B. deferred tax assets, less the net increase in deferred tax liabilities.
    C. deferred tax liabilities, less the net increase in deferred tax assets.
4. Analysts should treat deferred tax liabilities that are expected to reverse as:
    A. equity.
    B. liabilities.
    C. neither liabilities nor equity.
5. Deferred tax liabilities should be treated as equity when:
    A. they are not expected to reverse.
    B. the timing of tax payments is uncertain.
    C. the amount of tax payments is uncertain.
6. When both the timing and amount of tax payments are uncertain, analysts should treat deferred tax liabilities as:
    A. equity.
    B. liabilities.
    C. neither liabilities nor equity.
7. When accounting standards require recognition of an expense that is not permitted under tax laws, the result is a:
    A. deferred tax liability.
    B. temporary difference.
    C. permanent difference.
8. When certain expenditures result in tax credits that directly reduce taxes, the company will *most likely* record:
    A. a deferred tax asset.
    B. a deferred tax liability.
    C. no deferred tax asset or liability.
9. When accounting standards require an asset to be expensed immediately but tax rules require the item to be capitalized and amortized, the company will *most likely* record:
    A. a deferred tax asset.
    B. a deferred tax liability.
    C. no deferred tax asset or liability.
10. A company incurs a capital expenditure that may be amortized over five years for accounting purposes, but over four years for tax purposes. The company will *most likely* record:
    A. a deferred tax asset.
    B. a deferred tax liability.
    C. no deferred tax asset or liability.
11. A company receives advance payments from customers that are immediately taxable but will not be recognized for accounting purposes until the company fulfills its obligation. The company will *most likely* record:
    A. a deferred tax asset.
    B. a deferred tax liability.
    C. no deferred tax asset or liability.

The following information relates to Questions 12–14

Note I
Income Taxes

The components of earnings before income taxes are as follows ($ thousands):

	Year 3	Year 2	Year 1
Earnings before income taxes:			
United States	$88,157	$75,658	$59,973
Foreign	116,704	113,509	94,760
Total	$204,861	$189,167	$154,733

The components of the provision for income taxes are as follows ($ thousands):

	Year 3	Year 2	Year 1
Income taxes			
Current:			
Federal	$30,632	$22,031	$18,959
Foreign	28,140	27,961	22,263
	$58,772	$49,992	$41,222
Deferred:			
Federal	($4,752)	$5,138	$2,336
Foreign	124	1,730	621
	(4,628)	6,868	2,957
Total	$54,144	$56,860	$44,179

12. In Year 3, the company's US GAAP income statement recorded a provision for income taxes *closest* to:
    A. $30,632.
    B. $54,144.
    C. $58,772.
13. The company's effective tax rate was *highest* in:
    A. Year 1.
    B. Year 2.
    C. Year 3.
14. Compared to the company's effective tax rate on US income, its effective tax rate on foreign income was:
    A. lower in each year presented.
    B. higher in each year presented.
    C. higher in some periods and lower in others.

15. Zimt AG presents its financial statements in accordance with US GAAP. In Year 3, Zimt discloses a valuation allowance of $1,101 against total deferred tax assets of $19,201. In Year 2, Zimt disclosed a valuation allowance of $1,325 against total deferred tax assets of $17,325. The change in the valuation allowance most likely indicates that Zimt's:
    A. deferred tax liabilities were reduced in Year 3.
    B. expectations of future earning power has increased.
    C. expectations of future earning power has decreased.

16. Cinnamon, Inc. recorded a total deferred tax asset in Year 3 of $12,301, offset by a $12,301 valuation allowance. Cinnamon *most likely*:
    A. fully utilized the deferred tax asset in Year 3.
    B. has an equal amount of deferred tax assets and deferred tax liabilities.
    C. expects not to earn any taxable income before the deferred tax asset expires.

The following information relates to Questions 17–19

The tax effects of temporary differences that give rise to deferred tax assets and liabilities are as follows ($ thousands):

	Year 3	Year 2
Deferred tax assets:		
Accrued expenses	$8,613	$7,927
Tax credit and net operating loss carryforwards	2,288	2,554
LIFO and inventory reserves	5,286	4,327
Other	2,664	2,109
Deferred tax assets	18,851	16,917
Valuation allowance	(1,245)	(1,360)
Net deferred tax assets	$17,606	$15,557
Deferred tax liabilities:		
Depreciation and amortization	$(27,338)	$(29,313)
Compensation and retirement plans	(3,831)	(8,963)
Other	(1,470)	(764)
Deferred tax liabilities	(32,639)	(39,040)
Net deferred tax liability	$(15,033)	$(23,483)

17. A reduction in the statutory tax rate would *most likely* benefit the company's:
    A. income statement and balance sheet.
    B. income statement but not the balance sheet.
    C. balance sheet but not the income statement.

18. If the valuation allowance had been the same in Year 3 as it was in Year 2, the company would have reported $115 *higher*:
    A. net income.
    B. deferred tax assets.
    C. income tax expense.

19. Compared to the provision for income taxes in Year 3, the company's cash tax payments
    were:
    A. lower.
    B. higher.
    C. the same.

The following information relates to Questions 20–22

A company's provision for income taxes resulted in effective tax rates attributable to loss from
continuing operations before cumulative effect of change in accounting principles that varied
from the statutory federal income tax rate of 34 percent, as summarized in the table below.

Year Ended 30 June	Year 3	Year 2	Year 1
Expected federal income tax expense (benefit) from continuing operations at 34 percent	($112,000)	$768,000	$685,000
Expenses not deductible for income tax purposes	357,000	32,000	51,000
State income taxes, net of federal benefit	132,000	22,000	100,000
Change in valuation allowance for deferred tax assets	(150,000)	(766,000)	(754,000)
Income tax expense	$227,000	$56,000	$82,000

20. In Year 3, the company's net income (loss) was *closest* to:
    A. ($217,000).
    B. ($329,000).
    C. ($556,000).
21. The $357,000 adjustment in Year 3 *most likely* resulted in:
    A. an increase in deferred tax assets.
    B. an increase in deferred tax liabilities.
    C. no change to deferred tax assets and liabilities.
22. Over the three years presented, changes in the valuation allowance for deferred tax assets
    were *most likely* indicative of:
    A. decreased prospects for future profitability.
    B. increased prospects for future profitability.
    C. assets being carried at a higher value than their tax base.

CHAPTER **10**

NON-CURRENT (LONG-TERM) LIABILITIES

LEARNING OUTCOMES

After completing this chapter, you will be able to do the following:

- determine the initial recognition, initial measurement, and subsequent measurement of bonds;
- describe the effective interest method and calculate interest expense, amortization of bond discounts/premiums, and interest payments;
- explain the derecognition of debt;
- describe the role of debt covenants in protecting creditors;
- describe the financial statement presentation of and disclosures relating to debt;
- explain motivations for leasing assets instead of purchasing them;
- explain the financial reporting of leases from a lessee's perspective;
- explain the financial reporting of leases from a lessor's perspective;
- compare the presentation and disclosure of defined contribution and defined benefit pension plans;
- calculate and interpret leverage and coverage ratios.

SUMMARY OVERVIEW

Non-current liabilities arise from different sources of financing and different types of creditors. Bonds are a common source of financing from debt markets. Key points in accounting and reporting of non-current liabilities include the following:

- The sales proceeds of a bond issue are determined by discounting future cash payments using the market rate of interest at the time of issuance (effective interest rate). The reported interest expense on bonds is based on the effective interest rate.
- Future cash payments on bonds usually include periodic interest payments (made at the stated interest rate or coupon rate) and the principal amount at maturity.

- When the market rate of interest equals the coupon rate for the bonds, the bonds will sell at par (i.e., at a price equal to the face value). When the market rate of interest is higher than the bonds' coupon rate, the bonds will sell at a discount. When the market rate of interest is lower than the bonds' coupon rate, the bonds will sell at a premium.
- An issuer amortizes any issuance discount or premium on bonds over the life of the bonds.
- If a company redeems bonds before maturity, it reports a gain or loss on debt extinguishment computed as the net carrying amount of the bonds (including bond issuance costs under IFRS) less the amount required to redeem the bonds.
- Debt covenants impose restrictions on borrowers, such as limitations on future borrowing or requirements to maintain a minimum debt-to-equity ratio.
- The carrying amount of bonds is typically the amortized historical cost, which can differ from their fair value.
- Companies are required to disclose the fair value of financial liabilities, including debt. Although permitted to do so, few companies opt to report debt at fair values on the balance sheet.
- Beginning with fiscal year 2019, lessees report a right-of-use asset and a lease liability for all leases longer than one year. An exception under IFRS exists for leases when the underlying asset is of low value.
  - Subsequent to lease inception, the lessee's income statement will include both a depreciation expense on the right-of-use asset and an interest expense on the lease liability for all leases under IFRS and, under US GAAP for finance leases.
  - For lessee accounting, the distinction between finance leases and operating leases exists in US GAAP but not in IFRS. For operating leases under US GAAP, the lessee's income statement will show a single lease expense.
  - Under IFRS, a lessor classifies each lease as either a finance lease or an operating lease. A lease is classified as a finance lease if it "transfers substantially all the risks and rewards incidental to ownership of an underlying asset" and otherwise as an operating lease. For finance leases, but not for operating leases, the lessor derecognizes the underlying leased asset, and recognizes a lease receivable, and recognizes selling profit where applicable. For operating leases, the lessor does not derecognize the underlying asset and recognizes lease receipts as income.
  - Under US GAAP, a lessor classifies a lease in one of three categories: sales-type, direct financing, or operating. The lessor's classification and accounting for operating leases under US GAAP is similar to that under IFRS. For both sales-type and direct financing leases, the lessor derecognizes the underlying asset and recognizes a lease receivable; however, the lessor recognizes selling profit only if the lease is considered a sales-type lease.
- Two types of pension plans are defined contribution plans and defined benefits plans. In a defined contribution plan, the amount of contribution into the plan is specified (i.e., defined), and the amount of pension that is ultimately paid by the plan (received by the retiree) depends on the performance of the plan's assets. In a defined benefit plan, the amount of pension that is ultimately paid by the plan (received by the retiree) is defined, usually according to a benefit formula.
- Under a defined contribution pension plan, the cash payment made into the plan is recognised as pension expense.
- Under both IFRS and US GAAP, companies must report the difference between the defined benefit pension obligation and the pension assets as an asset or liability on the balance sheet. An underfunded defined benefit pension plan is shown as a non-current liability.

- Under IFRS, the change in the defined benefit plan net asset or liability is recognized as a cost of the period, with two components of the change (service cost and net interest expense or income) recognized in profit and loss and one component (remeasurements) of the change recognized in other comprehensive income.
- Under US GAAP, the change in the defined benefit plan net asset or liability is also recognised as a cost of the period with three components of the change (current service costs, interest expense on the beginning pension obligation, and expected return on plan assets) recognized in profit and loss and two components (past service costs and actuarial gains and losses) typically recognized in other comprehensive income.
- Solvency refers to a company's ability to meet its long-term debt obligations.
- In evaluating solvency, leverage ratios focus on the balance sheet and measure the amount of debt financing relative to equity financing.
- In evaluating solvency, coverage ratios focus on the income statement and cash flows and measure the ability of a company to cover its interest payments.

PROBLEMS

1. A company issues €1 million of bonds at face value. When the bonds are issued, the company will record a:
   A. cash inflow from investing activities.
   B. cash inflow from financing activities.
   C. cash inflow from operating activities.

2. At the time of issue of 4.50% coupon bonds, the effective interest rate was 5.00%. The bonds were *most likely* issued at:
   A. par.
   B. a discount.
   C. a premium.

3. Oil Exploration LLC paid $45,000 in printing, legal fees, commissions, and other costs associated with its recent bond issue. It is *most likely* to record these costs on its financial statements as:
   A. an asset under US GAAP and reduction of the carrying value of the debt under IFRS.
   B. a liability under US GAAP and reduction of the carrying value of the debt under IFRS.
   C. a cash outflow from investing activities under both US GAAP and IFRS.

4. A company issues $1,000,000 face value of 10-year bonds on January 1, 2015 when the market interest rate on bonds of comparable risk and terms is 5%. The bonds pay 6% interest annually on December 31. At the time of issue, the bonds payable reflected on the balance sheet is *closest* to:
   A. $926,399.
   B. $1,000,000.
   C. $1,077,217.

5. Midland Brands issues three-year bonds dated January 1, 2015 with a face value of $5,000,000. The market interest rate on bonds of comparable risk and term is 3%. If the bonds pay 2.5% annually on December 31, bonds payable when issued are most likely reported as *closest* to:
   A. $4,929,285.
   B. $5,000,000.
   C. $5,071,401.

6. A firm issues a bond with a coupon rate of 5.00% when the market interest rate is 5.50% on bonds of comparable risk and terms. One year later, the market interest rate increases to 6.00%. Based on this information, the effective interest rate is:
   A. 5.00%.
   B. 5.50%.
   C. 6.00%.

7. On January 1, 2010, Elegant Fragrances Company issues £1,000,000 face value, five-year bonds with annual interest payments of £55,000 to be paid each December 31. The market interest rate is 6.0 percent. Using the effective interest rate method of amortization, Elegant Fragrances is *most likely* to record:
   A. an interest expense of £55,000 on its 2010 income statement.
   B. a liability of £982,674 on the December 31, 2010 balance sheet.
   C. a £58,736 cash outflow from operating activity on the 2010 statement of cash flows.

8. Consolidated Enterprises issues €10 million face value, five-year bonds with a coupon rate of 6.5 percent. At the time of issuance, the market interest rate is 6.0 percent. Using the effective interest rate method of amortization, the carrying value after one year will be *closest* to:
   A. €10.17 million.
   B. €10.21 million.
   C. €10.28 million.

9. A company issues €10,000,000 face value of 10-year bonds dated January 1, 2015 when the market interest rate on bonds of comparable risk and terms is 6%. The bonds pay 7% interest annually on December 31. Based on the effective interest rate method, the interest expense on December 31, 2015 is *closest* to:
   A. €644,161.
   B. €700,000.
   C. €751,521.

10. A company issues $30,000,000 face value of five-year bonds dated January 1, 2015 when the market interest rate on bonds of comparable risk and terms is 5%. The bonds pay 4% interest annually on December 31. Based on the effective interest rate method, the carrying amount of the bonds on December 31, 2015 is *closest* to:
    A. $28,466,099.
    B. $28,800,000.
    C. $28,936,215.

11. Lesp Industries issues five-year bonds dated January 1, 2015 with a face value of $2,000, 000 and 3% coupon rate paid annually on December 31. The market interest rate on

bonds of comparable risk and term is 4%. The sales proceeds of the bonds are $1,910,964. Under the effective interest rate method, the interest expense in 2017 is *closest* to:
A. $77,096.
B. $77,780.
C. $77,807.

12. For a bond issued at a premium, using the effective interest rate method, the:
A. carrying amount increases each year.
B. amortization of the premium increases each year.
C. premium is evenly amortized over the life of the bond.

13. Comte Industries issues $3,000,000 worth of three-year bonds dated January 1, 2015. The bonds pay interest of 5.5% annually on December 31. The market interest rate on bonds of comparable risk and term is 5%. The sales proceeds of the bonds are $3,040,849. Under the straight-line method, the interest expense in the first year is *closest* to:
A. $150,000.
B. $151,384.
C. $152,042.

14. The management of Bank EZ repurchases its own bonds in the open market. They pay €6.5 million for bonds with a face value of €10.0 million and a carrying value of €9.8 million. The bank will *most likely* report:
A. other comprehensive income of €3.3 million.
B. other comprehensive income of €3.5 million.
C. a gain of €3.3 million on the income statement.

15. A company redeems $1,000,000 face value bonds with a carrying value of $990,000. If the call price is 104 the company will:
A. reduce bonds payable by $1,000,000.
B. recognize a loss on the extinguishment of debt of $50,000.
C. recognize a gain on the extinguishment of debt of $10,000.

16. Innovative Inventions, Inc. needs to raise €10 million. If the company chooses to issue zero-coupon bonds, its debt-to-equity ratio will *most likely*:
A. rise as the maturity date approaches.
B. decline as the maturity date approaches.
C. remain constant throughout the life of the bond.

17. Fairmont Golf issued fixed rate debt when interest rates were 6 percent. Rates have since risen to 7 percent. Using only the carrying amount (based on historical cost) reported on the balance sheet to analyze the company's financial position would *most likely* cause an analyst to:
A. overestimate Fairmont's economic liabilities.
B. underestimate Fairmont's economic liabilities.
C. underestimate Fairmont's interest coverage ratio.

18. Which of the following is an example of an affirmative debt covenant? The borrower is:
A. prohibited from entering into mergers.
B. prevented from issuing excessive additional debt.
C. required to perform regular maintenance on equipment pledged as collateral.

19. Debt covenants are *least likely* to place restrictions on the issuer's ability to:
    A. pay dividends.
    B. issue additional debt.
    C. issue additional equity.

20. Regarding a company's debt obligations, which of the following is *most likely* presented on the balance sheet?
    A. Effective interest rate.
    B. Maturity dates for debt obligations.
    C. The portion of long-term debt due in the next 12 months.

21. Compared to using a finance lease, a lessee that makes use of an operating lease will *most likely* report higher:
    A. debt.
    B. rent expense.
    C. cash flow from operating activity.

22. Which of the following is *most likely* a lessee's disclosure about operating leases?
    A. Lease liabilities.
    B. Future obligations by maturity.
    C. Net carrying amounts of leased assets.

23. For a lessor, the leased asset appears on the balance sheet and continues to be depreciated when the lease is classified as:
    A. a sales-type lease.
    B. an operating lease.
    C. a financing lease.

24. Under US GAAP, a lessor's reported revenues at lease inception will be *highest* if the lease is classified as:
    A. a sales-type lease.
    B. an operating lease.
    C. a direct financing lease.

25. A lessor will record interest income if a lease is classified as:
    A. a capital lease.
    B. an operating lease.
    C. either a capital or an operating lease.

26. Compared with a finance lease, an operating lease:
    A. is similar to renting an asset.
    B. is equivalent to the purchase of an asset.
    C. term is for the majority of the economic life of the asset.

27. Under US GAAP, which of the following would require the lessee to classify a lease as a capital lease?
    A. The term is 60% of the useful life of the asset.
    B. The lease contains an option to purchase the asset at fair value.
    C. The present value of the lease payments is 95% of the fair value.

28. A lessee that enters into a finance lease will report the:
    A. lease payable on its balance sheet.
    B. full lease payment on its income statement.
    C. full lease payment as an operating cash flow.

29. A company enters into a finance lease agreement to acquire the use of an asset for three years with lease payments of €19,000,000 starting next year. The leased asset has a fair market value of €49,000,000, and the present value of the lease payments is €47,250,188. Based on this information, the value of the lease payable reported on the company's balance sheet is *closest* to:
    A. €47,250,188.
    B. €49,000,000.
    C. €57,000,000.

30. Which of the following *best* describes reporting and disclosure requirements for a company that enters into an operating lease as the lessee? The operating lease obligation is:
    A. reported as a receivable on the balance sheet.
    B. disclosed in notes to the financial statements.
    C. reported as a component of debt on the balance sheet.

31. Cavalier Copper Mines has $840 million in total liabilities and $520 million in shareholders' equity. It discloses operating lease commitments over the next five years with a present value of $100 million. If the lease commitments are treated as debt, the debt-to-total-capital ratio is *closest* to:
    A. 0.58.
    B. 0.62.
    C. 0.64.

32. The following presents selected financial information for a company:

	$ Millions
Short-term borrowing	4,231
Current portion of long-term interest-bearing debt	29
Long-term interest-bearing debt	925
Average shareholders' equity	18,752
Average total assets	45,981

    The financial leverage ratio is *closest* to:
    A. 0.113.
    B. 0.277.
    C. 2.452.

33. An analyst evaluating three industrial companies calculates the following ratios:

	Company A	Company B	Company C
Debt-to-Equity	23.5%	22.5%	52.5%
Interest Coverage	15.6	49.5	45.5

The company with both the lowest financial leverage and the greatest ability to meet interest payments is:
A. Company A.
B. Company B.
C. Company C.

34. An analyst evaluating a company's solvency gathers the following information:

	$ Millions
Short-term interest-bearing debt	1,258
Long-term interest-bearing debt	321
Total shareholder's equity	4,285
Total assets	8,750
EBIT	2,504
Interest payments	52

The company's debt-to-assets ratio is *closest* to:
A. 0.18.
B. 0.27.
C. 0.37.

35. Penben Corporation has a defined benefit pension plan. At December 31, its pension obligation is €10 million, and pension assets are €9 million. Under either IFRS or US GAAP, the reporting on the balance sheet would be *closest* to which of the following?
A. €10 million is shown as a liability, and €9 million appears as an asset.
B. €1 million is shown as a net pension obligation.
C. Pension assets and obligations are not required to be shown on the balance sheet but only disclosed in footnotes.

36. The following information is associated with a company that offers its employees a defined benefit plan:

Fair value of fund's assets	$1,500,000,000
Estimated pension obligations	$2,600,000,000
Present value of estimated pension obligations	$1,200,000,000

Based on this information, the company's balance sheet will present a net pension:
A. asset of $300,000,000.
B. asset of $1,400,000,000.
C. liability of $1,100,000,000.

CHAPTER 11

FINANCIAL REPORTING QUALITY

LEARNING OUTCOMES

After completing this chapter, you will be able to do the following:

- distinguish between financial reporting quality and quality of reported results (including quality of earnings, cash flow, and balance sheet items);
- describe a spectrum for assessing financial reporting quality;
- distinguish between conservative and aggressive accounting;
- describe motivations that might cause management to issue financial reports that are not high quality;
- describe conditions that are conducive to issuing low-quality, or even fraudulent, financial reports;
- describe mechanisms that determine financial reporting quality and the potential limitations of those mechanisms;
- describe presentation choices, including non-GAAP measures, that could be used to influence an analyst's opinion;
- describe accounting methods (choices and estimates) that could be used to manage earnings, cash flow, and balance sheet items;
- describe accounting warning signs and methods for detecting manipulation of information in financial reports.

SUMMARY OVERVIEW

Financial reporting quality varies across companies. The ability to assess the quality of a company's financial reporting is an important skill for analysts. Indications of low-quality financial reporting can prompt an analyst to maintain heightened skepticism when reading a company's reports, to review disclosures critically when undertaking financial statement analysis, and to incorporate appropriate adjustments in assessments of past performance and forecasts of future performance.

- Financial reporting quality can be thought of as spanning a continuum from the highest (containing information that is relevant, correct, complete, and unbiased) to the lowest (containing information that is not just biased or incomplete but possibly pure fabrication).
- *Reporting quality*, the focus of this chapter, pertains to the information disclosed. High-quality reporting represents the economic reality of the company's activities during the reporting period and the company's financial condition at the end of the period.
- *Results quality* (commonly referred to as earnings quality) pertains to the earnings and cash generated by the company's actual economic activities and the resulting financial condition, relative to expectations of current and future financial performance. Quality earnings are regarded as being sustainable, providing a sound platform for forecasts.
- An aspect of financial reporting quality is the degree to which accounting choices are conservative or aggressive. "Aggressive" typically refers to choices that aim to enhance the company's reported performance and financial position by inflating the amount of revenues, earnings, and/or operating cash flow reported in the period; or by decreasing expenses for the period and/or the amount of debt reported on the balance sheet.
- Conservatism in financial reports can result from either (1) accounting standards that specifically require a conservative treatment of a transaction or an event or (2) judgments made by managers when applying accounting standards that result in conservative results.
- Managers may be motivated to issue less-than-high-quality financial reports in order to mask poor performance, to boost the stock price, to increase personal compensation, and/or to avoid violation of debt covenants.
- Conditions that are conducive to the issuance of low-quality financial reports include a cultural environment that result in fewer or less transparent financial disclosures, book/tax conformity that shifts emphasis toward legal compliance and away from fair presentation, and limited capital markets regulation.
- Mechanisms that discipline financial reporting quality include the free market and incentives for companies to minimize cost of capital, auditors, contract provisions specifically tailored to penalize misreporting, and enforcement by regulatory entities.
- Pro forma earnings (also commonly referred to as non-GAAP or non-IFRS earnings) adjust earnings as reported on the income statement. Pro forma earnings that exclude negative items are a hallmark of aggressive presentation choices.
- Companies are required to make additional disclosures when presenting any non-GAAP or non-IFRS metric.
- Managers' considerable flexibility in choosing their companies' accounting policies and in formulating estimates provides opportunities for aggressive accounting.
- Examples of accounting choices that affect earnings and balance sheets include inventory cost flow assumptions, estimates of uncollectible accounts receivable, estimated realizability of deferred tax assets, depreciation method, estimated salvage value of depreciable assets, and estimated useful life of depreciable assets.
- Cash from operations is a metric of interest to investors that can be enhanced by operating choices, such as stretching accounts payable, and potentially by classification choices.

PROBLEMS

1. In contrast to earnings quality, financial reporting quality *most likely* pertains to:
   A. sustainable earnings.
   B. relevant information.
   C. adequate return on investment.

2. The information provided by a low-quality financial report will *most likely*:
   A. decrease company value.
   B. indicate earnings are not sustainable.
   C. impede the assessment of earnings quality.

3. To properly assess a company's past performance, an analyst requires:
   A. high earnings quality.
   B. high financial reporting quality.
   C. both high earnings quality and high financial reporting quality.

4. Low quality earnings *most likely* reflect:
   A. low-quality financial reporting.
   B. company activities which are unsustainable.
   C. information that does not faithfully represent company activities.

5. Earnings that result from non-recurring activities *most likely* indicate:
   A. lower-quality earnings.
   B. biased accounting choices.
   C. lower-quality financial reporting.

6. Which attribute of financial reports would *most likely* be evaluated as optimal in the financial reporting spectrum?
   A. Conservative accounting choices
   B. Sustainable and adequate returns
   C. Emphasized pro forma earnings measures

7. Financial reports of the lowest level of quality reflect:
   A. fictitious events.
   B. biased accounting choices.
   C. accounting that is non-compliant with GAAP.

8. When earnings are increased by deferring research and development (R&D) investments until the next reporting period, this choice is considered:
   A. non-compliant accounting.
   B. earnings management as a result of a real action.
   C. earnings management as a result of an accounting choice.

9. A high-quality financial report may reflect:
   A. earnings smoothing.
   B. low earnings quality.
   C. understatement of asset impairment.

10. If a particular accounting choice is considered aggressive in nature, then the financial performance for the reporting period would *most likely*:
    A. be neutral.
    B. exhibit an upward bias.
    C. exhibit a downward bias.

11. Which of the following is *most likely* to reflect conservative accounting choices?
    A. Decreased reported earnings in later periods
    B. Increased reported earnings in the period under review
    C. Increased debt reported on the balance sheet at the end of the current period

12. Which of the following is *most likely* to be considered a potential benefit of accounting conservatism?
    A. A reduction in litigation costs
    B. Less biased financial reporting
    C. An increase in current period reported performance

13. Which of the following statements *most likely* describes a situation that would motivate a manager to issue low-quality financial reports?
    A. The manager's compensation is tied to stock price performance.
    B. The manager has increased the market share of products significantly.
    C. The manager has brought the company's profitability to a level higher than competitors.

14. Which of the following concerns would *most likely* motivate a manager to make conservative accounting choices?
    A. Attention to future career opportunities
    B. Expected weakening in the business environment
    C. Debt covenant violation risk in the current period

15. Which of the following conditions *best* explains why a company's manager would obtain legal, accounting, and board level approval prior to issuing low-quality financial reports?
    A. Motivation
    B. Opportunity
    C. Rationalization

16. A company is experiencing a period of strong financial performance. In order to increase the likelihood of exceeding analysts' earnings forecasts in the next reporting period, the company would *most likely* undertake accounting choices for the period under review that:
    A. inflate reported revenue.
    B. delay expense recognition.
    C. accelerate expense recognition.

17. Which of the following situations represents a motivation, rather than an opportunity, to issue low-quality financial reports?
    A. Poor internal controls
    B. Search for a personal bonus
    C. Inattentive board of directors

18. Which of the following situations will *most likely* motivate managers to inflate reported earnings?
    A. Possibility of bond covenant violation
    B. Earnings in excess of analysts' forecasts
    C. Earnings that are greater than the previous year

19. Which of the following *best* describes an opportunity for management to issue low-quality financial reports?
    A. Ineffective board of directors
    B. Pressure to achieve some performance level
    C. Corporate concerns about financing in the future

20. An audit opinion of a company's financial reports is *most likely* intended to:
    A. detect fraud.
    B. reveal misstatements.
    C. assure that financial information is presented fairly.

21. If a company uses a non-GAAP financial measure in an SEC filing, then the company must:
    A. give more prominence to the non-GAAP measure if it is used in earnings releases.
    B. provide a reconciliation of the non-GAAP measure and equivalent GAAP measure.
    C. exclude charges requiring cash settlement from any non-GAAP liquidity measures.

22. A company wishing to increase earnings in the reporting period may choose to:
    A. decrease the useful life of depreciable assets.
    B. lower estimates of uncollectible accounts receivables.
    C. classify a purchase as an expense rather than a capital expenditure.

23. Bias in revenue recognition would *least likely* be suspected if:
    A. the firm engages in barter transactions.
    B. reported revenue is higher than the previous quarter.
    C. revenue is recognized before goods are shipped to customers.

24. Which technique *most likely* increases the cash flow provided by operations?
    A. Stretching the accounts payable credit period
    B. Applying all non-cash discount amortization against interest capitalized
    C. Shifting classification of interest paid from financing to operating cash flows

25. Which of the following is an indication that a company may be recognizing revenue prematurely? Relative to its competitors, the company's:
    A. asset turnover is decreasing.
    B. receivables turnover is increasing.
    C. days sales outstanding is increasing.

26. Which of the following would *most likely* signal that a company may be using aggressive accrual accounting policies to shift current expenses to later periods? Over the last five-year period, the ratio of cash flow to net income has:
    A. increased each year.
    B. decreased each year.
    C. fluctuated from year to year.

27. An analyst reviewing a firm with a large reported restructuring charge to earnings should:
    A. view expenses reported in prior years as overstated.
    B. disregard it because it is solely related to past events.
    C. consider making pro forma adjustments to prior years' earnings.

CHAPTER 12

APPLICATIONS OF FINANCIAL STATEMENT ANALYSIS

LEARNING OUTCOMES

After completing this chapter, you will be able to do the following:

- evaluate a company's past financial performance and explain how a company's strategy is reflected in past financial performance;
- forecast a company's future net income and cash flow;
- describe the role of financial statement analysis in assessing the credit quality of a potential debt investment;
- describe the use of financial statement analysis in screening for potential equity investments;
- explain appropriate analyst adjustments to a company's financial statements to facilitate comparison with another company.

SUMMARY OVERVIEW

This chapter described selected applications of financial statement analysis, including the evaluation of past financial performance, the projection of future financial performance, the assessment of credit risk, and the screening of potential equity investments. In addition, the chapter introduced analyst adjustments to reported financials. In all cases, the analyst needs to have a good understanding of the financial reporting standards under which the financial statements were prepared. Because standards evolve over time, analysts must stay current in order to make good investment decisions.

The main points in the chapter are as follows:

- Evaluating a company's historical performance addresses not only what happened but also the causes behind the company's performance and how the performance reflects the company's strategy.
- The projection of a company's future net income and cash flow often begins with a top-down sales forecast in which the analyst forecasts industry sales and the company's market share.

By projecting profit margins or expenses and the level of investment in working and fixed capital needed to support projected sales, the analyst can forecast net income and cash flow.

- Projections of future performance are needed for discounted cash flow valuation of equity and are often needed in credit analysis to assess a borrower's ability to repay interest and principal of a debt obligation.
- Credit analysis uses financial statement analysis to evaluate credit-relevant factors, including tolerance for leverage, operational stability, and margin stability.
- When ratios constructed from financial statement data and market data are used to screen for potential equity investments, fundamental decisions include which metrics to use as screens, how many metrics to include, what values of those metrics to use as cutoff points, and what weighting to give each metric.
- Analyst adjustments to a company's reported financial statements are sometimes necessary (e.g., when comparing companies that use different accounting methods or assumptions). Adjustments can include those related to investments; inventory; property, plant, and equipment; and goodwill.

PROBLEMS

1. Projecting profit margins into the future on the basis of past results would be *most* reliable when the company:
   A. is in the commodities business.
   B. operates in a single business segment.
   C. is a large, diversified company operating in mature industries.

2. Galambos Corporation had an average receivables collection period of 19 days in 2003. Galambos has stated that it wants to decrease its collection period in 2004 to match the industry average of 15 days. Credit sales in 2003 were $300 million, and analysts expect credit sales to increase to $400 million in 2004. To achieve the company's goal of decreasing the collection period, the change in the average accounts receivable balance from 2003 to 2004 that must occur is *closest* to:
   A. −$420,000.
   B. $420,000.
   C. $836,000.

3. Credit analysts are likely to consider which of the following in making a rating recommendation?
   A. Business risk but not financial risk
   B. Financial risk but not business risk
   C. Both business risk and financial risk

4. When screening for potential equity investments based on return on equity, to control risk, an analyst would be *most likely* to include a criterion that requires:
   A. positive net income.
   B. negative net income.
   C. negative shareholders' equity.

5. One concern when screening for stocks with low price-to-earnings ratios is that companies with low P/Es may be financially weak. What criterion might an analyst include to avoid inadvertently selecting weak companies?
   A. Net income less than zero
   B. Debt-to-total assets ratio below a certain cutoff point
   C. Current-year sales growth lower than prior-year sales growth

6. When a database eliminates companies that cease to exist because of a merger or bankruptcy, this can result in:
   A. look-ahead bias.
   B. back-testing bias.
   C. survivorship bias.

7. In a comprehensive financial analysis, financial statements should be:
   A. used as reported without adjustment.
   B. adjusted after completing ratio analysis.
   C. adjusted for differences in accounting standards, such as international financial reporting standards and US generally accepted accounting principles.

8. When comparing a US company that uses the last in, first out (LIFO) method of inventory with companies that prepare their financial statements under international financial reporting standards (IFRS), analysts should be aware that according to IFRS, the LIFO method of inventory:
   A. is never acceptable.
   B. is always acceptable.
   C. is acceptable when applied to finished goods inventory only.

9. An analyst is evaluating the balance sheet of a US company that uses last in, first out (LIFO) accounting for inventory. The analyst collects the following data:

	Dec. 31, 2005	Dec. 31, 2006
Inventory reported on balance sheet	$500,000	$600,000
LIFO reserve	$50,000	$70,000
Average tax rate	30%	30%

After adjusting the amounts to convert to the first in, first out (FIFO) method, inventory at December 31, 2006 would be *closest* to:
   A. $600,000.
   B. $620,000.
   C. $670,000.

10. An analyst gathered the following data for a company ($ millions):

	Dec. 31, 2000	Dec. 31, 2001
Gross investment in fixed assets	$2.8	$2.8
Accumulated depreciation	$1.2	$1.6

The average age and average depreciable life of the company's fixed assets at the end of 2001 are *closest* to:

	Average Age	Average Depreciable Life
A.	1.75 years	7 years
B.	1.75 years	14 years
C.	4.00 years	7 years

11. To compute tangible book value, an analyst would:
    A. add goodwill to stockholders' equity.
    B. add all intangible assets to stockholders' equity.
    C. subtract all intangible assets from stockholders' equity.

12. Which of the following is an off-balance-sheet financing technique? The use of:
    A. capital leases.
    B. operating leases.
    C. the last in, first out inventory method.

13. To better evaluate the solvency of a company, an analyst would *most likely* add to total liabilities:
    A. the present value of future capital lease payments.
    B. the total amount of future operating lease payments.
    C. the present value of future operating lease payments.

CHAPTER 13

INTERCORPORATE INVESTMENTS

LEARNING OUTCOMES

After completing this chapter, you will be able to do the following:

- describe the classification, measurement, and disclosure under International Financial Reporting Standards (IFRS) for 1) investments in financial assets, 2) investments in associates, 3) joint ventures, 4) business combinations, and 5) special purpose and variable interest entities;
- distinguish between IFRS and US GAAP in the classification, measurement, and disclosure of investments in financial assets, investments in associates, joint ventures, business combinations, and special purpose and variable interest entities;
- analyze how different methods used to account for intercorporate investments affect financial statements and ratios.

SUMMARY OVERVIEW

Intercompany investments play a significant role in business activities and create significant challenges for the analyst in assessing company performance. Investments in other companies can take five basic forms: investments in financial assets, investments in associates, joint ventures, business combinations, and investments in special purpose and variable interest entities. Key concepts are as follows:

- Investments in financial assets are those in which the investor has no significant influence. They can be measured and reported as
  - fair value through profit or loss;
  - fair value through other comprehensive income; or
  - amortized cost.
  IFRS and US GAAP treat investments in financial assets in a similar manner.

- Investments in associates and joint ventures are those in which the investor has significant influence, but not control, over the investee's business activities. Because the investor can exert significant influence over financial and operating policy decisions, IFRS and US GAAP require the equity method of accounting because it provides a more objective basis for reporting investment income.
- The equity method requires the investor to recognize income as earned rather than when dividends are received.
- The equity investment is carried at cost, plus its share of post-acquisition income (after adjustments) less dividends received.
- The equity investment is reported as a single line item on the balance sheet and on the income statement.
- IFRS and US GAAP accounting standards require the use of the acquisition method to account for business combinations. Fair value of the consideration given is the appropriate measurement for identifiable assets and liabilities acquired in the business combination.
- Goodwill is the difference between the acquisition value and the fair value of the target's identifiable net tangible and intangible assets. Because it is considered to have an indefinite life, it is not amortized. Instead, it is evaluated at least annually for impairment. Impairment losses are reported on the income statement. IFRS use a one-step approach to determine and measure the impairment loss, whereas US GAAP uses a two-step approach.
- If the acquiring company acquires less than 100%, non-controlling (minority) shareholders' interests are reported on the consolidated financial statements. IFRS allows the non-controlling interest to be measured at either its fair value (full goodwill) or at the non-controlling interest's proportionate share of the acquiree's identifiable net assets (partial goodwill). US GAAP requires the non-controlling interest to be measured at fair value (full goodwill).
- Consolidated financial statements are prepared in each reporting period.
- Special purpose entities (SPEs) and variable interest entities (VIEs) are required to be consolidated by the entity which is expected to absorb the majority of the expected losses or receive the majority of expected residual benefits.

PROBLEMS

The following information relates to Questions 1–5

Cinnamon, Inc. is a diversified manufacturing company headquartered in the United Kingdom. It complies with IFRS. In 2017, Cinnamon held a 19 percent passive equity ownership interest in Cambridge Processing. In December 2017, Cinnamon announced that it would be increasing its ownership interest to 50 percent effective January 1, 2018 through a cash purchase. Cinnamon and Cambridge have no intercompany transactions.

Peter Lubbock, an analyst following both Cinnamon and Cambridge, is curious how the increased stake will affect Cinnamon's consolidated financial statements. He asks Cinnamon's CFO how the company will account for the investment, and is told that the decision has not yet been made. Lubbock decides to use his existing forecasts for both companies' financial statements to compare the outcomes of alternative accounting treatments.

Lubbock assembles abbreviated financial statement data for Cinnamon (Exhibit 1) and Cambridge (Exhibit 2) for this purpose.

EXHIBIT 1   Selected Financial Statement Information for Cinnamon, Inc. (£ Millions)

Year ending December 31	2017	2018*
Revenue	1,400	1,575
Operating income	126	142
Net income	62	69
December 31	2017	2018*
Total assets	1,170	1,317
Shareholders' equity	616	685

*Estimates made prior to announcement of increased stake in Cambridge.

EXHIBIT 2   Selected Financial Statement Information for Cambridge Processing (£ Millions)

Year ending December 31	2017	2018*
Revenue	1,000	1,100
Operating income	80	88
Net income	40	44
Dividends paid	20	22
December 31	2017	2018*
Total assets	800	836
Shareholders' equity	440	462

*Estimates made prior to announcement of increased stake by Cinnamon.

1. In 2018, if Cinnamon is deemed to have control over Cambridge, it will *most likely* account for its investment in Cambridge using:
   A. the equity method.
   B. the acquisition method.
   C. proportionate consolidation.

2. At December 31, 2018, Cinnamon's total shareholders' equity on its balance sheet would *most likely* be:
   A. highest if Cinnamon is deemed to have control of Cambridge.
   B. independent of the accounting method used for the investment in Cambridge.
   C. highest if Cinnamon is deemed to have significant influence over Cambridge.

3. In 2018, Cinnamon's net profit margin would be *highest* if:
   A. it is deemed to have control of Cambridge.
   B. it had not increased its stake in Cambridge.
   C. it is deemed to have significant influence over Cambridge.

4. At December 31, 2018, assuming control and recognition of goodwill, Cinnamon's reported debt to equity ratio will *most likely* be highest if it accounts for its investment in Cambridge using the:
   A. equity method.
   B. full goodwill method.
   C. partial goodwill method.

5. Compared to Cinnamon's operating margin in 2017, if it is deemed to have control of Cambridge, its operating margin in 2018 will *most likely* be:
   A. lower.
   B. higher.
   C. the same.

The following information relates to Questions 6–10

Zimt, AG is a consumer products manufacturer headquartered in Austria. It complies with IFRS. In 2017, Zimt held a 10 percent passive stake in Oxbow Limited. In December 2017, Zimt announced that it would be increasing its ownership to 50 percent effective January 1, 2018.

Franz Gelblum, an analyst following both Zimt and Oxbow, is curious how the increased stake will affect Zimt's consolidated financial statements. Because Gelblum is uncertain how the company will account for the increased stake, he uses his existing forecasts for both companies' financial statements to compare various alternative outcomes.

Gelblum gathers abbreviated financial statement data for Zimt (Exhibit 1) and Oxbow (Exhibit 2) for this purpose.

EXHIBIT 1   Selected Financial Statement Estimates for Zimt AG (€ Millions)

Year ending December 31	2017	2018*
Revenue	1,500	1,700
Operating income	135	153
Net income	66	75
31 December	2017	2018*
Total assets	1,254	1,421
Shareholders' equity	660	735

*Estimates made prior to announcement of increased stake in Oxbow.

EXHIBIT 2   Selected Financial Statement Estimates for Oxbow Limited (€ Millions)

Year ending December 31	2017	2018*
Revenue	1,200	1,350
Operating income	120	135
Net income	60	68
Dividends paid	20	22
December 31	2017	2018*
Total assets	1,200	1,283
Shareholders' equity	660	706

*Estimates made prior to announcement of increased stake by Zimt.

6. At December 31, 2018, Zimt's total assets balance would *most likely* be:
   A. highest if Zimt is deemed to have control of Oxbow.
   B. highest if Zimt is deemed to have significant influence over Oxbow.
   C. unaffected by the accounting method used for the investment in Oxbow.

7. Based on Gelblum's estimates, if Zimt is deemed to have significant influence over Oxbow, its 2018 net income (in € millions) would be *closest* to:
   A. €75.
   B. €109.
   C. €143.

8. Based on Gelblum's estimates, if Zimt is deemed to have joint control of Oxbow, and Zimt uses the proportionate consolidation method, its December 31, 2018 total liabilities (in € millions) will *most likely* be *closest* to:
   A. €686.
   B. €975.
   C. €1,263.

9. Based on Gelblum's estimates, if Zimt is deemed to have control over Oxbow, its 2018 consolidated sales (in € millions) will be *closest* to:
   A. €1,700.
   B. €2,375.
   C. €3,050.

10. Based on Gelblum's estimates, Zimt's net income in 2018 will *most likely* be:
    A. highest if Zimt is deemed to have control of Oxbow.
    B. highest if Zimt is deemed to have significant influence over Oxbow.
    C. independent of the accounting method used for the investment in Oxbow.

The following information relates to Questions 11–16

Burton Howard, CFA, is an equity analyst with Maplewood Securities. Howard is preparing a research report on Confabulated Materials, SA, a publicly traded company based in France that complies with IFRS 9. As part of his analysis, Howard has assembled data gathered from the financial statement footnotes of Confabulated's 2018 Annual Report and from discussions with company management. Howard is concerned about the effect of this information on Confabulated's future earnings.

Information about Confabulated's investment portfolio for the years ended December 31, 2017 and 2018 is presented in Exhibit 1. As part of his research, Howard is considering the possible effect on reported income of Confabulated's accounting classification for fixed income investments.

EXHIBIT 1   Confabulated's Investment Portfolio (€ Thousands)

Characteristic	Bugle AG	Cathay Corp	Dumas SA
Classification	FVPL	FVOCI	Amortized cost
Cost*	€25,000	€40,000	€50,000
Market value, December 31, 2017	29,000	38,000	54,000
Market value, December 31, 2018	28,000	37,000	55,000

* All securities were acquired at par value.

In addition, Confabulated's annual report discusses a transaction under which receivables were securitized through a special purpose entity (SPE) for Confabulated's benefit.

11. The balance sheet carrying value of Confabulated's investment portfolio (in € thousands) at December 31, 2018 is *closest* to:
    A. 112,000.
    B. 115,000.
    C. 118,000.

12. The balance sheet carrying value of Confabulated's investment portfolio at December 31, 2018 would have been higher if which of the securities had been reclassified as FVPL security?
    A. Bugle.
    B. Cathay.
    C. Dumas.

13. Compared to Confabulated's reported interest income in 2018, if Dumas had been classified as FVPL, the interest income would have been:
    A. lower.
    B. the same.
    C. higher.

14. Compared to Confabulated's reported earnings before taxes in 2018, if Dumas had been classified as a FVPL security, the earnings before taxes (in € thousands) would have been:
    A. the same.
    B. €1,000 lower.
    C. €3,000 higher.

15. Confabulated's reported interest income would be lower if the cost was the same but the par value (in € thousands) of:
    A. Bugle was €28,000.
    B. Cathay was €37,000.
    C. Dumas was €55,000.

16. Confabulated's special purpose entity is *most likely* to be:
    A. held off-balance sheet.
    B. consolidated on Confabulated's financial statements.
    C. consolidated on Confabulated's financial statements only if it is a "qualifying SPE."

The following information relates to Questions 17–22

BetterCare Hospitals, Inc. operates a chain of hospitals throughout the United States. The company has been expanding by acquiring local hospitals. Its largest acquisition, that of Statewide Medical, was made in 2001 under the pooling of interests method. BetterCare complies with US GAAP.

BetterCare is currently forming a 50/50 joint venture with Supreme Healthcare under which the companies will share control of several hospitals. BetterCare plans to use the equity method to account for the joint venture. Supreme Healthcare complies with IFRS and will use the proportionate consolidation method to account for the joint venture.

Erik Ohalin is an equity analyst who covers both companies. He has estimated the joint venture's financial information for 2018 in order to prepare his estimates of each company's earnings and financial performance. This information is presented in Exhibit 1.

EXHIBIT 1   Selected Financial Statement
Forecasts for Joint Venture ($ Millions)

Year ending December 31	2018
Revenue	1,430
Operating income	128
Net income	62
December 31	2018
Total assets	1,500
Shareholders' equity	740

Supreme Healthcare recently announced it had formed a special purpose entity through which it plans to sell up to $100 million of its accounts receivable. Supreme Healthcare has no voting interest in the SPE, but it is expected to absorb any losses that it may incur. Ohalin wants to estimate the impact this will have on Supreme Healthcare's consolidated financial statements.

17. Compared to accounting principles currently in use, the pooling method BetterCare used for its Statewide Medical acquisition has *most likely* caused its reported:
    A. revenue to be higher.
    B. total equity to be lower.
    C. total assets to be higher.

18. Based on Ohalin's estimates, the amount of joint venture revenue (in $ millions) included on BetterCare's consolidated 2018 financial statements should be *closest* to:
    A. $0.
    B. $715.
    C. $1,430.

19. Based on Ohalin's estimates, the amount of joint venture net income included on the consolidated financial statements of each venturer will *most likely* be:
    A. higher for BetterCare.
    B. higher for Supreme Healthcare.
    C. the same for both BetterCare and Supreme Healthcare.

20. Based on Ohalin's estimates, the amount of the joint venture's December 31, 2018 total assets (in $ millions) that will be included on Supreme Healthcare's consolidated financial statements will be *closest* to:
    A. $0.
    B. $750.
    C. $1,500.

21. Based on Ohalin's estimates, the amount of joint venture shareholders' equity at December 31, 2018 included on the consolidated financial statements of each venturer will *most likely* be:
    A. higher for BetterCare.
    B. higher for Supreme Healthcare.
    C. the same for both BetterCare and Supreme Healthcare.

22. If Supreme Healthcare sells its receivables to the SPE, its consolidated financial results will *most likely* show:
    A. a higher revenue for 2018.
    B. the same cash balance at December 31, 2018.
    C. the same accounts receivable balance at December 31, 2018.

The following information relates to Questions 23–28

Percy Byron, CFA, is an equity analyst with a UK-based investment firm. One firm Byron follows is NinMount PLC, a UK-based company. On December 31, 2008, NinMount paid £320 million to purchase a 50 percent stake in Boswell Company. The excess of the purchase price over the fair value of Boswell's net assets was attributable to previously unrecorded licenses. These licenses were estimated to have an economic life of six years. The fair value of Boswell's assets and liabilities other than licenses was equal to their recorded book values. NinMount and Boswell both use the pound sterling as their reporting currency and prepare their financial statements in accordance with IFRS.

Byron is concerned whether the investment should affect his "buy" rating on NinMount common stock. He knows NinMount could choose one of several accounting methods to report the results of its investment, but NinMount has not announced which method it will use. Byron forecasts that both companies' 2019 financial results (excluding any merger accounting adjustments) will be identical to those of 2018.

NinMount's and Boswell's condensed income statements for the year ended December 31, 2018, and condensed balance sheets at December 31, 2018, are presented in Exhibits 1 and 2, respectively.

EXHIBIT 1   NinMount PLC and Boswell Company Income Statements for the Year Ended December 31, 2018 (£ millions)

	NinMount	Boswell
Net sales	950	510
Cost of goods sold	(495)	(305)
Selling expenses	(50)	(15)
Administrative expenses	(136)	(49)
Depreciation & amortization expense	(102)	(92)
Interest expense	(42)	(32)
Income before taxes	125	17
Income tax expense	(50)	(7)
Net income	75	10

EXHIBIT 2 NinMount PLC and Boswell Company Balance Sheets at December 31, 2018 (£ millions)

	NinMount	Boswell
Cash	50	20
Receivables—net	70	45
Inventory	130	75
Total current assets	250	140
Property, plant, & equipment—net	1,570	930
Investment in Boswell	320	—
Total assets	2,140	1,070
Current liabilities	110	90
Long-term debt	600	400
Total liabilities	710	490
Common stock	850	535
Retained earnings	580	45
Total equity	1,430	580
Total liabilities and equity	2,140	1,070

Note: Balance sheets reflect the purchase price paid by NinMount, but do not yet consider the impact of the accounting method choice.

23. NinMount's current ratio on December 31, 2018 *most likely* will be highest if the results of the acquisition are reported using:
    A. the equity method.
    B. consolidation with full goodwill.
    C. consolidation with partial goodwill.

24. NinMount's long-term debt to equity ratio on December 31, 2018 *most likely* will be lowest if the results of the acquisition are reported using:
    A. the equity method.
    B. consolidation with full goodwill.
    C. consolidation with partial goodwill.

25. Based on Byron's forecast, if NinMount deems it has acquired control of Boswell, NinMount's consolidated 2019 depreciation and amortization expense (in £ millions) will be *closest* to:
    A. 102.
    B. 148.
    C. 204.

26. Based on Byron's forecast, NinMount's net profit margin for 2019 *most likely* will be highest if the results of the acquisition are reported using:
    A. the equity method.
    B. consolidation with full goodwill.
    C. consolidation with partial goodwill.

27. Based on Byron's forecast, NinMount's 2019 return on beginning equity *most likely* will be the same under:
   A. either of the consolidations, but different under the equity method.
   B. the equity method, consolidation with full goodwill, and consolidation with partial goodwill.
   C. none of the equity method, consolidation with full goodwill, or consolidation with partial goodwill.

28. Based on Byron's forecast, NinMount's 2019 total asset turnover ratio on beginning assets under the equity method is *most likely*:
   A. lower than if the results are reported using consolidation.
   B. the same as if the results are reported using consolidation.
   C. higher than if the results are reported using consolidation.

The following information relates to Questions 29–36

John Thronen is an analyst in the research department of an international securities firm. He is preparing a research report on Topmaker, Inc., a publicly traded company that complies with IFRS.

On January 1, 2018, Topmaker invested $11 million in Blanca Co. debt securities (with a 5.0% stated coupon on par value, and interest payable each December 31). The par value of the securities is $10 million, and the market interest rate in effect when the bonds were purchased was 4.0%. Topmaker designates the investment as amortized cost. As of December 31, 2018, the fair value of the securities is $12 million.

Blanca Co. wants to raise $40 million in capital by borrowing against its financial receivables. Blanca plans to create a special-purpose entity (SPE), invest $10 million in the SPE, have the SPE borrow $40 million, and then use the funds to purchase $50 million of receivables from Blanca. Blanca meets the definition of control and plans to consolidate the SPE. Blanca's balance sheet is presented in Exhibit 1.

EXHIBIT 1   Blanca Co. Balance Sheet at December 31, 2018 ($ millions)

Cash	20	Current liabilities	25
Accounts receivable	50	Noncurrent liabilities	30
Other assets	30	Shareholders' equity	45
Total assets	**100**	**Total liabilities and equity**	**100**

Also on January 1, 2018, Topmaker acquired a 15% equity interest with voting power in Rainer Co. for $300 million. Topmaker has representation on Rainer's board of directors and participates in Rainer's policymaking process. Thronen believes that Topmaker underestimated the goodwill and balance sheet value of its investment account in Rainer. To estimate these figures, Thronen gathers selected financial information for Rainer as of December 31, 2018 in Exhibit 2. The plant and equipment are depreciated on a straight-line basis and have 10 years of remaining life.

EXHIBIT 2   Selected Financial Data for Rainer Co., Year
Ending December 31, 2018 ($ millions)

	Book Value	Fair Value
Revenue	1,740	N/A
Net income	360	N/A
Dividends paid	220	N/A
Plant and equipment	2,900	3,160
Total assets	3,170	3,430
Liabilities	1,830	1,830
Net assets	1,340	1,600

During 2018, Rainer sold $60 million in inventory to Topmaker for $80 million. In 2019, Topmaker resold the entire inventory to a third party.

Thronen is concerned about possible goodwill impairment resulting from expected changes in the industry effective at the end of 2019. He calculates the impairment loss based on the projected consolidated balance sheet data shown in Exhibit 3, assuming that the cash-generating unit and reporting unit of Topmaker are the same.

EXHIBIT 3   Selected Financial Data for Topmaker, Inc., Estimated Year
Ending December 31, 2019 ($ millions)

Carrying value of cash-generating unit/reporting unit	15,200
Recoverable amount of cash-generating unit/reporting unit	14,900
Fair value of reporting unit	14,800
Identifiable net assets	14,400
Goodwill	520

Finally, Topmaker announces its plan to increase its ownership interest in Rainer to 80% effective January 1, 2020. It will account for the investment in Rainer using the partial goodwill method. Thronen estimates that the fair market value of the Rainer's shares on the expected date of exchange is $2 billion, with the identifiable assets valued at $1.5 billion.

29. The carrying value reported on the balance sheet of Topmaker's investment in Blanca's debt securities at December 31, 2018 is:
    A. $10,940,000.
    B. $11,000,000.
    C. $12,000,000.

30. Based on Exhibit 1 and Blanca's plans to borrow against its financial receivables, the consolidated balance sheet will show total assets of:
    A. $50,000,000.
    B. $140,000,000.
    C. $150,000,000.

31. Topmaker's influence on Rainer's business activities can be *best* described as:
    A. significant.
    B. controlling.
    C. shared control.

32. Based on Exhibit 2, the goodwill included in Topmaker's purchase of Rainer is:
    A. $21 million.
    B. $60 million.
    C. $99 million.

33. Based on Exhibit 2, the carrying value of Topmaker's investment in Rainer at the end of 2018 is *closest* to:
    A. $282 million.
    B. $317 million.
    C. $321 million.

34. Which of the following statements regarding the sale of inventory by Rainer to Topmaker is correct?
    A. The sale represents a downstream sale.
    B. Topmaker's unrealized profits are initially deferred.
    C. Profits will decline on Topmaker's 2018 income statement.

35. Based on Exhibit 3, Topmaker's impairment loss under IFRS is:
    A. $120 million.
    B. $300 million.
    C. $400 million.

36. The value of the minority interest at the acquisition date of January 1, 2020 is:
    A. $300 million.
    B. $400 million.
    C. $500 million.

CHAPTER 14

EMPLOYEE COMPENSATION: POST-EMPLOYMENT AND SHARE-BASED

LEARNING OUTCOMES

After completing this chapter, you will be able to do the following:

- describe the types of post-employment benefit plans and implications for financial reports;
- explain and calculate measures of a defined benefit pension obligation (i.e., present value of the defined benefit obligation and projected benefit obligation) and net pension liability (or asset);
- describe the components of a company's defined benefit pension costs;
- explain and calculate the effect of a defined benefit plan's assumptions on the defined benefit obligation and periodic pension cost;
- explain and calculate how adjusting for items of pension and other post-employment benefits that are reported in the notes to the financial statements affects financial statements and ratios;
- interpret pension plan note disclosures including cash flow related information;
- explain issues associated with accounting for share-based compensation;
- explain how accounting for stock grants and stock options affects financial statements, and the importance of companies' assumptions in valuing these grants and options.

SUMMARY OVERVIEW

This chapter discussed two different forms of employee compensation: post-employment benefits and share-based compensation. Although different, the two are similar in that they are forms of compensation outside of the standard salary arrangements. They also involve complex valuation, accounting, and reporting issues. Although IFRS and US GAAP are converging on accounting and reporting, it is important to note that differences in a country's social system, laws, and regulations can result in differences in a company's pension and share-based compensation plans that may be reflected in the company's earnings and financial reports.

Key points include the following:

- Defined contribution pension plans specify (define) only the amount of contribution to the plan; the eventual amount of the pension benefit to the employee will depend on the value of an employee's plan assets at the time of retirement.
- Balance sheet reporting is less analytically relevant for defined contribution plans because companies make contributions to defined contribution plans as the expense arises and thus no liabilities accrue for that type of plan.
- Defined benefit pension plans specify (define) the amount of the pension benefit, often determined by a plan formula, under which the eventual amount of the benefit to the employee is a function of length of service and final salary.
- Defined benefit pension plan obligations are funded by the sponsoring company contributing assets to a pension trust, a separate legal entity. Differences exist in countries' regulatory requirements for companies to fund defined benefit pension plan obligations.
- Both IFRS and US GAAP require companies to report on their balance sheet a pension liability or asset equal to the projected benefit obligation minus the fair value of plan assets. The amount of a pension asset that can be reported is subject to a ceiling.
- Under IFRS, the components of periodic pension cost are recognized as follows: Service cost is recognized in P&L, net interest income/expense is recognized in P&L, and remeasurements are recognized in OCI and are not amortized to future P&L.
- Under US GAAP, the components of periodic pension cost recognized in P&L include current service costs, interest expense on the pension obligation, and expected returns on plan assets (which reduces the cost). Other components of periodic pension cost—including past service costs, actuarial gains and losses, and differences between expected and actual returns on plan assets—are recognized in OCI and amortized to future P&L.
- Estimates of the future obligation under defined benefit pension plans and other post-employment benefits are sensitive to numerous assumptions, including discount rates, assumed annual compensation increases, expected return on plan assets, and assumed health care cost inflation.
- Employee compensation packages are structured to fulfill varied objectives, including satisfying employees' needs for liquidity, retaining employees, and providing incentives to employees.
- Common components of employee compensation packages are salary, bonuses, and share-based compensation.
- Share-based compensation serves to align employees' interests with those of the shareholders. It includes stocks and stock options.
- Share-based compensation has the advantage of requiring no current-period cash outlays.
- Share-based compensation expense is reported at fair value under IFRS and US GAAP.
- The valuation technique, or option pricing model, that a company uses is an important choice in determining fair value and is disclosed.
- Key assumptions and input into option pricing models include such items as exercise price, stock price volatility, estimated life of each award, estimated number of options that will be forfeited, dividend yield, and the risk-free rate of interest. Certain assumptions are highly subjective, such as stock price volatility or the expected life of stock options, and can greatly change the estimated fair value and thus compensation expense.

PROBLEMS

The following information relates to Questions 1–7

Kensington plc, a hypothetical company based in the United Kingdom, offers its employees a defined benefit pension plan. Kensington complies with IFRS. The assumed discount rate that the company used in estimating the present value of its pension obligations was 5.48 percent. Information on Kensington's retirement plans is presented in Exhibit 1.

EXHIBIT 1   Kensington plc Defined Benefit Pension Plan

(in millions)	2010
Components of periodic benefit cost	
Service cost	£228
Net interest (income) expense	273
Remeasurements	–18
Periodic pension cost	£483
Change in benefit obligation	
Benefit obligations at beginning of year	£28,416
Service cost	228
Interest cost	1,557
Benefits paid	–1,322
Actuarial gain or loss	0
Benefit obligations at end of year	£28,879
Change in plan assets	
Fair value of plan assets at beginning of year	£23,432
Actual return on plan assets	1,302
Employer contributions	693
Benefits paid	–1,322
Fair value of plan assets at end of year	£24,105
Funded status at beginning of year	–£4,984
Funded status at end of year	–£4,774

1. At year-end 2010, £28,879 million represents:
   A. the funded status of the plan.
   B. the defined benefit obligation.
   C. the fair value of the plan's assets.

2. For the year 2010, the net interest expense of £273 represents the interest cost on the:
   A. ending benefit obligation.
   B. beginning benefit obligation.
   C. beginning net pension obligation.

3. For the year 2010, the remeasurement component of Kensington's periodic pension cost represents:
   A. the change in the net pension obligation.
   B. actuarial gains and losses on the pension obligation.
   C. actual return on plan assets minus the amount of return on plan assets included in the net interest expense.

4. Which of the following is *closest* to the actual rate of return on beginning plan assets and the rate of return on beginning plan assets that is included in the interest income/expense calculation?
   A. The actual rate of return was 5.56 percent, and the rate included in interest income/expense was 5.48 percent.
   B. The actual rate of return was 1.17 percent, and the rate included in interest income/expense was 5.48 percent.
   C. Both the actual rate of return and the rate included in interest income/expense were 5.48 percent.

5. Which component of Kensington's periodic pension cost would be shown in OCI rather than P&L?
   A. Service cost
   B. Net interest (income) expense
   C. Remeasurements

6. The relationship between the periodic pension cost and the plan's funded status is *best* expressed in which of the following?
   A. Periodic pension cost of –£483 = Ending funded status of –£4,774 – Employer contributions of £693 – Beginning funded status of –£4,984.
   B. Periodic pension cost of £1,322 = Benefits paid of £1,322.
   C. Periodic pension cost of £210 = Ending funded status of –£4,774 – Beginning funded status of –£4,984.

7. An adjustment to Kensington's statement of cash flows to reclassify the company's excess contribution for 2010 would *most likely* entail reclassifying £210 million (excluding income tax effects) as an outflow related to:
   A. investing activities rather than operating activities.
   B. financing activities rather than operating activities.
   C. operating activities rather than financing activities.

The following information relates to Questions 8–12

XYZ SA, a hypothetical company, offers its employees a defined benefit pension plan. Information on XYZ's retirement plans is presented in Exhibit 2. It also grants stock options to executives. Exhibit 3 contains information on the volatility assumptions used to value stock options.

EXHIBIT 2   XYZ SA Retirement Plan Information 2009

Employer contributions	1,000
Current service costs	200
Past service costs	120
Discount rate used to estimate plan liabilities	7.00%
Benefit obligation at beginning of year	42,000
Benefit obligation at end of year	41,720
Actuarial loss due to increase in plan obligation	460
Plan assets at beginning of year	39,000
Plan assets at end of year	38,700
Actual return on plan assets	2,700
Expected rate of return on plan assets	8.00%

EXHIBIT 3   XYZ SA Volatility Assumptions Used to Value Stock Option Grants

Grant Year	Weighted Average Expected Volatility
2009 valuation assumptions	
2005–2009	21.50%
2008 valuation assumptions	
2004–2008	23.00%

8. The total periodic pension cost is *closest* to:
   A. 320.
   B. 1,020.
   C. 1,320.

9. The amount of periodic pension cost that would be reported in P&L under IFRS is *closest* to:
   A. 20.
   B. 530.
   C. 1,020.

10. Assuming the company chooses not to immediately recognize the actuarial loss and assuming there is no amortization of past service costs or actuarial gains and losses, the amount of periodic pension cost that would be reported in P&L under US GAAP is *closest* to:
    A. 20.
    B. 59.
    C. 530.

11. Under IFRS, the amount of periodic pension cost that would be reported in OCI is *closest* to:
    A. 20.
    B. 490.
    C. 1,020.

12. Compared to 2009 net income as reported, if XYZ had used the same volatility assumption for its 2009 option grants that it had used in 2008, its 2009 net income would have been:
   A. lower.
   B. higher.
   C. the same.

The following information relates to Questions 13–18

Stereo Warehouse is a US retailer that offers employees a defined benefit pension plan and stock options as part of its compensation package. Stereo Warehouse prepares its financial statements in accordance with US GAAP.

Peter Friedland, CFA, is an equity analyst concerned with earnings quality. He is particularly interested in whether the discretionary assumptions the company is making regarding compensation plans are contributing to the recent earnings growth at Stereo Warehouse. He gathers information from the company's regulatory filings regarding the pension plan assumptions in Exhibit 4 and the assumptions related to option valuation in Exhibit 5.

EXHIBIT 4   Assumptions Used for Stereo Warehouse Defined Benefit Plan

	2009	2008	2007
Expected long-term rate of return on plan assets	6.06%	6.14%	6.79%
Discount rate	4.85	4.94	5.38
Estimated future salary increases	4.00	4.44	4.25
Inflation	3.00	2.72	2.45

EXHIBIT 5   Option Valuation Assumptions

	2009	2008	2007
Risk-free rate	4.6%	3.8%	2.4%
Expected life	5.0 yrs	4.5 yrs	5.0 yrs
Dividend yield	1.0%	0.0%	0.0%
Expected volatility	29%	31%	35%

13. Compared to the 2009 reported financial statements, if Stereo Warehouse had used the same expected long-term rate of return on plan assets assumption in 2009 as it used in 2007, its year-end 2009 pension obligation would *most likely* have been:
   A. lower.
   B. higher.
   C. the same.

14. Compared to the reported 2009 financial statements, if Stereo Warehouse had used the same discount rate as it used in 2007, it would have *most likely* reported lower:
   A. net income.
   B. total liabilities.
   C. cash flow from operating activities.

15. Compared to the assumptions Stereo Warehouse used to compute its periodic pension cost in 2008, earnings in 2009 were *most favorably* affected by the change in the:
    A. discount rate.
    B. estimated future salary increases.
    C. expected long-term rate of return on plan assets.

16. Compared to the pension assumptions Stereo Warehouse used in 2008, which of the following pairs of assumptions used in 2009 is *most likely* internally inconsistent?
    A. Estimated future salary increases, inflation
    B. Discount rate, estimated future salary increases
    C. Expected long-term rate of return on plan assets, discount rate

17. Compared to the reported 2009 financial statements, if Stereo Warehouse had used the 2007 volatility assumption to value its employee stock options, it would have *most likely* reported higher:
    A. net income.
    B. compensation expense.
    C. deferred compensation liability.

18. Compared to the assumptions Stereo Warehouse used to value stock options in 2008, earnings in 2009 were most favorably affected by the change in the:
    A. expected life.
    B. risk-free rate.
    C. dividend yield.

The following information relates to Questions 19–25

The board of directors at Sallie-Kwan Industrials (SKI), a publicly traded company, is meeting with various committees following the release of audited financial statements prepared in accordance with IFRS. The finance committee (FC) is next on the agenda to review retirement benefits funding and make recommendations to the board.

SKI's three retirement benefit plans are described as follows:

Plan A

- Benefit: Annual payments for life equal to 1% of the employee's final salary for each year of service beyond the date of the plan's establishment
- The employer makes regular contributions to the plan in order to meet the future obligation
- Closed to new participants; benefits accrue for existing participants
- Fair value of assets: €5.98 billion
- Present value of obligation: €4.80 billion
- Present value of reductions in future contributions: €1.50 billion
- Ten-year vesting schedule; 70% of the participants are fully vested

Plan B

- Benefit: Discretionary retirement withdrawals; amounts depend on the plan's investment performance
- Employer makes its agreed-upon contribution to the plan on behalf of the employee in the same period during which the employee provides the service; SKI is current on this obligation

- The employee may also contribute to the plan during employment years
- Available to all employees after one year of service; 80% of the employees are fully vested

Plan C

- Benefit: Medical, prescription drug, and dental coverage for the retiree, spouse, and dependents under age 18
- 80% funded
- Available to all employees on day one of service

The FC chair reviews Plan A's funded status and the amount recorded on the balance sheet with the board, explaining that the current service cost change from last quarter has primarily resulted from a higher percentage of employees that are expected to leave before the full vesting period.

A board member inquires how Plan A's periodic pension costs affect SKI's operating performance. The FC chair reviews the adjustments needed to account for individual pension components that are considered operating costs and those considered non-operating costs, when calculating profit before taxation. Note 16 in the income statement lists the following: current service costs of €40 million, interest costs of €263 million, expected return on plan assets of €299 million, and actual return on plan assets of €205 million.

Next, the FC chairman presents the following case study data to illustrate SKI's current pension obligation for an average fully vested participant in Plan A with 10 years of prior service:

- Current annual salary: €100,000
- Years to retirement: 17
- Retirement life expectancy: 20 years
- Current plan assumptions:
  - Annual compensation increase: 6%
  - Discount rate: 4%
  - Compensation increases are awarded on the first day of the service year; no adjustments are made to reflect the possibility that the employee may leave the firm at an earlier date.

A discussion ensues regarding the effect on the pension obligation, for an average participant, of changing Plan A's annual compensation increase to 5%.

Lastly, the FC chair recommends that the board consider modifying some key assumptions affecting Plan A in response to recent market trends. The chair also reviews how these changes will alter SKI's plan obligation.

Recommendation 1: Change the assumed discount rate to 5%.
Recommendation 2: Increase the retirement life expectancy assumption by eight years.
Recommendation 3: Reduce investment risk by decreasing the expected return to 3%.

19. The participant bears the greatest amount of investment risk under which plan?
    A. Plan A
    B. Plan B
    C. Plan C

20. The plan for which the amount of SKI's financial obligation is defined in the current period with no obligation for future retirement benefits is:
    A. Plan A.
    B. Plan B.
    C. Plan C.

21. For Plan A, SKI should report a net pension:
    A. asset of €1.50 billion.
    B. asset of €1.18 billion.
    C. liability of €1.18 billion.

22. Based on the FC chair's explanation about the current service cost change, the present value of Plan A's obligation:
    A. decreased.
    B. stayed the same.
    C. increased.

23. Based on Note 16, after reclassifying pension components to reflect economic income or expense, the net adjustment to profit before taxation is:
    A. −€205 million.
    B. −€94 million.
    C. +€129 million.

24. Based on the case study illustration and the effect of changing the annual compensation rate, the annual unit credit for the average participant would decrease by an amount *closest* to:
    A. €4,349.
    B. €4,858.
    C. €5,446.

25. All else being equal, which of the following FC recommendations will increase the plan's obligation?
    A. Recommendation 1
    B. Recommendation 2
    C. Recommendation 3

The following information relates to Questions 26–32

Natalie Holmstead, a senior portfolio manager, works with Daniel Rickards, a junior analyst. Together they are evaluating the financial statements of Company XYZ (XYZ) with a focus on post-employment benefits. XYZ has a defined benefit pension plan and prepares financial statements according to IFRS requirements.

Rickards calculates the current service cost for a single employee's defined benefit pension obligation using the projected unit credit method. The employee is expected to work for 7 years before retiring and has 15 years of vested service. Rickards assumes a discount rate of 4.00% and a lump sum value of the employee's benefit at retirement of $393,949.

Next, Holmstead and Rickards discuss the present value of the defined benefit obligation (PVDBO). Rickards makes the following statements to clarify his understanding:

Statement 1   An increase in the PVDBO will result in an actuarial loss for the company.
Statement 2   The PVDBO measures the present value of future benefits earned by plan participants and includes plan assets.
Statement 3   The company should use the expected long-term rate of return on plan assets as the discount rate to calculate the PVDBO.

XYZ's pension plan offers benefits based on the employee's final year's salary. Rickards calculates the PVDBO as of the end of the current period, based on the information presented in Exhibit 1.

EXHIBIT 1   Select XYZ Defined Benefit Pension Plan Data

	Current Period	Prior Period
Assumed future compensation growth rate	2.5%	3.0%
Plan assets (in $ millions)	3,108	
Net pension liability (in $ millions)	525	
Present value of reductions of future contributions (in $ millions)	48	

Rickards adjusts the balance sheet and cash flow statement information presented in Exhibit 2 to better reflect the economic nature of certain items related to the pension plan.

EXHIBIT 2   Select XYZ Balance Sheet and
Cash Flow Data (in $ millions)

Item	Current Period
Total assets	24,130
Total liabilities	17,560
Total equity	6,570
Total pension cost	96
Pension contribution	66
Financing cash flow	2,323
Operating cash flow	−1,087
Effective tax rate	30%

Finally, Rickards examines the data in Exhibit 3 and calculates the effect of a 100-basis-point increase in health care inflation on XYZ's debt-to-equity ratio.

EXHIBIT 3   Sensitivity of Accumulated Post-Employment Benefit Obligations to Changes in Assumed Health Care Inflation (in $ millions)

Item	100-bp Increase	100-bp Decrease
Benefit obligation change	$93	−$76
Benefit expense change	$12	−$10

26. The current service cost is *closest* to:
    A. $14,152.
    B. $15,758.
    C. $17,907.

27. Which of Rickards's statements about the PVDBO is correct?
    A. Statement 1
    B. Statement 2
    C. Statement 3

28. Based on Exhibit 1, the PVDBO is *closest* to:
    A. $3,585 million.
    B. $3,633 million.
    C. $3,681 million.

29. Based on Exhibit 1 and the method XYZ uses to link pension benefits to salaries, the change in the compensation growth rate compared with the prior period will *most likely* result in:
    A. lower periodic pension cost.
    B. no change in the periodic pension cost.
    C. higher periodic pension cost.

30. Based on the change in the assumed future compensation growth rate presented in Exhibit 1, which of the following pension cost components is affected?
    A. Service cost
    B. Remeasurement
    C. Net interest expense/income

31. Based on Exhibit 2, Rickards should adjust the operating and financing cash flows by:
    A. $21 million.
    B. $30 million.
    C. $96 million.

32. Based on Exhibits 2 and 3, as well as Holmstead's assumption about future health care inflation, the debt-to-equity ratio calculated by Rickards for XYZ should be *closest* to:
    A. 2.69.
    B. 2.71.
    C. 2.73.

MULTINATIONAL
OPERATIONS

LEARNING OUTCOMES

After completing this chapter, you will be able to do the following:

- distinguish among presentation (reporting) currency, functional currency, and local currency;
- describe foreign currency transaction exposure, including accounting for and disclosures about foreign currency transaction gains and losses;
- analyze how changes in exchange rates affect the translated sales of the subsidiary and parent company;
- compare the current rate method and the temporal method, evaluate how each affects the parent company's balance sheet and income statement, and determine which method is appropriate in various scenarios;
- calculate the translation effects and evaluate the translation of a subsidiary's balance sheet and income statement into the parent company's presentation currency;
- analyze how the current rate method and the temporal method affect financial statements and ratios;
- analyze how alternative translation methods for subsidiaries operating in hyperinflationary economies affect financial statements and ratios;
- describe how multinational operations affect a company's effective tax rate;
- explain how changes in the components of sales affect the sustainability of sales growth;
- analyze how currency fluctuations potentially affect financial results, given a company's countries of operation.

SUMMARY OVERVIEW

The translation of foreign currency amounts is an important accounting issue for companies with multinational operations. Foreign exchange rate fluctuations cause the functional currency values of foreign currency assets and liabilities resulting from foreign currency transactions as well as from foreign subsidiaries to change over time. These changes in value give rise to foreign exchange differences that companies' financial statements must reflect. Determining how to measure these foreign exchange differences and whether to include them in the calculation of net income are the major issues in accounting for multinational operations.

- The local currency is the national currency of the country where an entity is located. The functional currency is the currency of the primary economic environment in which an entity operates. Normally, the local currency is an entity's functional currency. For accounting purposes, any currency other than an entity's functional currency is a foreign currency for that entity. The currency in which financial statement amounts are presented is known as the presentation currency. In most cases, the presentation currency will be the same as the local currency.
- When an export sale (import purchase) on an account is denominated in a foreign currency, the sales revenue (inventory) and foreign currency account receivable (account payable) are translated into the seller's (buyer's) functional currency using the exchange rate on the transaction date. Any change in the functional currency value of the foreign currency account receivable (account payable) that occurs between the transaction date and the settlement date is recognized as a foreign currency transaction gain or loss in net income.
- If a balance sheet date falls between the transaction date and the settlement date, the foreign currency account receivable (account payable) is translated at the exchange rate at the balance sheet date. The change in the functional currency value of the foreign currency account receivable (account payable) is recognized as a foreign currency transaction gain or loss in income. Analysts should understand that these gains and losses are unrealized at the time they are recognized and might or might not be realized when the transactions are settled.
- A foreign currency transaction gain arises when an entity has a foreign currency receivable and the foreign currency strengthens or it has a foreign currency payable and the foreign currency weakens. A foreign currency transaction loss arises when an entity has a foreign currency receivable and the foreign currency weakens or it has a foreign currency payable and the foreign currency strengthens.
- Companies must disclose the net foreign currency gain or loss included in income. They may choose to report foreign currency transaction gains and losses as a component of operating income or as a component of non-operating income. If two companies choose to report foreign currency transaction gains and losses differently, operating profit and operating profit margin might not be directly comparable between the two companies.
- To prepare consolidated financial statements, foreign currency financial statements of foreign operations must be translated into the parent company's presentation currency. The major conceptual issues related to this translation process are, What is the appropriate exchange rate for translating each financial statement item, and how should the resulting translation adjustment be reflected in the consolidated financial statements? Two different translation methods are used worldwide.
- Under the current rate method, assets and liabilities are translated at the current exchange rate, equity items are translated at historical exchange rates, and revenues and expenses are translated at the exchange rate that existed when the underlying transaction occurred. For practical reasons, an average exchange rate is often used to translate income items.
- Under the temporal method, monetary assets (and non-monetary assets measured at current value) and monetary liabilities (and non-monetary liabilities measured at current value) are translated at the current exchange rate. Non-monetary assets and liabilities not measured at current value and equity items are translated at historical exchange rates. Revenues and expenses, other than those expenses related to non-monetary assets, are translated at the exchange rate that existed when the underlying transaction occurred. Expenses related to non-monetary assets are translated at the exchange rates used for the related assets.
- Under both IFRS and US GAAP, the functional currency of a foreign operation determines the method to be used in translating its foreign currency financial statements into the

parent's presentation currency and whether the resulting translation adjustment is recognized in income or as a separate component of equity.

- The foreign currency financial statements of a foreign operation that has a foreign currency as its functional currency are translated using the current rate method, and the translation adjustment is accumulated as a separate component of equity. The cumulative translation adjustment related to a specific foreign entity is transferred to net income when that entity is sold or otherwise disposed of. The balance sheet risk exposure associated with the current rate method is equal to the foreign subsidiary's net asset position.

- The foreign currency financial statements of a foreign operation that has the parent's presentation currency as its functional currency are translated using the temporal method, and the translation adjustment is included as a gain or loss in income. US GAAP refer to this process as remeasurement. The balance sheet exposure associated with the temporal method is equal to the foreign subsidiary's net monetary asset/liability position (adjusted for non-monetary items measured at current value).

- IFRS and US GAAP differ with respect to the translation of foreign currency financial statements of foreign operations located in a highly inflationary country. Under IFRS, the foreign currency statements are first restated for local inflation and then translated using the current exchange rate. Under US GAAP, the foreign currency financial statements are translated using the temporal method, with no restatement for inflation.

- Applying different translation methods for a given foreign operation can result in very different amounts reported in the parent's consolidated financial statements.

- Companies must disclose the total amount of translation gain or loss reported in income and the amount of translation adjustment included in a separate component of stockholders' equity. Companies are not required to separately disclose the component of translation gain or loss arising from foreign currency transactions and the component arising from application of the temporal method.

- Disclosures related to translation adjustments reported in equity can be used to include these as gains and losses in determining an adjusted amount of income following a clean-surplus approach to income measurement.

- Foreign currency translation rules are well established in both IFRS and US GAAP. Fortunately, except for the treatment of foreign operations located in highly inflationary countries, the two sets of standards have no major differences in this area. The ability to understand the impact of foreign currency translation on the financial results of a company using IFRS should apply equally well in the analysis of financial statements prepared in accordance with US GAAP.

- An analyst can obtain information about the tax impact of multinational operations from companies' disclosure on effective tax rates.

- For a multinational company, sales growth is driven not only by changes in volume and price but also by changes in the exchange rates between the reporting currency and the currency in which sales are made. Arguably, growth in sales that comes from changes in volume or price is more sustainable than growth in sales that comes from changes in exchange rates.

PROBLEMS

The following information relates to Questions 1–6

Pedro Ruiz is an analyst for a credit rating agency. One of the companies he follows, Eurexim SA, is based in France and complies with International Financial Reporting Standards (IFRS). Ruiz has learned that Eurexim used EUR220 million of its own cash and borrowed an equal amount to open a subsidiary in Ukraine. The funds were converted into hryvnia (UAH) on December 31, 20X1 at an exchange rate of EUR1.00 = UAH6.70 and used to purchase UAH1,500 million in fixed assets and UAH300 million of inventories.

Ruiz is concerned about the effect that the subsidiary's results might have on Eurexim's consolidated financial statements. He calls Eurexim's Chief Financial Officer, but learns little. Eurexim is not willing to share sales forecasts and has not even made a determination as to the subsidiary's functional currency.

Absent more useful information, Ruiz decides to explore various scenarios to determine the potential impact on Eurexim's consolidated financial statements. Ukraine is not currently in a hyperinflationary environment, but Ruiz is concerned that this situation could change. Ruiz also believes the euro will appreciate against the hryvnia for the foreseeable future.

1. If Ukraine's economy becomes highly inflationary, Eurexim will *most likely* translate inventory by:
   A. restating for inflation and using the temporal method.
   B. restating for inflation and using the current exchange rate.
   C. using the temporal method with no restatement for inflation.

2. Given Ruiz's belief about the direction of exchange rates, Eurexim's gross profit margin would be *highest* if it accounts for the Ukraine subsidiary's inventory using:
   A. FIFO and the temporal method.
   B. FIFO and the current rate method.
   C. weighted-average cost and the temporal method.

3. If the euro is chosen as the Ukraine subsidiary's functional currency, Eurexim will translate its fixed assets using the:
   A. average rate for the reporting period.
   B. rate in effect when the assets were purchased.
   C. rate in effect at the end of the reporting period.

4. If the euro is chosen as the Ukraine subsidiary's functional currency, Eurexim will translate its accounts receivable using the:
   A. rate in effect at the transaction date.
   B. average rate for the reporting period.
   C. rate in effect at the end of the reporting period.

5. If the hryvnia is chosen as the Ukraine subsidiary's functional currency, Eurexim will translate its inventory using the:
   A. average rate for the reporting period.
   B. rate in effect at the end of the reporting period.
   C. rate in effect at the time the inventory was purchased.

6. Based on the information available and Ruiz's expectations regarding exchange rates, if the hryvnia is chosen as the Ukraine subsidiary's functional currency, Eurexim will *most likely* report:
   A. an addition to the cumulative translation adjustment.
   B. a translation gain or loss as a component of net income.
   C. a subtraction from the cumulative translation adjustment.

The following information relates to Questions 7–12

Consolidated Motors is a US-based corporation that sells mechanical engines and components used by electric utilities. Its Canadian subsidiary, Consol-Can, operates solely in Canada. It was created on December 31, 20X1, and Consolidated Motors determined at that time that it should use the US dollar as its functional currency.

Chief Financial Officer Monica Templeton was asked to explain to the board of directors how exchange rates affect the financial statements of both Consol-Can and the consolidated financial statements of Consolidated Motors. For the presentation, Templeton collects Consol-Can's balance sheets for the years ended 20X1 and 20X2 (Exhibit 1), as well as relevant exchange rate information (Exhibit 2).

EXHIBIT 1   Consol-Can Condensed Balance Sheet for Fiscal Years Ending December 31 (C$ millions)

Account	20X2	20X1
Cash	135	167
Accounts receivable	98	—
Inventory	77	30
Fixed assets	100	100
Accumulated depreciation	(10)	—
Total assets	400	297
Accounts payable	77	22
Long-term debt	175	175
Common stock	100	100
Retained earnings	48	—
Total liabilities and shareholders' equity	400	297

EXHIBIT 2   Exchange Rate Information

	US$/C$
Rate on December 31, 20X1	0.86
Average rate in 20X2	0.92
Weighted-average rate for inventory purchases	0.92
Rate on December 31, 20X2	0.95

Templeton explains that Consol-Can uses the FIFO inventory accounting method and that purchases of C$300 million and the sell-through of that inventory occurred evenly throughout 20X2. Her presentation includes reporting the translated amounts in US dollars for each item, as well as associated translation-related gains and losses. The board responds with several questions.

• Would there be a reason to change the functional currency to the Canadian dollar?
• Would there be any translation effects for Consolidated Motors if the functional currency for Consol-Can were changed to the Canadian dollar?

- Would a change in the functional currency have any impact on financial statement ratios for the parent company?
- What would be the balance sheet exposure to translation effects if the functional currency were changed?

7. After translating Consol-Can's inventory and long-term debt into the parent company's currency (US$), the amounts reported on Consolidated Motor's financial statements on December 31, 20X2 would be *closest* to (in millions):
   A. $71 for inventory and $161 for long-term debt.
   B. $71 for inventory and $166 for long-term debt.
   C. $73 for inventory and $166 for long-term debt.

8. After translating Consol-Can's December 31, 20X2 balance sheet into the parent company's currency (US$), the translated value of retained earnings will be *closest* to:
   A. $41 million.
   B. $44 million.
   C. $46 million.

9. In response to the board's first question, Templeton would *most likely* reply that such a change would be justified if:
   A. the inflation rate in the United States became hyperinflationary.
   B. management wanted to flow more of the gains through net income.
   C. Consol-Can were making autonomous decisions about operations, investing, and financing.

10. In response to the board's second question, Templeton should reply that if the change is made, the consolidated financial statements for Consolidated Motors would begin to recognize:
    A. realized gains and losses on monetary assets and liabilities.
    B. realized gains and losses on non-monetary assets and liabilities.
    C. unrealized gains and losses on non-monetary assets and liabilities.

11. In response to the board's third question, Templeton should note that the change will *most likely* affect:
    A. the cash ratio.
    B. fixed asset turnover.
    C. receivables turnover.

12. In response to the board's fourth question, the balance sheet exposure (in C$ millions) would be *closest* to:
    A. −19.
    B. 148.
    C. 400.

The following information relates to Questions 13–18

Romulus Corp. is a US-based company that prepares its financial statements in accordance with US GAAP. Romulus Corp. has two European subsidiaries: Julius and Augustus. Anthony Marks, CFA, is an analyst trying to forecast Romulus's 20X2 results. Marks has prepared separate forecasts for both Julius and Augustus, as well as for Romulus's other operations (prior to consolidating the results.) He is now considering the impact of currency translation on the results of both the subsidiaries and the parent company's consolidated financials. His research has provided the following insights:

- The results for Julius will be translated into US dollars using the current rate method.
- The results for Augustus will be translated into US dollars using the temporal method.
- Both Julius and Augustus use the FIFO method to account for inventory.
- Julius had year-end 20X1 inventory of €340 million. Marks believes Julius will report €2,300 in sales and €1,400 in cost of sales in 20X2.

Marks also forecasts the 20X2 year-end balance sheet for Julius (Exhibit 1). Data and forecasts related to euro/dollar exchange rates are presented in Exhibit 2.

EXHIBIT 1   Forecasted Balance Sheet Data for Julius, December 31, 20X2 (€ millions)

Cash	50
Accounts receivable	100
Inventory	700
Fixed assets	1,450
Total assets	2,300
Liabilities	700
Common stock	1,500
Retained earnings	100
Total liabilities and shareholder equity	2,300

EXHIBIT 2   Exchange Rates ($/€)

December 31, 20X1	1.47
December 31, 20X2	1.61
20X2 average	1.54
Rate when fixed assets were acquired	1.25
Rate when 20X1 inventory was acquired	1.39
Rate when 20X2 inventory was acquired	1.49

13. Based on the translation method being used for Julius, the subsidiary is *most likely:*
    A. a sales outlet for Romulus's products.
    B. a self-contained, independent operating entity.
    C. using the US dollar as its functional currency.

14. To account for its foreign operations, Romulus has *most likely* designated the euro as the functional currency for:
    A. Julius only.
    B. Augustus only.
    C. both Julius and Augustus.

15. When Romulus consolidates the results of Julius, any unrealized exchange rate holding gains on monetary assets should be:
    A. reported as part of operating income.
    B. reported as a non-operating item on the income statement.
    C. reported directly to equity as part of the cumulative translation adjustment.

16. When Marks translates his forecasted balance sheet for Julius into US dollars, total assets as of December 31, 20X2 (dollars in millions) will be *closest* to:
    A. $1,429.
    B. $2,392.
    C. $3,703.

17. When Marks converts his forecasted income statement data for Julius into US dollars, the 20X2 gross profit margin will be *closest* to:
    A. 39.1%.
    B. 40.9%.
    C. 44.6%.

18. Relative to the gross margins the subsidiaries report in local currency, Romulus's consolidated gross margin *most likely*:
    A. will not be distorted by currency translations.
    B. would be distorted if Augustus were using the same translation method as Julius.
    C. will be distorted because of the translation and inventory accounting methods Augustus is using.

The following information relates to Questions 19–24

Redline Products, Inc. is a US-based multinational with subsidiaries around the world. One such subsidiary, Acceletron, operates in Singapore, which has seen mild but not excessive rates of inflation. Acceletron was acquired in 2000 and has never paid a dividend. It records inventory using the FIFO method.

Chief Financial Officer Margot Villiers was asked by Redline's board of directors to explain how the functional currency selection and other accounting choices affect Redline's consolidated financial statements. Villiers gathers Acceletron's financial statements denominated in Singapore dollars (SGD) in Exhibit 1 and the US dollar/Singapore dollar exchange rates in Exhibit 2. She does not intend to identify the functional currency actually in use but rather to use Acceletron as an example of how the choice of functional currency affects the consolidated statements.

EXHIBIT 1   Selected Financial Data for
Acceletron, December 31, 2007 (SGD millions)

Cash	SGD125
Accounts receivable	230
Inventory	500
Fixed assets	1,640
Accumulated depreciation	(205)
Total assets	SGD2,290

EXHIBIT 1 (Continued)

Accounts payable	185
Long-term debt	200
Common stock	620
Retained earnings	1,285
Total liabilities and equity	2,290
Total revenues	SGD4,800
Net income	SGD450

EXHIBIT 2   Exchange Rates Applicable to Acceletron

Exchange Rate in Effect at Specific Times	USD per SGD
Rate when first SGD1 billion of fixed assets were acquired	0.568
Rate when remaining SGD640 million of fixed assets were acquired	0.606
Rate when long-term debt was issued	0.588
December 31, 2006	0.649
Weighted-average rate when inventory was acquired	0.654
Average rate in 2007	0.662
December 31, 2007	0.671

19. Compared with using the Singapore dollar as Acceletron's functional currency for 2007, if the US dollar were the functional currency, it is *most likely* that Redline's consolidated:
    A. inventories will be higher.
    B. receivable turnover will be lower.
    C. fixed asset turnover will be higher.

20. If the US dollar were chosen as the functional currency for Acceletron in 2007, Redline could reduce its balance sheet exposure to exchange rates by:
    A. selling SGD30 million of fixed assets for cash.
    B. issuing SGD30 million of long-term debt to buy fixed assets.
    C. issuing SGD30 million in short-term debt to purchase marketable securities.

21. Redline's consolidated gross profit margin for 2007 would be *highest* if Acceletron accounted for inventory using:
    A. FIFO, and its functional currency were the US dollar.
    B. LIFO, and its functional currency were the US dollar.
    C. FIFO, and its functional currency were the Singapore dollar.

22. If the current rate method is used to translate Acceletron's financial statements into US dollars, Redline's consolidated financial statements will *most likely* include Acceletron's:
    A. USD3,178 million in revenues.
    B. USD118 million in long-term debt.
    C. negative translation adjustment to shareholder equity.

23. If Acceletron's financial statements are translated into US dollars using the temporal method, Redline's consolidated financial statements will *most likely* include Acceletron's:
    A. USD336 million in inventory.
    B. USD956 million in fixed assets.
    C. USD152 million in accounts receivable.

24. When translating Acceletron's financial statements into US dollars, Redline is *least likely* to use an exchange rate of USD per SGD:
    A. 0.671.
    B. 0.588.
    C. 0.654.

The following information relates to Questions 25–33

Adrienne Yu is an analyst with an international bank. She analyzes Ambleu S.A. ("Ambleu"), a multinational corporation, for a client presentation. Ambleu complies with IFRS, and its presentation currency is the Norvoltian krone (NVK). Ambleu's two subsidiaries, Ngcorp and Cendaró, have different functional currencies: Ngcorp uses the Bindiar franc (FB) and Cendaró uses the Crenland guinea (CRG).

Yu first analyzes the following three transactions to assess foreign currency transaction exposure:

Transaction 1:	Cendaró sells goods to a non-domestic customer that pays in dollars on the purchase date.
Transaction 2:	Ngcorp obtains a loan in Bindiar francs on June 1, 2016 from a European bank with the Norvoltian krone as its presentation currency.
Transaction 3:	Ambleu imports inventory from Bindiar under 45-day credit terms, and the payment is to be denominated in Bindiar francs.

Yu then reviews Transactions 2 and 3. She determines the method that Ambleu would use to translate Transaction 2 into its December 31, 2016 consolidated financial statements. While analyzing Transaction 3, Yu notes that Ambleu purchased inventory on June 1, 2016 for FB27,000/ton. Ambleu pays for the inventory on July 15, 2016. Exhibit 1 presents selected economic data for Bindiar and Crenland.

EXHIBIT 1   Selected Economic Data for Bindiar and Crenland

Date	Spot FB/NVK Exchange Rate	Bindiar Inflation Rate (%)	Spot CRG/ NVK Exchange Rate	Crenland Inflation Rate (%)	Crenland GPI
Dec 31, 2015	—	—	5.6780	—	100.0
Jun 1, 2016	4.1779	—	—	—	—
Jul 15, 2016	4.1790	—	—	—	—
Dec 31, 2016	4.2374	3.1	8.6702	40.6	140.6
Average 2016	4.3450	—	—	—	—
Dec 31, 2017	4.3729	2.1	14.4810	62.3	228.2
Average 2017	4.3618	—	11.5823	—	186.2

Prior to reviewing the 2016 and 2017 consolidated financial statements of Ambleu, Yu meets with her supervisor, who asks Yu the following two questions:

Question 1:   Would a foreign currency translation loss reduce Ambleu's net sales growth?

Question 2:   According to IFRS, what disclosures should be included relating to Ambleu's treatment of foreign currency translation for Ngcorp?

To complete her assignment, Yu analyzes selected information and notes from Ambleu's 2016 and 2017 consolidated financial statements, presented in Exhibit 2.

EXHIBIT 2   Selected Information and Notes from Consolidated Financial Statements of Ambleu S.A. (in NVK millions)

Income Statement	2017	2016	Balance Sheet	2017	2016
Revenue [1]	1,069	1,034	Cash[3]	467	425
Profit before tax	294	269	Intangibles [4]	575	570
Income tax expense [2]	–96	–94	—	—	—
Net profit	198	175	—	—	—

Note 1: Cendaro's revenue for 2017 is CRG125.23 million.

Note 2:

Reconciliation of Income Tax Expense	2017 (in NVK millions)	2016 (in NVK millions)
Income tax at Ambleu's domestic tax rate	102	92
Effect of tax rates on non-domestic jurisdictions	–14	–9
Unrecognized current year tax losses	8	11
Income tax expense	96	94

Note 3: The parent company transferred NVK15 million to Cendaró on January 1, 2016 to purchase a patent from a competitor for CRG85.17 million.

Note 4: The 2016 consolidated balance sheet includes Ngcorp's total intangible assets of NVK3 million, which were added to Ngcorp's balance sheet on July 15, 2016.

25. Which transaction would generate foreign currency transaction exposure for Ambleu?
    A. Transaction 1
    B. Transaction 2
    C. Transaction 3

26. Yu's determination regarding Transaction 2 should be based on the currency of the:
    A. loan.
    B. bank.
    C. borrower.

27. Based on Exhibit 1, what is the foreign exchange gain resulting from Transaction 3 on the December 31, 2016 financial statements?
    A. NVK1.70 per ton
    B. NVK90.75 per ton
    C. NVK248.54 per ton

28. What is the *best* response to Question 1?
    A. Yes
    B. No, because it would reduce organic sales growth
    C. No, because it would reduce net price realization and mix

29. Based on Exhibit 1, the *best* response to Question 2 is that Ambleu should disclose:
    A. a restatement for local inflation.
    B. that assets carried at historical cost are translated at historical rates.
    C. the amount of foreign exchange differences included in net income.

30. Based on Exhibit 1 and Note 1 in Exhibit 2, the amount that Ambleu should include in its December 31, 2017 revenue from Cendaró is *closest* to:
    A. NVK10.60 million.
    B. NVK13.25 million.
    C. NVK19.73 million.

31. Based on Exhibit 2 and Note 2, the change in Ambleu's consolidated income tax rate from 2016 to 2017 *most likely* resulted from a:
    A. decrease in Ambleu's domestic tax rate.
    B. more profitable business mix in its subsidiaries.
    C. stronger Norvoltian krone relative to the currencies of its subsidiaries.

32. Based on Exhibit 1 and Note 3 in Exhibit 2, the cumulative translation loss recognized by Ambleu related to the patent purchase on the December 31, 2017 financial statements is *closest* to:
    A. NVK0.39 million.
    B. NVK1.58 million
    C. NVK9.12 million.

33. Based on Exhibit 1 and Note 4 in Exhibit 2, the total intangible assets on Ngcorp's balance sheet as of December 31, 2016 are *closest* to:
    A. FB12.54 million.
    B. FB12.71 million.
    C. FB13.04 million.

The following information relates to Questions 34–40

Triofind, Inc. (Triofind), based in the country of Norvolt, provides wireless services to various countries, including Norvolt, Borliand, Abuelio, and Certait. The company's presentation currency is the Norvolt euro (NER), and Triofind complies with IFRS. Triofind has two wholly owned subsidiaries, located in Borliand and Abuelio. The Borliand subsidiary (Triofind-B) was established on June 30, 2016, by Triofind both investing NER1,000,000, which was converted into Borliand dollars (BRD), and borrowing an additional BRD500,000.

Marie Janssen, a financial analyst in Triofind's Norvolt headquarters office, translates Triofind-B's financial statements using the temporal method. Non-monetary assets are measured at cost under the lower of cost or market rule. Spot BRD/NER exchange rates are presented in Exhibit 1, and the balance sheet for Triofind-B is presented in Exhibit 2.

EXHIBIT 1   Spot BRD/NER Exchange Rates

Date	BRD per NER
June 30, 2016	1.15
Weighted-average rate when inventory was acquired (2016)	1.19
December 31, 2016	1.20
Weighted-average rate when inventory was acquired (2017)	1.18
June 30, 2017	1.17

EXHIBIT 2   Triofind-B Balance Sheet for 2016 and 2017 (BRD)

Assets	December 31, 2016	June 30, 2017	Liabilities and Stockholders' Equity	December 31, 2016	June 30, 2017
Cash	900,000	1,350,000	Notes payable	500,000	500,000
Inventory	750,000	500,000	Common stock	1,150,000	1,150,000
			Retained earnings		200,000
Total	1,650,000	1,850,000	Total	1,650,000	1,850,000

Janssen next analyzes Triofind's Abuelio subsidiary (Triofind-A), which uses the current rate method to translate its results into Norvolt euros. Triofind-A, which prices its goods in Abuelio pesos (ABP), sells mobile phones to a customer in Certait on May 31, 2017 and receives payment of 1 million Certait rand (CRD) on July 31, 2017.

On May 31, 2017, Triofind-A also received NER50,000 from Triofind and used the funds to purchase a new warehouse in Abuelio. Janssen translates the financial statements of Triofind-A as of July 31, 2017 and must determine the appropriate value for the warehouse in Triofind's presentation currency. She observes that the cumulative Abuelio inflation rate exceeded 100% from 2015 to 2017. Spot exchange rates and inflation data are presented in Exhibit 3.

EXHIBIT 3   Spot Exchange Rates and Inflation Data for Triofind-A

Date	NER per CRD	NER per ABP	Abuelio Monthly Inflation Rate (%)
May 31, 2017	0.2667	0.0496	—
June 30, 2017	0.2703	0.0388	25
July 31, 2017	0.2632	0.0312	22

Janssen gathers corporate tax rate data and company disclosure information to include in Triofind's annual report. She determines that the corporate tax rates for Abuelio, Norvolt, and Borliand are 35%, 34%, and 0%, respectively, and that Norvolt exempts the non-domestic income of multinationals from taxation. Triofind-B constitutes 25% of Triofind's net income, and Triofind-A constitutes 15%. Janssen also gathers data on components of net sales growth in different countries, presented in Exhibit 4.

EXHIBIT 4   Components of Net Sales Growth (%) Fiscal Year 2017

Country	Contribution from Volume Growth	Contribution from Price Growth	Foreign Currency Exchange	Net Sales Growth
Abuelio	7	6	–2	11
Borliand	4	5	4	13
Norvolt	7	3	—	10

34. Based on Exhibits 1 and 2 and Janssen's translation method, total assets for Triofind-B translated into Triofind's presentation currency as of December 31, 2016 are *closest* to:
    A. NER1,375,000.
    B. NER1,380,252.
    C. NER1,434,783.

35. Based on Exhibits 1 and 2, the translation adjustment for Triofind-B's liabilities into Triofind's presentation currency for the six months ended December 31, 2016 is:
    A. negative.
    B. zero.
    C. positive.

36. Based on Exhibits 1 and 2 and Janssen's translation method, retained earnings for Triofind-B translated into Triofind's presentation currency as of June 30, 2017 are *closest* to:
    A. NER150,225.
    B. NER170,940.
    C. NER172,414.

37. The functional currency for Triofind-A's sale of mobile phones to a customer in Certait is the:
    A. Certait real.
    B. Norvolt euro.
    C. Abuelio peso.

38. Based on Exhibit 3, the value of the new warehouse in Abuelio on Triofind's balance sheet as of July 31, 2017 is *closest* to:
    A. NER31,452.
    B. NER47,964.
    C. NER50,000.

39. Relative to its domestic tax rate, Triofind's effective tax rate is *most likely*:
    A. lower.
    B. the same.
    C. higher.

40. Based on Exhibit 4, the country with the highest sustainable sales growth is:
    A. Norvolt.
    B. Abuelio.
    C. Borliand.

CHAPTER 16

ANALYSIS OF FINANCIAL INSTITUTIONS

LEARNING OUTCOMES

After completing this chapter, you will be able to do the following:

- describe how financial institutions differ from other companies;
- describe key aspects of financial regulations of financial institutions;
- explain the CAMELS (capital adequacy, asset quality, management, earnings, liquidity, and sensitivity) approach to analyzing a bank, including key ratios and its limitations;
- describe other factors to consider in analyzing a bank;
- analyze a bank based on financial statements and other factors;
- describe key ratios and other factors to consider in analyzing an insurance company.

SUMMARY OVERVIEW

- Financial institutions' systemic importance results in heavy regulation of their activities.
- Systemic risk refers to the risk of impairment in some part of the financial system that then has the potential to spread throughout other parts of the financial system and thereby to negatively affect the entire economy.
- The Basel Committee, a standing committee of the Bank for International Settlements, includes representatives from central banks and bank supervisors from around the world.
- The Basel Committee's international regulatory framework for banks includes minimum capital requirements, minimum liquidity requirements, and stable funding requirements.
- Among the international organizations that focus on financial stability are the Financial Stability Board, the International Association of Insurance Supervisors, the International Association of Deposit Insurers, and the International Organization of Securities Commissions.
- Another distinctive feature of financial institutions (compared to manufacturing or merchandising companies) is that their productive assets are predominantly financial assets, such as loans and securities, creating greater direct exposures to a variety of risks, such as credit risk, liquidity risk, market risk, and interest rate risk. In general, the values of their assets are relatively close to fair market values.

- A widely used approach to analyzing a bank, CAMELS, considers a bank's **C**apital adequacy, **A**sset quality, **M**anagement capabilities, **E**arnings sufficiency, **L**iquidity position, and **S**ensitivity to market risk.
- "**C**apital adequacy," described in terms of the proportion of the bank's assets that is funded with capital, indicates that a bank has enough capital to absorb potential losses without severely damaging its financial position.
- "**A**sset quality" includes the concept of quality of the bank's assets—credit quality and diversification—and the concept of overall sound risk management.
- "**M**anagement capabilities" refers to the bank management's ability to identify and exploit appropriate business opportunities and to simultaneously manage associated risks.
- "**E**arnings" refers to the bank's return on capital relative to cost of capital and also includes the concept of earnings quality.
- "**L**iquidity" refers to the amount of liquid assets held by the bank relative to its near-term expected cash flows. Under Basel III, liquidity also refers to the stability of the bank's funding sources.
- "**S**ensitivity to market risk" pertains to how adverse changes in markets (including interest rate, exchange rate, equity, and commodity markets) could affect the bank's earnings and capital position.
- In addition to the CAMELS components, important attributes deserving analysts' attention include government support, the banking entity's mission, corporate culture and competitive environment, off-balance-sheet items, segment information, currency exposure, and risk disclosures.
- Insurance companies are typically categorized as property and casualty (P&C) or life and health (L&H).
- Insurance companies earn revenues from premiums (amounts paid by the purchaser of insurance products) and from investment income earned on the float (amounts collected as premiums and not yet paid out as benefits).
- P&C insurers' policies are usually short term, and the final cost will usually be known within a year of a covered event, whereas L&H insurers' policies are usually longer term. P&C insurers' claims are more variable, whereas L&H insurers' claims are more predictable.
- For both types of insurance companies, important areas for analysis include business profile, earnings characteristics, investment returns, liquidity, and capitalization. In addition, analysis of P&C companies' profitability includes analysis of loss reserves and the combined ratio.

PROBLEMS

The following information relates to Questions 1–7

Viktoria Smith is a recently hired junior analyst at Aries Investments. Smith and her supervisor, Ingrid Johansson, meet to discuss some of the firm's investments in banks and insurance companies.

Johansson asks Smith to explain why the evaluation of banks is different from the evaluation of non-financial companies. Smith tells Johansson the following:

Statement 1: As intermediaries, banks are more likely to be systemically important than non-financial companies.

Statement 2: The assets of banks mostly consist of deposits, which are exposed to different risks than the tangible assets of non-financial companies.

Smith and Johansson also discuss key aspects of financial regulations, particularly the framework of Basel III. Johansson tells Smith:

"Basel III specifies the minimum percentage of its risk-weighted assets that a bank must fund with equity. This requirement of Basel III prevents a bank from assuming so much financial leverage that it is unable to withstand loan losses or asset write-downs."

Johansson tells Smith that she uses the CAMELS approach to evaluate banks, even though it has some limitations. To evaluate P&C insurance companies, Johansson tells Smith that she places emphasis on the efficiency of spending on obtaining new premiums. Johansson and Smith discuss differences between P&C and L&H insurance companies. Smith notes the following differences:

Difference 1: L&H insurers' claims are more predictable than P&C insurers' claims.

Difference 2: P&C insurers' policies are usually short term, whereas L&H insurers' policies are usually longer term.

Difference 3: Relative to L&H insurers, P&C insurers often have lower capital requirements and can also seek higher returns offered by riskier investments.

Johansson asks Smith to review key performance ratios for three P&C insurers in which Aries is invested. The ratios are presented in Exhibit 1.

EXHIBIT 1 Key Performance Ratios for Selected P&C Insurers

	Insurer A	Insurer B	Insurer C
Loss and loss adjustment expense ratio	68.8%	65.9%	64.1%
Underwriting expense ratio	33.7%	37.8%	32.9%
Combined ratio	102.5%	103.7%	97.0%

Johansson also asks Smith to review key performance ratios for ABC Bank, a bank in which Aries is invested. The ratios are presented in Exhibit 2.

EXHIBIT 2 Key Performance Ratios for ABC Bank*

	2017	2016	2015
Common equity Tier 1 capital ratio	10.7%	11.5%	12.1%
Tier 1 capital ratio	11.5%	12.6%	13.4%
Total capital ratio	14.9%	14.8%	14.9%
Liquidity coverage ratio	123.6%	121.4%	119.1%
Net stable funding ratio	114.9%	113.2%	112.7%
Total trading VaR (all market risk factors)	$11	$13	$15
Total trading and credit portfolio VaR	$15	$18	$21

*Note: VaR amounts are in millions and are based on a 99% confidence interval and a single-day holding period.

1. Which of Smith's statements regarding banks is correct?
   A. Only Statement 1
   B. Only Statement 2
   C. Both Statement 1 and Statement 2

2. The aspect of the Basel III framework that Johansson describes to Smith relates to minimum:
   A. capital requirements.
   B. liquidity requirements.
   C. amounts of stable funding requirements.

3. One limitation of the approach used by Johansson to evaluate banks is that it fails to address a bank's:
   A. sensitivity to market risk.
   B. management capabilities.
   C. competitive environment.

4. The best indicator of the operations of a P&C insurance company emphasized by Johansson when evaluating P&C insurance companies is the:
   A. combined ratio.
   B. underwriting loss ratio.
   C. underwriting expense ratio.

5. Which of the differences between P&C insurers and L&H insurers noted by Smith is *incorrect*?
   A. Difference 1
   B. Difference 2
   C. Difference 3

6. Based on Exhibit 1, Smith should conclude that the insurer with the most efficient underwriting operation is:
   A. Insurer A.
   B. Insurer B.
   C. Insurer C.

7. Based on Exhibit 2, Smith and Johansson should conclude that over the past three years, ABC Bank's:
   A. liquidity position has declined.
   B. capital adequacy has improved.
   C. sensitivity to market risk has improved.

The following information relates to Questions 8–14

Ivan Paulinic, an analyst at a large wealth management firm, meets with his supervisor to discuss adding financial institution equity securities to client portfolios. Paulinic focuses on Vermillion Insurance (Vermillion), a property and casualty company, and Cobalt Life Insurance (Cobalt). To evaluate Vermillion further, Paulinic compiles the information presented in Exhibit 1.

EXHIBIT 1   Select Financial Ratios for Vermillion Insurance

Ratio	2017	2016
Loss and loss adjustment expense	59.1%	61.3%
Underwriting expense	36.3%	35.8%
Combined	95.4%	97.1%
Dividend	2.8%	2.6%

In addition to the insurance companies, Paulinic gathers data on three national banks that meet initial selection criteria but require further review. This information is shown in Exhibits 2, 3, and 4.

EXHIBIT 2   Select Balance Sheet Data for National Banks—Trading: Contribution to Total Revenues

Bank	2017	2013	2009	2005
N-bank	4.2%	7.0%	10.1%	8.9%
R-bank	8.3%	9.1%	17.0%	7.9%
T-bank	5.0%	5.0%	11.9%	6.8%

Focusing on N-bank and T-bank, Paulinic prepares the following data.

EXHIBIT 3   2017 Select Data for N-bank and T-bank

	N-bank		T-bank	
	2017	2016	2017	2016
Average daily trading VaR ($ millions)	11.3	12.6	21.4	20.5
Annual trading revenue/average daily trading VaR	160×	134×	80×	80×

Paulinic investigates R-bank's risk management practices with respect to the use of credit derivatives to enhance earnings, following the 2008 financial crisis. Exhibit 4 displays R-bank's exposure over the last decade to credit derivatives not classified as hedges.

EXHIBIT 4   R-bank's Exposure to Freestanding Credit Derivatives

Credit Derivative Balances	2017	2012	2007
Notional amount ($ billions)	13.4	15.5	305.1

All of the national banks under consideration primarily make long-term loans and source a significant portion of their funding from retail deposits. Paulinic and the rest of the research team note that the central bank is unwinding a long period of monetary easing as evidenced by two recent increases in the overnight funding rate. Paulinic informs his supervisor that:

Statement 1:   Given the recently reported stronger-than-anticipated macroeconomic data, there is an imminent risk that the yield curve will invert.

Statement 2:   N-bank is very active in the 30-day reverse repurchase agreement market during times when the bank experiences significant increases in retail deposits.

8. Paulinic's analysis of the two insurance companies *most likely* indicates that:
   A. Cobalt has more-predictable claims than Vermillion.
   B. Cobalt has a higher capital requirement than Vermillion.
   C. Vermillion's calculated risk-based capital is more sensitive than Cobalt's to interest rate risk.

9. Based only on the information in Exhibit 1, in 2017 Vermillion *most likely*:
   A. experienced a decrease in overall efficiency.
   B. improved its ability to estimate insured risks.
   C. was more efficient in obtaining new premiums.

10. Based only on Exhibit 2, which of the following statements is correct?
    A. The quality of earnings for R-bank was the highest in 2009.
    B. Relative to the other banks, N-bank has the highest quality of earnings in 2017.
    C. Trading represented a sustainable revenue source for T-bank between 2005 and 2013.

11. Based only on Exhibit 3, Paulinic should conclude that:
    A. trading activities are riskier at T-bank than N-bank.
    B. trading revenue per unit of risk has improved more at N-bank than T-bank.
    C. compared with duration, the metric used is a better measure of interest rate risk.

12. Based only on Exhibit 4, R-bank's use of credit derivatives since 2007 *most likely*:
    A. increased posted collateral.
    B. decreased the volatility of earnings from trading activities.
    C. indicates consistent correlations among the relevant risks taken.

13. Based on Statement 1, the net interest margin for the three banks' *most likely* will:
    A. decrease.
    B. remain unchanged.
    C. increase.

14. Based on Statement 2, the financial ratio *most* directly affected is the:
    A. Tier 2 capital ratio.
    B. net stable funding ratio.
    C. liquidity coverage ratio.

The following information relates to Questions 15–20

Judith Yoo is a financial sector analyst writing an industry report. In the report, Yoo discusses the relative global systemic risk across industries, referencing Industry A (international property and casualty insurance), Industry B (credit unions), and Industry C (global commercial banks).

Part of Yoo's analysis focuses on Company XYZ, a global commercial bank, and its CAMELS rating, risk management practices, and performance. First, Yoo considers the firm's capital adequacy as measured by the key capital ratios (common equity Tier 1 capital, total Tier 1 capital, and total capital) in Exhibit 1.

EXHIBIT 1   Company XYZ: Excerpt from Annual Report Disclosure

At December 31 Regulatory capital	2017 $m	2016 $m	2015 $m
Common equity Tier 1 capital	146,424	142,367	137,100
Additional Tier 1 capital	22,639	20,443	17,600
Tier 2 capital	22,456	27,564	38,200
Total regulatory capital	191,519	190,374	192,900

EXHIBIT 1   (Continued)

At December 31 Regulatory capital	2017 $m	2016 $m	2015 $m
Risk-weighted assets (RWAs) by risk type			
Credit risk	960,763	989,639	968,600
Market risk	44,100	36,910	49,600
Operational risk	293,825	256,300	224,300
Total RWAs	1,298,688	1,282,849	1,242,500

Yoo turns her attention to Company XYZ's asset quality using the information in Exhibit 2.

EXHIBIT 2   Company XYZ: Asset Composition

At December 31	2017 $m	2016 $m	2015 $m
Total liquid assets	361,164	354,056	356,255
Investments	434,256	367,158	332,461
Consumer loans	456,957	450,576	447,493
Commercial loans	499,647	452,983	403,058
Goodwill	26,693	26,529	25,705
Other assets	151,737	144,210	121,780
Total assets	1,930,454	1,795,512	1,686,752

To assess Company XYZ's risk management practices, Yoo reviews the consumer loan credit quality profile in Exhibit 3 and the loan loss analysis in Exhibit 4.

EXHIBIT 3   Company XYZ: Consumer Loan Profile by Credit Quality

At December 31	2017 $m	2016 $m	2015 $m
Strong credit quality	338,948	327,345	320,340
Good credit quality	52,649	54,515	54,050
Satisfactory credit quality	51,124	55,311	56,409
Substandard credit quality	23,696	24,893	27,525
Past due but not impaired	2,823	2,314	2,058
Impaired	8,804	9,345	10,235
Total gross amount	478,044	473,723	470,617
Impairment allowances	−5,500	−4,500	−4,000
Total	472,544	469,223	466,617

EXHIBIT 4   Company XYZ: Loan Loss Analysis Data

At December 31	2017 $m	2016 $m	2015 $m
Consumer loans			
Allowance for loan losses	11,000	11,500	13,000
Provision for loan losses	3,000	2,000	1,300
Charge-offs	3,759	3,643	4,007
Recoveries	1,299	1,138	1,106
Net charge-offs	2,460	2,505	2,901
Commercial loans			
Allowance for loan losses	1,540	1,012	169
Provision for loan losses	1,100	442	95
Charge-offs	1,488	811	717
Recoveries	428	424	673
Net charge-offs	1,060	387	44

Finally, Yoo notes the following supplementary information from Company XYZ's annual report:

• Competition in the commercial loan space has become increasingly fierce, leading XYZ managers to pursue higher-risk strategies to increase market share.
• The net benefit plan obligation has steadily decreased during the last three years.
• Company XYZ awards above-average equity-based compensation to its top managers.

15. Which of the following industries *most likely* has the highest level of global systemic risk?
    A. Industry A
    B. Industry B
    C. Industry C

16. Based on Exhibit 1, Company XYZ's capital adequacy over the last three years, as measured by the three key capital ratios, signals conditions that are:
    A. mixed.
    B. declining.
    C. improving.

17. Based only on Exhibit 2, asset composition from 2015 to 2017 indicates:
    A. declining liquidity.
    B. increasing risk based on the proportion of total loans to total assets.
    C. decreasing risk based on the proportion of investments to total assets.

18. Based on Exhibit 3, the trend in impairment allowances is reflective of the changes in:
    A. impaired assets.
    B. strong credit quality assets.
    C. past due but not impaired assets.

19. Based on Exhibit 4, a loan loss analysis for the last three years indicates that:
    A. Company XYZ has become less conservative in its provisioning for consumer loans.
    B. the provision for commercial loan losses has trailed the actual net charge-off experience.
    C. the cushion between the allowance and the net commercial loan charge-offs has declined.

20. Which of the following supplemental factors is consistent with a favorable assessment of Company XYZ's financial outlook?
    A. Competitive environment
    B. Net benefit plan obligation
    C. Equity-based compensation policy

CHAPTER 17

EVALUATING QUALITY OF FINANCIAL REPORTS

LEARNING OUTCOMES

After completing this chapter, you will be able to do the following:

- demonstrate the use of a conceptual framework for assessing the quality of a company's financial reports;
- explain potential problems that affect the quality of financial reports;
- describe how to evaluate the quality of a company's financial reports;
- evaluate the quality of a company's financial reports;
- describe the concept of sustainable (persistent) earnings;
- describe indicators of earnings quality;
- explain mean reversion in earnings and how the accruals component of earnings affects the speed of mean reversion;
- evaluate the earnings quality of a company;
- describe indicators of cash flow quality;
- evaluate the cash flow quality of a company;
- describe indicators of balance sheet quality;
- evaluate the balance sheet quality of a company;
- describe sources of information about risk.

SUMMARY OVERVIEW

Assessing the quality of financial reports—both reporting quality and results quality—is an important analytical skill.

- The quality of financial reporting can be thought of as spanning a continuum from the highest quality to the lowest.
- Potential problems that affect the quality of financial reporting broadly include revenue and expense recognition on the income statement; classification on the statement of cash flows;

and the recognition, classification, and measurement of assets and liabilities on the balance sheet.
- Typical steps involved in evaluating financial reporting quality include an understanding of the company's business and industry in which the company is operating; comparison of the financial statements in the current period and the previous period to identify any significant differences in line items; an evaluation of the company's accounting policies, especially any unusual revenue and expense recognition compared with those of other companies in the same industry; financial ratio analysis; examination of the statement of cash flows with particular focus on differences between net income and operating cash flows; perusal of risk disclosures; and review of management compensation and insider transactions.
- High-quality earnings increase the value of the company more than low-quality earnings, and the term "high-quality earnings" assumes that reporting quality is high.
- Low-quality earnings are insufficient to cover the company's cost of capital and/or are derived from non-recurring, one-off activities. In addition, the term "low-quality earnings" can be used when the reported information does not provide a useful indication of the company's performance.
- Various alternatives have been used as indicators of earnings quality: recurring earnings, earnings persistence and related measures of accruals, beating benchmarks, and after-the-fact confirmations of poor-quality earnings, such as enforcement actions and restatements.
- Earnings that have a significant accrual component are less persistent and thus may revert to the mean more quickly.
- A company that consistently reports earnings that exactly meet or only narrowly beat benchmarks can raise questions about its earnings quality.
- Cases of accounting malfeasance have commonly involved issues with revenue recognition, such as premature recognition of revenues or the recognition of fraudulent revenues.
- Cases of accounting malfeasance have involved misrepresentation of expenditures as assets rather than as expenses or misrepresentation of the timing or amount of expenses.
- Bankruptcy prediction models, used in assessing financial results quality, quantify the likelihood that a company will default on its debt and/or declare bankruptcy.
- Similar to the term "earnings quality," when reported cash flows are described as being high quality, it means that the company's underlying economic performance was satisfactory in terms of increasing the value of the firm, and it also implies that the company had high reporting quality (i.e., that the information calculated and disclosed by the company was a good reflection of economic reality). Cash flow can be described as "low quality" either because the reported information properly represents genuinely bad economic performance or because the reported information misrepresents economic reality.
- For the balance sheet, high financial *reporting* quality is indicated by completeness, unbiased measurement, and clear presentation.
- A balance sheet with significant amounts of off-balance-sheet debt would lack the completeness aspect of financial reporting quality.
- Unbiased measurement is a particularly important aspect of financial reporting quality for assets and liabilities for which valuation is subjective.
- A company's financial statements can provide useful indicators of financial or operating risk.
- The management commentary (also referred to as the management discussion and analysis, or MD&A) can give users of the financial statements information that is helpful in assessing the company's risk exposures and approaches to managing risk.

- Required disclosures regarding, for example, changes in senior management or inability to make a timely filing of required financial reports can be a warning sign of problems with financial reporting quality.
- The financial press can be a useful source of information about risk when, for example, a financial reporter uncovers financial reporting issues that had not previously been recognized. An analyst should undertake additional investigation of any issue identified.

PROBLEMS

The following information relates to Questions 1–4

Mike Martinez is an equity analyst who has been asked to analyze Stellar, Inc. by his supervisor, Dominic Anderson. Stellar exhibited strong earnings growth last year; however, Anderson is skeptical about the sustainability of the company's earnings. He wants Martinez to focus on Stellar's financial reporting quality and earnings quality.

After conducting a thorough review of the company's financial statements, Martinez concludes the following:

Conclusion 1:	Although Stellar's financial statements adhere to generally accepted accounting principles (GAAP), Stellar understates earnings in periods when the company is performing well and overstates earnings in periods when the company is struggling.
Conclusion 2:	Stellar most likely understated the value of amortizable intangibles when recording the acquisition of Solar, Inc. last year. No goodwill impairment charges have been taken since the acquisition.
Conclusion 3:	Over time, the accruals component of Stellar's earnings is large relative to the cash component.
Conclusion 4:	Stellar reported an unusually sharp decline in accounts receivable in the current year, and an increase in long-term trade receivables.

1. Based on Martinez's conclusions, Stellar's financial statements are *best* categorized as:
   A. non-GAAP compliant.
   B. GAAP compliant, but with earnings management.
   C. GAAP compliant and decision useful, with sustainable and adequate returns.

2. Based on Conclusion 2, after the acquisition of Solar, Stellar's earnings are *most likely*:
   A. understated.
   B. fairly stated.
   C. overstated.

3. In his follow-up analysis relating to Conclusion 3, Martinez should focus on Stellar's:
   A. total accruals.
   B. discretionary accruals.
   C. non-discretionary accruals.

4. What will be the impact on Stellar in the current year if Martinez's belief in Conclusion 4 is correct? Compared with the previous year, Stellar's:
   A. current ratio will increase.
   B. days sales outstanding (DSO) will decrease.
   C. accounts receivable turnover will decrease.

The following information relates to Questions 5–12

Ioana Matei is a senior portfolio manager for an international wealth management firm. She directs research analyst Teresa Pereira to investigate the earnings quality of Miland Communications and Globales, Inc.

Pereira first reviews industry data and the financial reports of Miland Communications for the past few years. Pereira then makes the following three statements about Miland:

Statement 1: Miland shortened the depreciable lives for capital assets.
Statement 2: Revenue growth has been higher than that of industry peers.
Statement 3: Discounts to customers and returns from customers have decreased.

Pereira also observes that Miland has experienced increasing inventory turnover, increasing receivables turnover, and net income greater than cash flow from operations. She estimates the following regression model to assess Miland's earnings persistence:

$$\text{Earnings}_{t+1} = \alpha + \beta_1 \text{Cash flow}_t + \beta_2 \text{Accruals}_t + \varepsilon$$

Pereira and Matei discuss quantitative models such as the Beneish model, used to assess the likelihood of misreporting. Pereira makes the following two statements to Matei:

Statement 4: An advantage of using quantitative models is that they can determine cause and effect between model variables.
Statement 5: A disadvantage of using quantitative models is that their predictive power declines over time because many managers have learned to test the detectability of manipulation tactics by using the model.

Pereira collects the information in Exhibit 1 to use the Beneish model to assess Miland's likelihood of misreporting.

EXHIBIT 1   Selected Beneish Model Data for Miland Communications

	Last Year	Current Year
Days' sales receivable index (DSR)	0.90	1.20
Leverage index (LEVI)	0.75	0.95
Sales, general, and administrative expenses index (SGAI)	0.60	0.75

Pereira concludes her investigation of Miland by examining the company's reported pre-tax income of $5.4 billion last year. This amount includes $1.2 billion of acquisition and divestiture-related expenses, $0.5 billion of restructuring expenses, and $1.1 billion of other non-operating expenses. Pereira determines that the acquisition and divestiture-related expenses as well as restructuring expenses are non-recurring expenses, but other expenses are recurring expenses.

Matei then asks Pereira to review last year's financial statements for Globales, Inc. and assess the effect of two possible misstatements. Upon doing so, Pereira judges that Globales improperly recognized EUR50 million of revenue and improperly capitalized EUR100 million of its cost of revenue. She then estimates the effect of these two misstatements on net income, assuming a tax rate of 25%.

Pereira compares Globales, Inc.'s financial statements with those of an industry competitor. Both firms have similar, above-average returns on equity (ROE), although Globales has a higher cash flow component of earnings. Pereira applies the mean reversion principle in her forecasts of the two firms' future ROE.

5. Which of Pereira's statements describes an accounting warning sign of potential overstatement or non-sustainability of operating and/or net income?
   A. Statement 1
   B. Statement 2
   C. Statement 3

6. Which of Pereira's statements about Miland Communications is *most likely* a warning sign of potential earnings manipulation?
   A. The trend in inventory turnover
   B. The trend in receivables turnover
   C. The amount of net income relative to cash flow from operations

7. Based on the regression model used by Pereira, earnings persistence for Miland would be highest if:
   A. β_1 is less than 0.
   B. β_1 is greater than β_2.
   C. β_2 is greater than β_1.

8. Which of Pereira's statements regarding the use of quantitative models to assess the likelihood of misreporting is correct?
   A. Only Statement 4
   B. Only Statement 5
   C. Both Statement 4 and Statement 5

9. Based on Exhibit 1, which variable in the Beneish model has a year-over-year change that would increase Miland's likelihood of manipulation?
   A. DSR
   B. LEVI
   C. SGAI

10. Based on Pereira's determination of recurring and non-recurring expenses for Miland, the company's recurring or core pre-tax earnings last year is *closest* to:
    A. $4.3 billion.
    B. $4.8 billion.
    C. $7.1 billion.

11. After adjusting the Globales, Inc. income statement for the two possible misstatements, the decline in net income is *closest* to:
    A. EUR37.5 million.
    B. EUR112.5 million.
    C. EUR150.0 million.

12. Pereira should forecast that the ROE for Globales is likely to decline:
    A. more slowly than that of the industry competitor.
    B. at the same rate as the industry competitor.
    C. more rapidly than that of the industry competitor.

The following information relates to Questions 13–19

Emmitt Dodd is a portfolio manager for Upsilon Advisers. Dodd meets with Sonya Webster, the firm's analyst responsible for the machinery industry, to discuss three established companies: BIG Industrial, Construction Supply, and Dynamic Production. Webster provides Dodd with research notes for each company that reflect trends during the last three years:

BIG Industrial:

Note 1: Operating income has been much lower than operating cash flow (OCF).
Note 2: Accounts payable has increased, while accounts receivable and inventory have substantially decreased.
Note 3: Although OCF was positive, it was just sufficient to cover capital expenditures, dividends, and debt repayments.

Construction Supply:

Note 4: Operating margins have been relatively constant.
Note 5: The growth rate in revenue has exceeded the growth rate in receivables.
Note 6: OCF was stable and positive, close to its reported net income, and just sufficient to cover capital expenditures, dividends, and debt repayments.

Dynamic Production:

Note 7: OCF has been more volatile than that of other industry participants.
Note 8: OCF has fallen short of covering capital expenditures, dividends, and debt repayments.

Dodd asks Webster about the use of quantitative tools to assess the likelihood of misreporting. Webster tells Dodd she uses the Beneish model, and she presents the estimated *M*-scores for each company in Exhibit 1.

EXHIBIT 1   Beneish Model *M*-scores

Company	2017	2016	Change in *M*-score
BIG Industrial	−1.54	−1.82	0.28
Construction Supply	−2.60	−2.51	−0.09
Dynamic Production	−1.86	−1.12	−0.74

Webster tells Dodd that Dynamic Production was required to restate its 2016 financial statements as a result of its attempt to inflate sales revenue. Customers of Dynamic Production were encouraged to take excess product in 2016, and they were then allowed to return purchases in the subsequent period, without penalty.

Webster's industry analysis leads her to believe that innovations have caused some of the BIG Industrial's inventory to become obsolete. Webster expresses concern to Dodd that although the notes to the financial statements for BIG Industrial are informative about its inventory cost methods, its inventory is overstated.

The BIG Industrial income statement reflects a profitable 49% unconsolidated equity investment. Webster calculates the return on sales of BIG Industrial based on the reported income statement. Dodd notes that industry peers consolidate similar investments. Dodd asks Webster to use a comparable method of calculating the return on sales for BIG Industrial.

13. Which of Webster's notes about BIG Industrial provides an accounting warning sign of a potential reporting problem?
    A. Only Note 1
    B. Only Note 2
    C. Both Note 1 and Note 2

14. Do either of Webster's Notes 4 or 5 about Construction Supply describe an accounting warning sign of potential overstatement or non-sustainability of operating income?
    A. No
    B. Yes, Note 4 provides a warning sign
    C. Yes, Note 5 provides a warning sign

15. Based on Webster's research notes, which company would *most likely* be described as having high-quality cash flow?
    A. BIG Industrial
    B. Construction Supply
    C. Dynamic Production

16. Based on the Beneish model results for 2017 in Exhibit 1, which company has the highest probability of being an earnings manipulator?
    A. BIG Industrial
    B. Construction Supply
    C. Dynamic Production

17. Based on the information related to its restatement, Dynamic Production reported poor operating cash flow quality in 2016 by understating:
    A. inventories.
    B. net income.
    C. trade receivables.

18. Webster's concern about BIG Industrial's inventory suggests poor reporting quality, *most likely* resulting from a lack of:
    A. completeness.
    B. clear presentation.
    C. unbiased measurement.

19. In response to Dodd's request, Webster's recalculated return on sales will *most likely*:
    A. decrease.
    B. remain the same.
    C. increase.

CHAPTER 18

INTEGRATION OF FINANCIAL STATEMENT ANALYSIS TECHNIQUES

LEARNING OUTCOMES

After completing this chapter, you will be able to do the following:

- demonstrate the use of a framework for the analysis of financial statements, given a particular problem, question, or purpose (e.g., valuing equity based on comparables, critiquing a credit rating, obtaining a comprehensive picture of financial leverage, evaluating the perspectives given in management's discussion of financial results);
- identify financial reporting choices and biases that affect the quality and comparability of companies' financial statements and explain how such biases may affect financial decisions;
- evaluate the quality of a company's financial data and recommend appropriate adjustments to improve quality and comparability with similar companies, including adjustments for differences in accounting standards, methods, and assumptions;
- evaluate how a given change in accounting standards, methods, or assumptions affects financial statements and ratios;
- analyze and interpret how balance sheet modifications, earnings normalization, and cash flow statement related modifications affect a company's financial statements, financial ratios, and overall financial condition.

SUMMARY OVERVIEW

The case study demonstrates the use of a financial analysis framework in investment decision making. Although each analysis undertaken may have a different focus, purpose, and context that result in the application of different techniques and tools, the case demonstrates the use of a common financial statement analysis framework. The analyst starts with a global, summarized view of a company and its attributes and digs below the surface of the financial statements to find economic truths that are not apparent from a superficial review. In the case of Nestlé, the analyst applied disaggregation techniques to review the company's performance in terms of ROE and then successively examined the drivers of ROE in increasing detail to evaluate management's skills in capital allocation.

An economic decision is reached, which is consistent with the primary reason for performing financial analysis: to facilitate an economic decision.

PROBLEMS

The following information relates to Questions 1–7

Quentin Abay, CFA, is an analyst for a private equity firm interested in purchasing Bickchip Enterprises, a conglomerate. His first task is to determine the trends in ROE and the main drivers of the trends using DuPont analysis. To do so he gathers the data in Exhibit 1.

EXHIBIT 1   Selected Financial Data for Bickchip Enterprises (€ Thousands)

	2020	2019	2018
Revenue	72,448	66,487	55,781
Earnings before interest and tax	6,270	4,710	3,609
Earnings before tax	5,101	4,114	3,168
Net income	4,038	3,345	2,576
Asset turnover	0.79	0.76	0.68
Assets/Equity	3.09	3.38	3.43

After conducting the DuPont analysis, Abay believes that his firm could increase the ROE without operational changes. Further, Abay thinks that ROE could improve if the company divested segments that were generating the lowest returns on capital employed (total assets less non-interest-bearing liabilities). Segment EBIT margins in 2020 were 11 percent for Automation Equipment, 5 percent for Power and Industrial, and 8 percent for Medical Equipment. Other relevant segment information is presented in Exhibit 2.

EXHIBIT 2   Segment Data for Bickchip Enterprises (€ Thousands)

Operating Segments	Capital Employed			Capital Expenditures (Excluding Acquisitions)		
	2020	2019	2018	2020	2019	2018
Automation Equipment	10,705	6,384	5,647	700	743	616
Power and Industrial	15,805	13,195	12,100	900	849	634
Medical Equipment	22,870	22,985	22,587	908	824	749
	49,380	42,564	40,334	2,508	2,416	1,999

Abay is also concerned with earnings quality, so he intends to calculate Bickchip's cash-flow-based accruals ratio and the ratio of operating cash flow before interest and taxes to operating income. To do so, he prepares the information in Exhibit 3.

EXHIBIT 3   Earnings Quality Data for Bickchip Enterprises (€ Thousands)

	2020	2019	2018
Net income	4,038	3,345	2,576
Net cash flow provided by (used in) operating activity[a]	9,822	5,003	3,198
Net cash flow provided by (used in) investing activity	(10,068)	(4,315)	(5,052)
Net cash flow provided by (used in) financing activity[b]	(5,792)	1,540	(2,241)
Average net operating assets	43,192	45,373	40,421
[a] includes cash paid for taxes of:	(1,930)	(1,191)	(1,093)
[b] includes cash paid for interest of:	(1,169)	(596)	(441)

1. Over the three-year period presented in Exhibit 1, Bickchip's return on equity is *best* described as:
   A. stable.
   B. trending lower.
   C. trending higher.

2. Based on the DuPont analysis, Abay's belief regarding ROE is *most likely* based on:
   A. leverage.
   B. profit margins.
   C. asset turnover.

3. Based on Abay's criteria, the business segment *best* suited for divestiture is:
   A. medical equipment.
   B. power and industrial.
   C. automation equipment.

4. Bickchip's cash-flow-based accruals ratio in 2020 is *closest* to:
   A. 9.9%.
   B. 13.4%.
   C. 23.3%.

5. The cash-flow-based accruals ratios from 2018 to 2020 indicate:
   A. improving earnings quality.
   B. deteriorating earnings quality.
   C. no change in earnings quality.

6. The ratio of operating cash flow before interest and taxes to operating income for Bickchip for 2020 is *closest* to:
   A. 1.6.
   B. 1.9.
   C. 2.1.

7. Based on the ratios for operating cash flow before interest and taxes to operating income, Abay should conclude that:
   A. Bickchip's earnings are backed by cash flow.
   B. Bickchip's earnings are not backed by cash flow.
   C. Abay can draw no conclusion due to the changes in the ratios over time.

SOLUTIONS

PART II

SOLUTIONS

CHAPTER 1

INTRODUCTION TO FINANCIAL STATEMENT ANALYSIS

SOLUTIONS

1. B is correct. This is the role of financial reporting. The role of financial statement analysis is to evaluate the financial reports.

2. C is correct. In general, analysts seek to examine the past and current performance and financial position of a company in order to form expectations about its future performance and financial position.

3. B is correct. The primary role of financial statement analysis is to use financial reports prepared by companies to evaluate their past, current, and potential performance and financial position for the purpose of making investment, credit, and other economic decisions.

4. A is correct. The balance sheet portrays the company's financial position on a specified date. The income statement and statement of cash flows present different aspects of performance during the period.

5. B is correct. Profitability is the performance aspect measured by the income statement. The balance sheet portrays the financial position. The statement of cash flows presents a different aspect of performance.

6. A is correct. Owners' equity is the owners' residual interest in (i.e., residual claim on) the company's assets after deducting its liabilities, which is information presented on the balance sheet.

7. B is correct. A company's profitability is best evaluated using the income statement. The income statement presents information on the financial results of a company's business activities over a period of time by communicating how much revenue was generated and the expenses incurred to generate that revenue.

8. C is correct. A company's revenues and expenses are presented on the income statement, which is used to evaluate a company's financial results (or profitability) from business activities over a period of time. A company's financial position is best evaluated by using the balance sheet. A company's sources of cash flow are best evaluated using the cash flow statement.

9. C is correct. The notes disclose choices in accounting policies, methods, and estimates.

10. A is correct. Information about management and director compensation is not found in the auditor's report. Disclosure of management compensation is required in the proxy statement, and some aspects of management compensation are disclosed in the notes to the financial statements.

11. B is correct. These are components of management commentary.

12. C is correct. The notes provide information that is essential to understanding the information provided in the primary statements.

13. C is correct. An unqualified opinion is a "clean" opinion and indicates that the financial statements present the company's performance and financial position fairly, in accordance with a specified set of accounting standards.

14. B is correct. A qualified audit opinion is one in which there is some scope limitation or exception to accounting standards. Exceptions are described in the audit report with additional explanatory paragraphs so that the analyst can determine the importance of the exception.

15. B is correct. The independent audit report provides reasonable assurance that the financial statements are fairly presented, meaning that there is a high probability that the audited financial statements are free from material error, fraud, or illegal acts that have a direct effect on the financial statements.

16. B is correct. Interim reports are typically provided semiannually or quarterly and present the four basic financial statements and condensed notes. They are not audited. Unqualified is a type of audit opinion.

17. B is correct. When performing financial statement analysis, analysts should review all company sources of information as well as information from external sources regarding the economy, the industry, the company, and peer (comparable) companies.

18. C is correct. Ratios are an output of the process data step but are an input into the analyze/interpret data step.

19. A is correct. The follow-up phase involves gathering information and repeating the analysis to determine whether it is necessary to update reports and recommendations.

CHAPTER 2

FINANCIAL REPORTING STANDARDS

SOLUTIONS

1. C is correct. Financial statements provide information, including information about the entity's financial position, performance, and changes in financial position, to users. They do not typically provide information about users.

2. B is correct. The IASB is currently charged with developing International Financial Reporting Standards.

3. B is correct. The FASB is responsible for the Accounting Standards Codification™, the single source of nongovernmental authoritative US generally accepted accounting principles.

4. C is correct. A core objective of IOSCO is to ensure that markets are fair, efficient, and transparent. The other core objectives are to reduce, not eliminate, systemic risk and to protect investors, not all users of financial statements.

5. A is correct. Accuracy is not an enhancing qualitative characteristic. Faithful representation, not accuracy, is a fundamental qualitative characteristic.

6. A is correct. Understandability is an enhancing qualitative characteristic of financial information—not a constraint.

7. C is correct. The *Conceptual Framework* identifies two important underlying assumptions of financial statements: accrual basis and going concern. Going concern is the assumption that the entity will continue to operate for the foreseeable future. Enterprises with the intent to liquidate or materially curtail operations would require different information for a fair presentation.

8. B is correct. Accrual basis reflects the effects of transactions and other events being recognized when they occur, not when the cash flows. These effects are recorded and reported in the financial statements of the periods to which they relate.

9. C is correct. The fundamental qualitative characteristic of faithful representation is contributed to by completeness, neutrality, and freedom from error.

10. B is correct. Historical cost is the consideration paid to acquire an asset.

11. C is correct. The amount that would be received in an orderly disposal is realizable value.

12. B is correct. There is no statement of changes in income. Under IAS No. 1, a complete set of financial statements includes a statement of financial position, a statement of comprehensive income, a statement of changes in equity, a statement of cash flows, and notes comprising a summary of significant accounting policies and other explanatory information.

13. B is correct. The elements of financial statements related to the measure of performance are income and expenses.

14. A is correct. The elements of financial statements related to the measurement of financial position are assets, liabilities, and equity.

15. A is correct. A discussion of the impact would be the most meaningful, although B would also be useful.

CHAPTER 3

UNDERSTANDING INCOME STATEMENTS

SOLUTIONS

1. C is correct. IAS No. 1 states that expenses may be categorized by either nature or function.
2. C is correct. Cost of goods sold is a classification by function. The other two expenses represent classifications by nature.
3. C is correct. Gross margin is revenue minus cost of goods sold. Answer A represents net income, and B represents operating income.
4. B is correct. Under IFRS, income includes increases in economic benefits from increases in assets, enhancement of assets, and decreases in liabilities.
5. B is correct. Net revenue is revenue for goods sold during the period less any returns and allowances, or $1,000,000 minus $100,000 = $900,000.
6. A is correct. Apex is not the owner of the goods and should only report its net commission as revenue.
7. C is correct. Under the converged accounting standards, the incremental costs of obtaining a contract and certain costs incurred to fulfill a contract must be capitalized. If a company expensed these incremental costs in the years prior to adopting the converged standards, all else being equal, its profitability will appear higher under the converged standards.
8. B is correct. Under the first in, first out (FIFO) method, the first 10,000 units sold came from the October purchases at £10, and the next 2,000 units sold came from the November purchases at £11.
9. C is correct. Under the weighted average cost method:

October purchases	10,000 units	$100,000
November purchases	5,000 units	$55,000
Total	15,000 units	$155,000

$155,000/15,000 units = $10.3333 × 12,000 units = $124,000.

10. B is correct. The last in, first out (LIFO) method is not permitted under IFRS. The other two methods are permitted.

11. A is correct. Straight-line depreciation would be ($600,000 − $50,000)/10, or $55,000.

12. C is correct. Double-declining balance depreciation would be $600,000 × 20 percent (twice the straight-line rate). The residual value is not subtracted from the initial book value to calculate depreciation. However, the book value (carrying amount) of the asset will not be reduced below the estimated residual value.

13. C is correct. This would result in the highest amount of depreciation in the first year and hence the lowest amount of net income relative to the other choices.

14. A is correct. A fire may be infrequent, but it would still be part of continuing operations and would be reported in the profit and loss statement. Discontinued operations relate to a decision to dispose of an operating division.

15. C is correct. If a company changes an accounting policy, the financial statements for all fiscal years shown in a company's financial report are presented, if practical, as if the newly adopted accounting policy had been used throughout the entire period; this retrospective application of the change makes the financial results of any prior years included in the report comparable. Notes to the financial statements describe the change and explain the justification for the change.

16. C is correct. The weighted average number of shares outstanding for 2009 is 1,050,000. Basic earnings per share would be $1,000,000 divided by 1,050,000, or $0.95.

17. B is correct. The formula to calculate diluted EPS is as follows:

Diluted EPS = (Net income − Preferred dividends)/[Weighted average number of shares outstanding + (New shares that would have been issued at option exercise − Shares that could have been purchased with cash received upon exercise) × (Proportion of year during which the financial instruments were outstanding)].

The underlying assumption is that outstanding options are exercised, and then the proceeds from the issuance of new shares are used to repurchase shares already outstanding:

Proceeds from option exercise = 100,000 × $20 = $2,000,000

Shares repurchased = $2,000,000/$25 = 80,000

The net increase in shares outstanding is thus 100,000 − 80,000 = 20,000. Therefore, the diluted EPS for CWC = ($12,000,000 − $800,000)/2,020,000 = $5.54.

18. A is correct. Basic and diluted EPS are equal for a company with a simple capital structure. A company that issues only common stock, with no financial instruments that are potentially convertible into common stock has a simple capital structure. Basic EPS is calculated using the weighted average number of shares outstanding.

19. B is correct. LB has warrants in its capital structure; if the exercise price is less than the weighted average market price during the year, the effect of their conversion is to increase the weighted average number of common shares outstanding, causing diluted EPS to be lower than basic EPS. If the exercise price is equal to the weighted average market price, the number of shares issued equals the number of shares repurchased. Therefore, the weighted average number of common shares outstanding is not affected, and diluted EPS equals basic EPS. If the exercise price is greater than the weighted average market price, the effect of their conversion is anti-dilutive. As such, they are not included in the calculation of basic EPS. LB's basic EPS is $1.22 [= ($3,350,000 − $430,000)/2,400,000]. Stock dividends are treated as having been issued retroactively to the beginning of the period.

20. A is correct. With stock options, the treasury stock method must be used. Under that method, the company would receive $100,000 (10,000 × $10) and would repurchase 6,667 shares ($100,000/$15). The shares for the denominator would be:

Shares outstanding	1,000,000
Options exercises	10,000
Treasury shares purchased	(6,667)
Denominator	1,003,333

21. C is correct.

   Diluted EPS = (Net income)/(Weighted average number of shares outstanding + New common shares that would have been issued at conversion)

   = $200,000,000/[50,000,000 + (2,000,000 × 2)]

   = $3.70

   The diluted EPS assumes that the preferred dividend is not paid and that the shares are converted at the beginning of the period.

22. A is correct. When a company has stock options outstanding, diluted EPS is calculated as if the financial instruments had been exercised and the company had used the proceeds from the exercise to repurchase as many shares as possible at the weighted average market price of common stock during the period. As a result, the conversion of stock options increases the number of common shares outstanding but has no effect on net income available to common shareholders. The conversion of convertible debt increases the net income available to common shareholders by the after-tax amount of interest expense saved. The conversion of convertible preferred shares increases the net income available to common shareholders by the amount of preferred dividends paid; the numerator becomes the net income.

23. B is correct. Common size income statements facilitate comparison across time periods (time-series analysis) and across companies (cross-sectional analysis) by stating each line item of the income statement as a percentage of revenue. The relative performance of different companies can be more easily assessed because scaling the numbers removes the effect of size. A common size income statement states each line item on the income statement as a percentage of revenue. The standardization of each line item makes a common size income statement useful for identifying differences in companies' strategies.

24. C is correct. Comprehensive income includes both net income and other comprehensive income.

   Other comprehensive income = Unrealized gain on available-for-sale securities − Unrealized loss on derivatives accounted for as hedges + Foreign currency translation gain on consolidation

   = $5 million − $3 million + $2 million

   = $4 million

Alternatively,

Comprehensive income – Net income = Other comprehensive income

Comprehensive income = (Ending shareholders equity – Beginning shareholders equity) + Dividends

= ($493 million – $475 million) + $1 million

= $18 million + $1 million = $19 million

Net income is $15 million, so other comprehensive income is $4 million.

25. A is correct. Other comprehensive income includes items that affect shareholders' equity but are not reflected in the company's income statement. In consolidating the financial statements of foreign subsidiaries, the effects of translating the subsidiaries' balance sheet assets and liabilities at current exchange rates are included as other comprehensive income.

CHAPTER 4

UNDERSTANDING
BALANCE SHEETS

SOLUTIONS

1. B is correct. Assets are resources controlled by a company as a result of past events.
2. A is correct. Assets = Liabilities + Equity and, therefore, Assets − Liabilities = Equity.
3. A is correct. A classified balance sheet is one that classifies assets and liabilities as current or non-current and provides a subtotal for current assets and current liabilities. A liquidity-based balance sheet broadly presents assets and liabilities in order of liquidity.
4. B is correct. The balance sheet omits important aspects of a company's ability to generate future cash flows, such as its reputation and management skills. The balance sheet measures some assets and liabilities based on historical cost and measures others based on current value. Market value of shareholders' equity is updated continuously. Shareholders' equity reported on the balance sheet is updated for reporting purposes and represents the value that was current at the end of the reporting period.
5. B is correct. Balance sheet information is as of a specific point in time, and items measured at current value reflect the value that was current at the end of the reporting period. For all financial statement items, an item should be recognized in the financial statements only if it is probable that any future economic benefit associated with the item will flow to or from the entity and if the item has a cost or value that can be measured with reliability.
6. B is correct. Payments due within one operating cycle of the business, even if they will be settled more than one year after the balance sheet date, are classified as current liabilities. Payment received in advance of the delivery of a good or service creates an obligation or liability. If the obligation is to be fulfilled at least one year after the balance sheet date, it is recorded as a non-current liability, such as deferred revenue or deferred income. Payments that the company has the unconditional right to defer for at least one year after the balance sheet may be classified as non-current liabilities.
7. A is correct. A liquidity-based presentation, rather than a current/non-current presentation, may be used by such entities as banks if broadly presenting assets and liabilities in order of liquidity is reliable and more relevant.

8. B is correct. Goodwill is a long-term asset, and the others are all current assets.

9. C is correct. Both the cost of inventory and property, plant, and equipment include delivery costs, or costs incurred in bringing them to the location for use or resale.

10. A is correct. Current liabilities are those liabilities, including debt, due within one year. Preferred refers to a class of stock. Convertible refers to a feature of bonds (or preferred stock) allowing the holder to convert the instrument into common stock.

11. B is correct. The cash received from customers represents an asset. The obligation to provide a product in the future is a liability called "unearned income" or "unearned revenue." As the product is delivered, revenue will be recognized, and the liability will be reduced.

12. C is correct. A contra asset account is netted against (i.e., reduces) the balance of an asset account. The allowance for doubtful accounts reduces the balance of accounts receivable. Accumulated depreciation, not depreciation expense, is a contra asset account. Sales returns and allowances create a contra account that reduce sales, not an asset.

13. C is correct. Under IFRS, inventories are carried at historical cost, unless net realizable value of the inventory is less. Under US GAAP, inventories are carried at the lower of cost or market.

14. C is correct. Paying rent in advance will reduce cash and increase prepaid expenses, both of which are assets.

15. C is correct. Accrued liabilities are expenses that have been reported on a company's income statement but have not yet been paid.

16. A is correct. Initially, goodwill is measured as the difference between the purchase price paid for an acquisition and the fair value of the acquired, not acquiring, company's net assets (identifiable assets less liabilities).

17. C is correct. Impairment write-downs reduce equity in the denominator of the debt-to-equity ratio but do not affect debt, so the debt-to-equity ratio is expected to increase. Impairment write-downs reduce total assets but do not affect revenue. Thus, total asset turnover is expected to increase.

18. B is correct. Vertical common-size analysis involves stating each balance sheet item as a percentage of total assets. Total assets are the sum of total liabilities (£35 million) and total stockholders' equity (£55 million), or £90 million. Total liabilities are shown on a vertical common-size balance sheet as (£35 million/£90 million) ≈ 39%.

19. B is correct. For financial assets classified as trading securities, unrealized gains and losses are reported on the income statement and flow to shareholders' equity as part of retained earnings.

20. C is correct. For financial assets classified as available for sale, unrealized gains and losses are not recorded on the income statement and instead are part of *other* comprehensive income. Accumulated other comprehensive income is a component of shareholders' equity.

21. A is correct. Financial assets classified as held to maturity are measured at amortized cost. Gains and losses are recognized only when realized.

22. B is correct. The non-controlling interest in consolidated subsidiaries is shown separately as part of shareholders' equity.

23. C is correct. The item "retained earnings" is a component of shareholders' equity.

24. B is correct. Share repurchases reduce the company's cash (an asset). Shareholders' equity is reduced because there are fewer shares outstanding and treasury stock is an offset to owners' equity.

25. B is correct. Common-size analysis (as presented in the chapter) provides information about composition of the balance sheet and changes over time. As a result, it can provide information about an increase or decrease in a company's financial leverage.

26. A is correct. The current ratio provides a comparison of assets that can be turned into cash relatively quickly and liabilities that must be paid within one year. The other ratios are more suited to longer-term concerns.
27. A is correct. The cash ratio determines how much of a company's near-term obligations can be settled with existing amounts of cash and marketable securities.
28. C is correct. The debt-to-equity ratio, a solvency ratio, is an indicator of financial risk.
29. B is correct. The quick ratio ([Cash + Marketable securities + Receivables] ÷ Current liabilities) is 1.07 ([= €4,011 + €990 + €5,899] ÷ €10,210). As noted in the text, the largest components of the current financial assets are loans and other financial receivables. Thus, financial assets are included in the quick ratio but not the cash ratio.
30. B is correct. The financial leverage ratio (Total assets ÷ Total equity) is 1.66 (= €42,497 ÷ €25,540).
31. C is correct. The presence of goodwill on Company A's balance sheet signifies that it has made one or more acquisitions in the past. The current, cash, and quick ratios are lower for Company A than for the sector average. These lower liquidity ratios imply above-average liquidity risk. The total debt, long-term debt-to-equity, debt-to-equity, and financial leverage ratios are lower for Company B than for the sector average. These lower solvency ratios imply below-average solvency risk.

   Current ratio is (35/35) = 1.00 for Company A, versus (48/28) = 1.71 for the sector average.

   Cash ratio is (5 + 5)/35 = 0.29 for Company A, versus (7 + 2)/28 = 0.32 for the sector average.

   Quick ratio is (5 + 5 + 5)/35 = 0.43 for Company A, versus (7 + 2 + 12)/28 = 0.75 for the sector average.

   Total debt ratio is (55/100) = 0.55 for Company B, versus (63/100) = 0.63 for the sector average.

   Long-term debt-to-equity ratio is (20/45) = 0.44 for Company B, versus (28/37) = 0.76 for the sector average.

   Debt-to-equity ratio is (55/45) = 1.22 for Company B, versus (63/37) = 1.70 for the sector average.

   Financial leverage ratio is (100/45) = 2.22 for Company B, versus (100/37) = 2.70 for the sector average.

32. A is correct. The quick ratio is defined as (Cash and cash equivalents + Marketable securities + receivables) ÷ Current liabilities. For Company A, this calculation is (5 + 5 + 5)/35 = 0.43.
33. C is correct. The financial leverage ratio is defined as Total assets ÷ Total equity. For Company B, total assets are 100, and total equity is 45; hence, the financial leverage ratio is 100/45 = 2.22.
34. A is correct. The cash ratio is defined as (Cash + Marketable securities)/Current liabilities. Company A's cash ratio, (5 + 5)/35 = 0.29, is higher than (5 + 0)/25 = 0.20 for Company B.

CHAPTER 5

UNDERSTANDING CASH FLOW STATEMENTS

SOLUTIONS

1. B is correct. Operating, investing, and financing are the three major classifications of activities in a cash flow statement. Revenues, expenses, and net income are elements of the income statement. Inflows, outflows, and net flows are items of information in the statement of cash flows.

2. B is correct. Purchases and sales of long-term assets are considered investing activities. Note that if the transaction had involved the exchange of a building for other than cash (for example, for another building, common stock of another company, or a long-term note receivable), it would have been considered a significant non-cash activity.

3. B is correct. The purchase and sale of securities considered cash equivalents and securities held for trading are considered operating activities even for companies in which this activity is not a primary business activity.

4. C is correct. Payment of dividends is a financing activity under US GAAP. Payment of interest and receipt of dividends are included in operating cash flows under US GAAP. Note that IFRS allow companies to include receipt of interest and dividends as either operating or investing cash flows and to include payment of interest and dividends as either operating or financing cash flows.

5. C is correct. Non-cash transactions, if significant, are reported as supplementary information, not in the investing or financing sections of the cash flow statement.

6. C is correct. Because no cash is involved in non-cash transactions, these transactions are not incorporated in the cash flow statement. However, non-cash transactions that significantly affect capital or asset structures are required to be disclosed either in a separate note or a supplementary schedule to the cash flow statement.

7. C is correct. Interest expense is always classified as an operating cash flow under US GAAP but may be classified as either an operating or financing cash flow under IFRS.

8. C is correct. Taxes on income are required to be separately disclosed under IFRS and US GAAP. The disclosure may be in the cash flow statement or elsewhere.

9. A is correct. The operating section may be prepared under the indirect method. The other sections are always prepared under the direct method.

10. A is correct. Under the indirect method, the operating section would begin with net income and adjust it to arrive at operating cash flow. The other two items would appear in the operating section under the direct method.

11. C is correct. The primary argument in favor of the direct method is that it provides information on the specific sources of operating cash receipts and payments. Arguments for the indirect method include that it mirrors a forecasting approach and it is easier and less costly

12. C is correct. The amount of cash collected from customers during the quarter is equal to beginning accounts receivable plus revenues minus ending accounts receivable: $66 million + $72 million − $55 million = $83 million. A reduction in accounts receivable indicates that cash collected during the quarter was greater than revenue on an accrual basis.

13. B is correct. An addition to net income is made when there is a loss on the retirement of debt, which is a non-operating loss. A gain on the sale of an asset and a decrease in deferred tax liability are both subtracted from net income.

14. A is correct. Revenues of $100 million minus the increase in accounts receivable of $10 million equal $90 million cash received from customers. The increase in accounts receivable means that the company received less in cash than it reported as revenue.

15. A is correct.

Operating cash flows = Cash received from customers − (Cash paid to suppliers + Cash paid to employees + Cash paid for other operating expenses + Cash paid for interest + Cash paid for income taxes)

Cash received from customers = Revenue + Decrease in accounts receivable

= $37 + $3 = $40 million

Cash paid to suppliers = Cost of goods sold + Increase in inventory + Decrease in accounts payable

= $16 + $4 + $2 = $22 million

Therefore, the company's operating cash flow = $40 − $22 − Cash paid for salaries − Cash paid for interest − Cash paid for taxes = $40 − $22 − $6 − $2 − $4 = $6 million.

16. C is correct. Cost of goods sold of $80 million plus the increase in inventory of $5 million equals purchases from suppliers of $85 million. The increase in accounts payable of $2 million means that the company paid $83 million in cash ($85 million minus $2 million) to its suppliers.

17. A is correct. Cost of goods sold of $75 million less the decrease in inventory of $6 million equals purchases from suppliers of $69 million. The increase in accounts payable of $2 million means that the company paid $67 million in cash ($69 million minus $2 million).

18. C is correct. Beginning salaries payable of $3 million plus salaries expense of $20 million minus ending salaries payable of $1 million equals $22 million. Alternatively, the expense of $20 million plus the $2 million decrease in salaries payable equals $22 million.

19. C is correct. Cash received from customers = Sales + Decrease in accounts receivable = 254.6 + 4.9 = 259.5. Cash paid to suppliers = Cost of goods sold + Increase in inventory − Increase in accounts payable = 175.9 + 8.8 − 2.6 = 182.1.

20. C is correct. Interest expense of $19 million less the increase in interest payable of $3 million equals interest paid of $16 million. Tax expense of $6 million plus the decrease in taxes payable of $4 million equals taxes paid of $10 million.

21. B is correct. All dollar amounts are in millions. Net income (NI) for 2018 is $35. This amount is the increase in retained earnings, $25, plus the dividends paid, $10. Depreciation of $25 is added back to net income, and the increases in accounts receivable, $5, and in inventory, $3, are subtracted from net income because they are uses of cash. The decrease in accounts payable is also a use of cash and, therefore, a subtraction from net income. Thus, cash flow from operations is $25 + $10 + $25 − $5 − $3 − $7 = $45.

22. A is correct. Selling price (cash inflow) minus book value equals gain or loss on sale; therefore, gain or loss on sale plus book value equals selling price (cash inflow). The amount of loss is given—$2 million. To calculate the book value of the equipment sold, find the historical cost of the equipment and the accumulated depreciation on the equipment.

    • Beginning balance of equipment of $100 million plus equipment purchased of $10 million minus ending balance of equipment of $105 million equals the historical cost of equipment sold, or $5 million.
    • Beginning accumulated depreciation of $40 million plus depreciation expense for the year of $8 million minus ending balance of accumulated depreciation of $46 million equals accumulated depreciation on the equipment sold, or $2 million.
    • Therefore, the book value of the equipment sold was $5 million minus $2 million, or $3 million.
    • Because the loss on the sale of equipment was $2 million, the amount of cash received must have been $1 million.

23. A is correct. The increase of $42 million in common stock and additional paid-in capital indicates that the company issued stock during the year. The increase in retained earnings of $15 million indicates that the company paid $10 million in cash dividends during the year, determined as beginning retained earnings of $100 million plus net income of $25 million minus ending retained earnings of $115 million, which equals $10 million in cash dividends.

24. B is correct. To derive operating cash flow, the company would make the following adjustments to net income: Add depreciation (a non-cash expense) of $2 million; add the decrease in accounts receivable of $3 million; add the increase in accounts payable of $5 million; and subtract the increase in inventory of $4 million. Total additions would be $10 million, and total subtractions would be $4 million, which gives net additions of $6 million.

25. C is correct. An overall assessment of the major sources and uses of cash should be the first step in evaluating a cash flow statement.

26. B is correct. The primary source of cash is operating activities. Cash flow provided by operating activity totaled €13,796 million in the most recent year. The primary use of cash is investing activities (total of €10,245 million). Dividends paid are classified as a financing activity.

27. A is correct. The amount of cash paid to suppliers is calculated as follows:

    = Cost of goods sold − Decrease in inventory − Increase in accounts payable

    = $27,264 − $501 − $1,063

    = $25,700.

28. B is correct. An appropriate method to prepare a common-size cash flow statement is to show each line item on the cash flow statement as a percentage of net revenue. An alternative way to prepare a statement of cash flows is to show each item of cash inflow as a percentage of total inflows and each item of cash outflows as a percentage of total outflows.

29. B is correct. Free cash flow to the firm can be computed as operating cash flows plus after-tax interest expense less capital expenditures.

30. A is correct. This ratio is an interest coverage ratio, measuring a company's ability to meet its interest obligations and indicating a company's solvency. This coverage ratio is based on cash flow information; another common coverage ratio uses a measure based on the income statement (earnings before interest, taxes, depreciation, and amortization).

CHAPTER 6

FINANCIAL ANALYSIS TECHNIQUES

SOLUTIONS

1. C is correct. Cross-sectional analysis involves the comparison of companies with each other for the same time period. Technical analysis uses price and volume data as the basis for investment decisions. Time-series or trend analysis is the comparison of financial data across different time periods.

2. C is correct. Solvency ratios are used to evaluate the ability of a company to meet its long-term obligations. An analyst is more likely to use activity ratios to evaluate how efficiently a company uses its assets. An analyst is more likely to use liquidity ratios to evaluate the ability of a company to meet its short-term obligations.

3. A is correct. The current ratio is a liquidity ratio. It compares the net amount of current assets expected to be converted into cash within the year with liabilities falling due in the same period. A current ratio of 1.0 would indicate that the company would have just enough current assets to pay current liabilities.

4. C is correct. The fixed charge coverage ratio is a coverage ratio that relates known fixed charges or obligations to a measure of operating profit or cash flow generated by the company. Coverage ratios, a category of solvency ratios, measure the ability of a company to cover its payments related to debt and leases.

5. C is correct. The analyst is *unlikely* to reach the conclusion given in Statement C because days of sales outstanding increased from 23 days in FY1 to 25 days in FY2 to 28 days in FY3, indicating that the time required to collect receivables has increased over the period. This is a negative factor for Spherion's liquidity. By contrast, days of inventory on hand dropped over the period FY1 to FY3, a positive for liquidity. The company's increase in days payable, from 35 days to 40 days, shortened its cash conversion cycle, thus also contributing to improved liquidity.

6. A is correct. The company is becoming increasingly less solvent, as evidenced by its debt-to-equity ratio increasing from 0.35 to 0.50 from FY3 to FY5. The amount of a company's debt and equity do not provide direct information about the company's liquidity position.

   Debt to equity:

$$FY5: 2,000/4,000 = 0.5000$$
$$FY4: 1,900/4,500 = 0.4222$$
$$FY3: 1,750/5,000 = 0.3500$$

7. C is correct. The decline in the company's equity indicates that the company may be incurring losses, paying dividends greater than income, or repurchasing shares. Recall that Beginning equity + New shares issuance − Shares repurchased + Comprehensive income − Dividends = Ending equity. The book value of a company's equity is not affected by changes in the market value of its common stock. An increased amount of lending does not necessarily indicate that lenders view a company as increasingly creditworthy. Creditworthiness is not evaluated based on how much a company has increased its debt but rather on its willingness and ability to pay its obligations. (Its financial strength is indicated by its solvency, liquidity, profitability, efficiency, and other aspects of credit analysis.)

8. C is correct. The company's problems with its inventory management system causing duplicate orders would likely result in a higher amount of inventory and would, therefore, result in a decrease in inventory turnover. A more efficient inventory management system and a write off of inventory at the beginning of the period would both likely decrease the average inventory for the period (the denominator of the inventory turnover ratio), thus increasing the ratio rather than decreasing it.

9. B is correct. A write off of receivables would decrease the average amount of accounts receivable (the denominator of the receivables turnover ratio), thus increasing this ratio. Customers with weaker credit are more likely to make payments more slowly or to pose collection difficulties, which would likely increase the average amount of accounts receivable and thus decrease receivables turnover. Longer payment terms would likely increase the average amount of accounts receivable and thus decrease receivables turnover.

10. A is correct. The average accounts receivable balances (actual and desired) must be calculated to determine the desired change. The average accounts receivable balance can be calculated as an average day's credit sales times the DSO. For the most recent fiscal year, the average accounts receivable balance is $15.62 million [= ($300,000,000/365) × 19]. The desired average accounts receivable balance for the next fiscal year is $16.03 million (= ($390,000,000/365) × 15). This is an increase of $0.41 million (= 16.03 million − 15.62 million). An alternative approach is to calculate the turnover and divide sales by turnover to determine the average accounts receivable balance. Turnover equals 365 divided by DSO. Turnover is 19.21 (= 365/19) for the most recent fiscal year and is targeted to be 24.33 (= 365/15) for the next fiscal year. The average accounts receivable balances are $15.62 million (= $300,000,000/19.21), and $16.03 million (= $390,000,000/24.33). The change is an increase in receivables of $0.41 million

11. A is correct. Company A's current ratio of 4.0 (= $40,000/$10,000) indicates it is more liquid than Company B, whose current ratio is only 1.2 (= $60,000/$50,000). Company B is more solvent, as indicated by its lower debt-to-equity ratio of 30 percent (= $150,000/$500,000) compared with Company A's debt-to-equity ratio of 200 percent (= $60,000/$30,000).

12. C is correct. The company's efficiency deteriorated, as indicated by the decline in its total asset turnover ratio from 1.11 {= 4,390/[(4,384 + 3,500)/2]} for FY10 to 0.87 {= 11,366/[(12,250 + 13,799)/2]} for FY14. The decline in the total asset turnover ratio resulted from an increase in average total assets from GBP3,942 [= (4,384 + 3,500)/2] for FY10 to GBP13,024.5 for FY14, an increase of 230 percent, compared with an increase in revenue from GBP4,390 in FY10 to GBP11,366 in FY14, an increase of only 159 percent. The current ratio is not an indicator of efficiency.

13. B is correct. Comparing FY14 with FY10, the company's solvency deteriorated, as indicated by a decrease in interest coverage from 10.6 (= 844/80) in FY10 to 8.4 (= 1,579/188) in FY14. The debt-to-asset ratio increased from 0.14 (= 602/4,384) in FY10 to 0.27 (= 3,707/13,799) in FY14. This is also indicative of deteriorating solvency. In isolation, the amount of profits does not provide enough information to assess solvency.

14. C is correct. Comparing FY14 with FY10, the company's liquidity improved, as indicated by an increase in its current ratio from 0.71 [= (316 + 558)/1,223] in FY10 to 0.75 [= (682 + 1,634)/3,108] in FY14. Note, however, comparing only current investments with the level of current liabilities shows a decline in liquidity from 0.26 (= 316/1,223) in FY10 to 0.22 (= 682/3,108) in FY14. Debt-to-assets ratio and interest coverage are measures of solvency not liquidity.

15. B is correct. Comparing FY14 with FY10, the company's profitability deteriorated, as indicated by a decrease in its net profit margin from 11.0 percent (= 484/4,390) to 5.7 percent (= 645/11,366). Debt-to-assets ratio is a measure of solvency not an indicator of profitability. Growth in shareholders' equity, in isolation, does not provide enough information to assess profitability.

16. C is correct. Assuming no changes in other variables, an increase in average assets (an increase in the denominator) would decrease ROA. A decrease in either the effective tax rate or interest expense, assuming no changes in other variables, would increase ROA.

17. C is correct. The company's net profit margin has decreased, and its financial leverage has increased. ROA = Net profit margin × Total asset turnover. ROA decreased over the period despite the increase in total asset turnover; therefore, the net profit margin must have decreased.

    ROE = Return on assets × Financial leverage. ROE increased over the period despite the drop in ROA; therefore, financial leverage must have increased.

18. C is correct. The increase in the average tax rate in FY12, as indicated by the decrease in the value of the tax burden (the tax burden equals one minus the average tax rate), offset the improvement in efficiency indicated by higher asset turnover) leaving ROE unchanged. The EBIT margin, measuring profitability, was unchanged in FY12, and no information is given on liquidity.

19. C is correct. The difference between the two companies' ROE in 2010 is very small and is mainly the result of Company A's increase in its financial leverage, indicated by the increase in its Assets/Equity ratio from 2 to 4. The impact of efficiency on ROE is identical for the two companies, as indicated by both companies' asset turnover ratios of 1.5. Furthermore, if Company A had purchased newer equipment to replace older, depreciated equipment, then the company's asset turnover ratio (computed as sales/assets) would have declined, assuming constant sales. Company A has experienced a significant decline in its operating margin, from 10 percent to 7 percent, which, all else equal, would not suggest that it is selling more products with higher profit margins.

20. A is correct. The P/E ratio measures the "multiple" that the stock market places on a company's EPS.

21. B is correct. In general, a creditor would consider a decrease in debt to total assets as positive news. A higher level of debt in a company's capital structure increases the risk of default and will, in general, result in higher borrowing costs for the company to compensate lenders for assuming greater credit risk. A decrease in either interest coverage or return on assets is likely to be considered negative news.

22. B is correct. The results of an analyst's financial analysis are integral to the process of developing forecasts, along with the analysis of other information and judgment of the analysts. Forecasts are not limited to a single point estimate but should involve a range of possibilities.

CHAPTER 7

INVENTORIES

SOLUTIONS

1. C is correct. Transportation costs incurred to ship inventory to customers are an expense and may not be capitalized in inventory. (Transportation costs incurred to bring inventory to the business location can be capitalized in inventory.) Storage costs required as part of production, as well as costs incurred as a result of normal waste of materials, can be capitalized in inventory. (Costs incurred as a result of abnormal waste must be expensed.)

2. B is correct. Inventory expense includes costs of purchase, costs of conversion, and other costs incurred in bringing the inventories to their present location and condition. It does not include storage costs not required as part of production.

3. A is correct. IFRS allow the inventories of producers and dealers of agricultural and forest products, agricultural produce after harvest, and minerals and mineral products to be carried at net realizable value even if above historical cost. (US GAAP treatment is similar.)

4. A is correct. A perpetual inventory system updates inventory values and quantities and cost of goods sold continuously to reflect purchases and sales. The ending inventory of 800 units consists of 300 units at $20 and 500 units at $17.

$$(300 \times \$20) + (500 \times \$17) = \$14,500$$

5. A is correct. In an environment with falling inventory costs and declining inventory levels, periodic LIFO will result in a higher ending inventory value and lower cost of goods sold versus perpetual LIFO and perpetual FIFO methods. This results in a lower inventory turnover ratio, which is calculated as follows:

Inventory turnover ratio = Cost of goods sold/Ending inventory

The inventory turnover ratio using periodic LIFO is $39,000/$16,000 = 244% or 2.44 times.

The inventory turnover ratio using perpetual LIFO is 279% or 2.79 times, which is provided in Table 2 (= 40,500/14,500 from previous question).

The inventory turnover for perpetual FIFO is $41,400/$13,600 = 304% or 3.04 times.

6. B is correct. During a period of rising inventory costs, a company using the FIFO method will allocate a lower amount to cost of goods sold and a higher amount to ending inventory as compared with the LIFO method. The inventory turnover ratio is the ratio of cost of sales to ending inventory. A company using the FIFO method will produce a lower inventory turnover ratio as compared with the LIFO method. The current ratio (current assets/current liabilities) and the gross profit margin [gross profit/sales = (sales less cost of goods sold)/sales] will be higher under the FIFO method than under the LIFO method in periods of rising inventory unit costs.

7. A is correct. LIFO reserve is the FIFO inventory value less the LIFO inventory value. In periods of rising inventory unit costs, the carrying amount of inventory under FIFO will always exceed the carrying amount of inventory under LIFO. The LIFO reserve may increase over time as a result of the increasing difference between the older costs used to value inventory under LIFO and the more recent costs used to value inventory under FIFO. When inventory unit levels are decreasing, the company will experience a LIFO liquidation, reducing the LIFO reserve.

8. A is correct. When the number of units sold exceeds the number of units purchased, a company using LIFO will experience a LIFO liquidation. If inventory unit costs have been rising from period-to-period and a LIFO liquidation occurs, it will produce an increase in gross profit as a result of the lower inventory carrying amounts of the liquidated units (lower cost per unit of the liquidated units).

9. B is correct. The adjusted COGS under the FIFO method is equal to COGS under the LIFO method less the increase in LIFO reserve:

$$COGS \ (FIFO) = COGS \ (LIFO) - \text{Increase in LIFO reserve}$$

$$COGS \ (FIFO) = £50,800 - (£4,320 - £2,600)$$

$$COGS \ (FIFO) = £49,080$$

10. B is correct. Under IFRS, the reversal of write-downs is required if net realizable value increases. The inventory will be reported on the balance sheet at £1,000,000. The inventory is reported at the lower of cost or net realizable value. Under US GAAP, inventory is carried at the lower of cost or market value. After a write-down, a new cost basis is determined, and additional revisions may only reduce the value further. The reversal of write-downs is not permitted.

11. A is correct. IFRS require the reversal of inventory write-downs if net realizable values increase; US GAAP do not permit the reversal of write-downs.

12. C is correct. Activity ratios (for example, inventory turnover and total asset turnover) will be positively affected by a write-down to net realizable value because the asset base (denominator) is reduced. On the balance sheet, the inventory carrying amount is written down to its net realizable value and the loss in value (expense) is generally reflected on the income statement in cost of goods sold, thus reducing gross profit, operating profit, and net income.

13. B is correct. Cinnamon uses the weighted average cost method, so in 2018, 5,000 units of inventory were 2017 units at €10 each, and 50,000 were 2008 purchases at €11. The weighted average cost of inventory during 2008 was thus $(5,000 \times 10) + (50,000 \times 11) =$ $50,000 + 550,000 = €600,000$, and the weighted average cost was approximately €10.91 = €600,000/55,000. Cost of sales was €10.91 × 45,000, which is approximately €490,950.

14. C is correct. Zimt uses the FIFO method, and thus the first 5,000 units sold in 2018 depleted the 2017 inventory. Of the inventory purchased in 2018, 40,000 units were sold, and 10,000 remain, valued at €11 each, for a total of €110,000.

15. A is correct. Zimt uses the FIFO method, so its cost of sales represents units purchased at a (no longer available) lower price. Nutmeg uses the LIFO method, so its cost of sales is approximately equal to the current replacement cost of inventory.

16. B is correct. Nutmeg uses the LIFO method, and thus some of the inventory on the balance sheet was purchased at a (no longer available) lower price. Zimt uses the FIFO method, so the carrying value on the balance sheet represents the most recently purchased units and thus approximates the current replacement cost.

17. B is correct. In a declining price environment, the newest inventory is the lowest-cost inventory. In such circumstances, using the LIFO method (selling the newer, cheaper inventory first) will result in lower cost of sales and higher profit.

18. B is correct. In a rising price environment, inventory balances will be higher for the company using the FIFO method. Accounts payable are based on amounts due to suppliers, not the amounts accrued based on inventory accounting.

19. C is correct. The write-down reduced the value of inventory and increased cost of sales in 2017. The higher numerator and lower denominator mean that the inventory turnover ratio as reported was too high. Gross margin and the current ratio were both too low.

20. A is correct. The reversal of the write-down shifted cost of sales from 2018 to 2017. The 2017 cost of sales was higher because of the write-down, and the 2018 cost of sales was lower because of the reversal of the write-down. As a result, the reported 2018 profits were overstated. Inventory balance in 2018 is the same because the write-down and reversal cancel each other out. Cash flow from operations is not affected by the non-cash write-down, but the higher profits in 2018 likely resulted in higher taxes and thus lower cash flow from operations.

21. B is correct. LIFO will result in lower inventory and higher cost of sales. Gross margin (a profitability ratio) will be lower, the current ratio (a liquidity ratio) will be lower, and inventory turnover (an efficiency ratio) will be higher.

22. A is correct. LIFO will result in lower inventory and higher cost of sales in periods of rising costs compared to FIFO. Consequently, LIFO results in a lower gross profit margin than FIFO.

23. B is correct. The LIFO method increases cost of sales, thus reducing profits and the taxes thereon.

24. A is correct. US GAAP do not permit inventory write-downs to be reversed.

25. B is correct. Both US GAAP and IFRS require disclosure of the amount of inventories recognized as an expense during the period. Only US GAAP allows the LIFO method and requires disclosure of any material amount of income resulting from the liquidation of LIFO inventory. US GAAP does not permit the reversal of prior-year inventory write-downs.

26. B is correct. A significant increase (attributable to increases in unit volume rather than increases in unit cost) in raw materials and/or work-in-progress inventories may signal that the company expects an increase in demand for its products. If the growth of finished goods inventories is greater than the growth of sales, it could indicate a decrease in demand and a decrease in future earnings. A substantial increase in finished goods inventories while raw materials and work-in-progress inventories are declining may signal a decrease in demand for the company's products.

27. B is correct. During a period of rising inventory prices, a company using the LIFO method will have higher cost of cost of goods sold and lower inventory compared with a company using the FIFO method. The inventory turnover ratio will be higher for the company using the LIFO method, thus making it appear more efficient. Current assets and

gross profit margin will be lower for the company using the LIFO method, thus making it appear less liquid and less profitable.

28. B is correct. In an environment of declining inventory unit costs and constant or increasing inventory quantities, FIFO (in comparison with weighted average cost or LIFO) will have higher cost of goods sold (and net income) and lower inventory. Because both inventory and net income are lower, total equity is lower, resulting in a higher debt-to-equity ratio.

29. C is correct. The storage costs for inventory awaiting shipment to customers are not costs of purchase, costs of conversion, or other costs incurred in bringing the inventories to their present location and condition, and are not included in inventory. The storage costs for the chocolate liquor occur during the production process and are thus part of the conversion costs. Excise taxes are part of the purchase cost.

30. C is correct. The carrying amount of inventories under FIFO will more closely reflect current replacement values because inventories are assumed to consist of the most recently purchased items. FIFO is an acceptable, but not preferred, method under IFRS. Weighted average cost, not FIFO, is the cost formula that allocates the same per unit cost to both cost of sales and inventory.

31. B is correct. Inventory turnover = Cost of sales/Average inventory = 41,043/7,569.5 = 5.42. Average inventory is (8,100 + 7,039)/2 = 7,569.5.

32. B is correct. For comparative purposes, the choice of a competitor that reports under IFRS is requested because LIFO is permitted under US GAAP.

33. A is correct. The carrying amount of the ending inventory may differ because the perpetual system will apply LIFO continuously throughout the year, liquidating layers as sales are made. Under the periodic system, the sales will start from the last layer in the year. Under FIFO, the sales will occur from the same layers regardless of whether a perpetual or periodic system is used. Specific identification identifies the actual products sold and remaining in inventory, and there will be no difference under a perpetual or periodic system.

34. B is correct. The cost of sales is closest to CHF 4,550. Under FIFO, the inventory acquired first is sold first. Using Exhibit 4, a total of 310 cartons were available for sale (100 + 40 + 70 + 100) and 185 cartons were sold (50 + 100 + 35), leaving 125 in ending inventory. The FIFO cost would be as follows:

$$100 \text{ (beginning inventory)} \times 22 = 2,200$$
$$40 \text{ (February 4, 2009)} \times 25 = 1,000$$
$$45 \text{ (July 23, 2009)} \times 30 = 1,350$$
$$\text{Cost of sales} = 2,200 + 1,000 + 1,350 = \text{CHF } 4,550$$

35. A is correct. Gross profit will most likely increase by CHF 7,775. The net realizable value has increased and now exceeds the cost. The write-down from 2017 can be reversed. The write-down in 2017 was 9,256 [92,560 × (4.05 − 3.95)]. IFRS require the reversal of any write-downs for a subsequent increase in value of inventory previously written down. The reversal is limited to the lower of the subsequent increase or the original write-down. Only 77,750 kilograms remain in inventory; the reversal is 77,750 × (4.05 − 3.95) = 7,775. The amount of any reversal of a write-down is recognized as a reduction in cost of sales. This reduction results in an increase in gross profit.

36. C is correct. Using the FIFO method to value inventories when prices are rising will allocate more of the cost of goods available for sale to ending inventories (the most recent

purchases, which are at higher costs, are assumed to remain in inventory) and less to cost of sales (the oldest purchases, which are at lower costs, are assumed to be sold first).

37. C is correct. Karp's inventory under FIFO equals Karp's inventory under LIFO plus the LIFO reserve. Therefore, as of December 31, 2018, Karp's inventory under FIFO equals:

$$\text{Inventory (FIFO method)} = \text{Inventory (LIFO method)} + \text{LIFO reserve}$$
$$= \$620 \text{ million} + 155 \text{ million}$$
$$= \$775 \text{ million}$$

38. B is correct. Karp's cost of goods sold (COGS) under FIFO equals Karp's cost of goods sold under LIFO minus the increase in the LIFO reserve. Therefore, for the year ended December 31, 2018, Karp's cost of goods sold under FIFO equals:

$$\text{COGS (FIFO method)} = \text{COGS (LIFO method)} - \text{Increase in LIFO reserve}$$
$$= \$2,211 \text{ million} - (155 \text{ million} - 117 \text{ million})$$
$$= \$2,173 \text{ million}$$

39. A is correct. Karp's net income (NI) under FIFO equals Karp's net income under LIFO plus the after-tax increase in the LIFO reserve. For the year ended December 31, 2018, Karp's net income under FIFO equals:

$$\text{NI (FIFO method)} = \text{NI (LIFO method)} + \text{Increase in LIFO reserve} \times (1 - \text{Tax rate})$$
$$= \$247 \text{ million} + 38 \text{ million} \times (1 - 20\%)$$
$$= \$277.4 \text{ million}$$

Therefore, the increase in net income is:

$$\text{Increase in NI} = \text{NI (FIFO method)} - \text{NI (LIFO method)}$$
$$= \$277 \text{ million} - 247 \text{ million}$$
$$= \$30.4 \text{ million}$$

40. B is correct. Karp's retained earnings (RE) under FIFO equals Karp's retained earnings under LIFO plus the after-tax LIFO reserve. Therefore, for the year ended December 31, 2018, Karp's retained earnings under FIFO equals:

$$\text{RE (FIFO method)} = \text{RE (LIFO method)} + \text{LIFO reserve} \times (1 - \text{Tax rate})$$
$$= \$787 \text{ million} + 155 \text{ million} \times (1 - 20\%)$$
$$= \$911 \text{ million}$$

Therefore, the increase in retained earnings is:

$$\text{Increase in RE} = \text{RE (FIFO method)} - \text{RE (LIFO method)}$$
$$= \$911 \text{ million} - 787 \text{ million}$$
$$= \$124 \text{ million}$$

41. A is correct. The cash ratio (cash and cash equivalents ÷ current liabilities) would be lower because cash would have been less under FIFO. Karp's income before taxes would have been higher under FIFO, and consequently taxes paid by Karp would have also been higher, and cash would have been lower. There is no impact on current liabilities. Both Karp's current ratio and gross profit margin would have been higher if FIFO had been used. The current ratio would have been higher because inventory

under FIFO increases by a larger amount than the cash decreases for taxes paid. Because the cost of goods sold under FIFO is lower than under LIFO, the gross profit margin would have been higher.

42. B is correct. If Karp had used FIFO instead of LIFO, the debt-to-equity ratio would have decreased. No change in debt would have occurred, but shareholders' equity would have increased as a result of higher retained earnings.

43. B is correct. Crux's adjusted inventory turnover ratio must be computed using cost of goods sold (COGS) under FIFO and excluding charges for increases in valuation allowances.

COGS (adjusted) = COGS (LIFO method) − Charges included in cost of goods sold for inventory write-downs − Change in LIFO reserve

= $3,120 million − 13 million − (55 million − 72 million)

= $3,124 million

Note: Minus the change in LIFO reserve is equivalent to plus the decrease in LIFO reserve. The adjusted inventory turnover ratio is computed using average inventory under FIFO.

Ending inventory (FIFO) = Ending inventory (LIFO) + LIFO reserve

Ending inventory 2018 (FIFO) = $480 + 55 = $535

Ending inventory 2017 (FIFO) = $465 + 72 = $537

Average inventory = ($535 + 537)/2 = $536

Therefore, adjusted inventory turnover ratio equals:

Inventory turnover ratio = COGS/Average inventory = $3,124/$536 = 5.83

44. B is correct. Rolby's adjusted net profit margin must be computed using net income (NI) under FIFO and excluding charges for increases in valuation allowances.

NI (adjusted) = NI (FIFO method) + Charges, included in cost of goods sold for inventory write-downs, after tax

= $327 million + 15 million × (1 − 30%)

= $337.5 million

Therefore, adjusted net profit margin equals:

Net profit margin = NI/Revenues = $337.5/$5,442 = 6.20%

45. A is correct. Mikko's adjusted debt-to-equity ratio is lower because the debt (numerator) is unchanged and the adjusted shareholders' equity (denominator) is higher. The adjusted shareholders' equity corresponds to shareholders' equity under FIFO, excluding charges for increases in valuation allowances. Therefore, adjusted shareholders' equity is higher than reported (unadjusted) shareholders' equity.

46. C is correct. Mikko's and Crux's gross margin ratios would better reflect the current gross margin of the industry than Rolby because both use LIFO. LIFO recognizes as cost of goods sold the cost of the most recently purchased units; therefore, it better reflects replacement cost. However, Mikko's gross margin ratio best reflects the current gross margin

of the industry because Crux's LIFO reserve is decreasing. This could reflect a LIFO liquidation by Crux, which would distort gross profit margin.

47. B is correct. The FIFO method shows a higher gross profit margin than the LIFO method in an inflationary scenario, because FIFO allocates to cost of goods sold the cost of the oldest units available for sale. In an inflationary environment, these units are the ones with the lowest cost.

48. A is correct. An inventory write-down increases cost of sales and reduces profit and reduces the carrying value of inventory and assets. This has a negative effect on profitability and solvency ratios. However, activity ratios appear positively affected by a write-down because the asset base, whether total assets or inventory (denominator), is reduced. The numerator, sales, in total asset turnover is unchanged, and the numerator, cost of sales, in inventory turnover is increased. Thus, turnover ratios are higher and appear more favorable as the result of the write-down.

49. B is correct. Finished goods least accurately reflect current prices because some of the finished goods are valued under the "last-in, first-out" ("LIFO") basis. The costs of the newest units available for sale are allocated to cost of goods sold, leaving the oldest units (at lower costs) in inventory. ZP values raw materials and work in process using the weighted average cost method. While not fully reflecting current prices, some inflationary effect will be included in the inventory values.

50. C is correct. FIFO inventory = Reported inventory + LIFO reserve = ¥608,572 + 10,120 = ¥618,692. The LIFO reserve is disclosed in Note 2 of the notes to consolidated financial statements.

51. A is correct. The inventory turnover ratio would be lower. The average inventory would be higher under FIFO, and cost of products sold would be lower by the increase in LIFO reserve. LIFO is not permitted under IFRS.

    Inventory turnover ratio = Cost of products sold ÷ Average inventory

    2018 inventory turnover ratio as reported = 10.63 = ¥5,822,805/[(608,572 + 486,465)/2].

    2018 inventory turnover ratio adjusted to FIFO as necessary = 10.34 = [¥5,822,805 − (19,660 − 10,120)]/[(608,572 + 10,120 + 486,465 + 19,660)/2].

52. A is correct. No LIFO liquidation occurred during 2018; the LIFO reserve increased from ¥10,120 million in 2008 to ¥19,660 million in 2018. Management stated in the MD&A that the decrease in inventories reflected the impacts of decreased sales volumes and fluctuations in foreign currency translation rates.

53. C is correct. Finished goods and raw materials inventories are lower in 2018 when compared to 2017. Reduced levels of inventory typically indicate an anticipated business contraction.

54. B is correct. The decrease in LIFO inventory in 2018 would typically indicate that more inventory units were sold than produced or purchased. Accordingly, one would expect a liquidation of some of the older LIFO layers and the LIFO reserve to decrease. In actuality, the LIFO reserve *increased* from ¥10,120 million in 2017 to ¥19,660 million in 2009. This is not to be expected and is likely caused by the increase in prices of raw materials, other production materials, and parts of foreign currencies as noted in the MD&A. An analyst should seek to confirm this explanation.

55. B is correct. If prices have been decreasing, write-downs under FIFO are least likely to have a significant effect because the inventory is valued at closer to the new, lower prices. Typically, inventories valued using LIFO are less likely to incur inventory write-downs than inventories valued using weighted average cost or FIFO. Under LIFO, the *oldest* costs are reflected in the inventory carrying value on the balance sheet. Given increasing inventory costs, the inventory carrying values under the LIFO method are already conservatively presented at the oldest and lowest costs. Thus, it is far less likely that inventory write-downs will occur under LIFO; and if a write-down does occur, it is likely to be of a lesser magnitude.

CHAPTER 8

LONG-LIVED ASSETS

SOLUTIONS

1. B is correct. Only costs necessary for the machine to be ready to use can be capitalized. Therefore, Total capitalized costs = 12,980 + 1,200 + 700 + 100 = $14,980.

2. C is correct. When property and equipment are purchased, the assets are recorded on the balance sheet at cost. Costs for the assets include all expenditures required to prepare the assets for their intended use. Any other costs are expensed. Costs to train staff for using the machine are not required to prepare the property and equipment for their intended use, and these costs are expensed.

3. B is correct. When a company constructs an asset, borrowing costs incurred directly related to the construction are generally capitalized. If the asset is constructed for sale, the borrowing costs are classified as inventory.

4. A is correct. Borrowing costs can be capitalized under IFRS until the tangible asset is ready for use. Also, under IFRS, income earned on temporarily investing the borrowed monies decreases the amount of borrowing costs eligible for capitalization. Therefore, Total capitalized interest = (500 million × 14% × 2 years) − 10 million = 130 million.

5. B is correct. A product patent with a defined expiration date is an intangible asset with a finite useful life. A copyright with no expiration date is an intangible asset with an indefinite useful life. Goodwill is no longer considered an intangible asset under IFRS and is considered to have an indefinite useful life.

6. C is correct. An intangible asset with a finite useful life is amortized, whereas an intangible asset with an indefinite useful life is not.

7. A is correct. The costs to internally develop intangible assets are generally expensed when incurred.

8. C is correct. Under both International Financial Reporting Standards (IFRS) and US GAAP, if an item is acquired in a business combination and cannot be recognized as a tangible asset or identifiable intangible asset, it is recognized as goodwill. Under US GAAP, assets arising from contractual or legal rights and assets that can be separated from the acquired company are recognized separately from goodwill.

9. A is correct. In the fiscal year when long-lived equipment is purchased, the assets on the balance sheet increase, and depreciation expense on the income statement increases because of the new long-lived asset.

10. B is correct. Company Z's return on equity based on year-end equity value will be 6.1%. Company Z will have an additional £200,000 of expenses compared with Company X. Company Z expensed the printer for £300,000 rather than capitalizing the printer and having a depreciation expense of £100,000 like Company X. Company Z's net income and shareholders' equity will be £150,000 lower (= £200,000 × 0.75) than that of Company X.

$$\text{ROE} = \left(\frac{\text{Net income}}{\text{Shareholders' Equity}} \right)$$

$$= £600,000/£9,850,000$$

$$= 0.61 = 6.1\%$$

11. A is correct. If the company uses the straight-line method, the depreciation expense will be one-fifth (20 percent) of the depreciable cost in Year 1. If it uses the units-of-production method, the depreciation expense will be 19 percent (2,000/10,500) of the depreciable cost in Year 1. Therefore, if the company uses the straight-line method, its depreciation expense will be higher, and its net income will be lower.

12. C is correct. The operating income or earnings before interest and taxes will be lowest for the method that results in the highest depreciation expense. The double-declining balance method results in the highest depreciation expense in the first year of use.

   Depreciation expense:

   Straight line = €1,500/5 = €300.

   Double-declining balance = €1,500 × 0.40 = €600.

   Units of production = €1,500 × 0.15 = €225.

13. C is correct. If Martinez wants to minimize tax payments in the first year of the machine's life, he should use an accelerated method, such as the double-declining balance method.

14. A is correct. Using the straight-line method, depreciation expense amounts to

   Depreciation expense = (1,200,000 − 200,000)/8 years = 125,000.

15. B is correct. Using the units-of-production method, depreciation expense amounts to

   Depreciation expense = (1,200,000 − 200,000) × (135,000/800,000) = 168,750.

16. A is correct. The straight-line method is the method that evenly distributes the cost of an asset over its useful life because amortization is the same amount every year.

17. A is correct. A higher residual value results in a lower total depreciable cost and, therefore, a lower amount of amortization in the first year after acquisition (and every year after that).

18. C is correct. Shifting at the end of Year 2 from double-declining balance to straight-line depreciation methodology results in depreciation expense being the same in each of Years 3, 4, and 5. Shifting to the straight-line methodology at the beginning of Year 3 results in a greater depreciation expense in Year 4 than would have been calculated using the double-declining balance method.

Depreciation expense Year 4 (Using double-declining balance method all five years)

= 2 × Annual depreciation % using straight-line method × Carrying amount at end of Year 3

= 40% × $43,200

Depreciation expense Year 4 with switch to straight-line method in Year 3

= 1/3 × Remaining depreciable cost at start of Year 3

= 1/3 × $72,000

= $24,000

19. B is correct. Using the straight-line method, accumulated amortization amounts to

$$\text{Accumulated amortization} = [(2,300,000 - 500,000)/3 \text{ years}] \times 2 \text{ years}$$
$$= 1,200,000$$

20. B is correct. Using the units-of-production method, depreciation expense amounts to

$$\text{Depreciation expense} = 5,800,000 \times (20,000/175,000) = 662,857$$

21. B is correct. As shown in the following calculations, under the double-declining balance method, the annual amortization expense in Year 4 is closest to ¥9.9 million.

Annual amortization expense = 2 × Straight-line amortization rate × Net book value.

Amortization expense Year 4 = 33.3% × ¥29.6 million = ¥9.9 million.

22. A is correct. As shown in the following calculations, at the end of Year 4, the difference between the net book values calculated using straight-line versus double-declining balance is closest to €81,400.

Net book value end of Year 4 using straight-line method = €600,000 − [4 × (€600,000/6)] = €200,000.

Net book value end of Year 4 using double-declining balance method = €600,000 $(1 - 33.33\%)^4 \approx$ €118,600.

23. B is correct. In this case, the value increase brought about by the revaluation should be recorded directly in equity. The reason is that under IFRS, an increase in value brought about by a revaluation can only be recognized as a profit to the extent that it reverses a revaluation decrease of the same asset previously recognized in the income statement.

24. B is correct. The impairment loss equals £3,100,000.

Impairment = max(Fair value less costs to sell; Value in use) − Net carrying amount

= max(16,800,000 − 800,000; 14,500,000) − 19,100,000

= −3,100,000.

25. B is correct. Under IFRS, an impairment loss is measured as the excess of the carrying amount over the asset's recoverable amount. The recoverable amount is the higher of the asset's fair value less costs to sell and its value in use. Value in use is a discounted measure of expected future cash flows. Under US GAAP, assessing recoverability is separate from measuring the impairment loss. If the asset's carrying amount exceeds its undiscounted expected future cash flows, the asset's carrying amount is considered unrecoverable, and the impairment loss is measured as the excess of the carrying amount over the asset's fair value.

26. B is correct. The result on the sale of the vehicle equals

    Gain or loss on the sale = Sale proceeds − Carrying amount

    $= $ Sale proceeds − (Acquisition cost − Accumulated depreciation)

    $= 85{,}000 − \{100{,}000 − [((100{,}000 − 10{,}000)/9 \text{ years}) \times 3 \text{ years}]\}$

    $= 15{,}000.$

27. A is correct. Gain or loss on the sale = Sale proceeds − Carrying amount. Rearranging this equation, Sale proceeds = Carrying amount + Gain or loss on sale. Thus, Sale price = (12 million − 2 million) + (−3.2 million) = 6.8 million.

28. C is correct. The carrying amount of the asset on the balance sheet is reduced by the amount of the impairment loss, and the impairment loss is reported on the income statement.

29. A is correct. The gain or loss on the sale of long-lived assets is computed as the sales proceeds minus the carrying amount of the asset at the time of sale. This is true under the cost and revaluation models of reporting long-lived assets. In the absence of impairment losses, under the cost model, the carrying amount will equal historical cost net of accumulated depreciation.

30. B is correct. IFRS do not require acquisition dates to be disclosed.

31. A is correct. IFRS do not require fair value of intangible assets to be disclosed.

32. C is correct. Under US GAAP, companies are required to disclose the estimated amortization expense for the next five fiscal years. Under US GAAP, there is no reversal of impairment losses. Disclosure of the useful lives—finite or indefinite and additional related details—is required under IFRS.

33. B is correct. Investment property earns rent. Investment property and property, plant, and equipment are tangible and long-lived.

34. C is correct. When a company uses the fair value model to value investment property, changes in the fair value of the property are reported in the income statement—not in other comprehensive income.

35. A is correct. Investment property earns rent. Inventory is held for resale, and property, plant, and equipment are used in the production of goods and services.

36. C is correct. A company will change from the fair value model to either the cost model or revaluation model when the company transfers investment property to property, plant, and equipment.

37. A is correct. Under both the revaluation model for property, plant, and equipment and the fair model for investment property, the asset's fair value must be able to be measured reliably. Under the fair value model, net income is affected by all changes in the asset's fair value. Under the revaluation model, any increase in an asset's value to the extent that it reverses a previous revaluation decrease will be recognized on the income statement and increase net income.

38. A is correct. Under IFRS, when using the cost model for its investment properties, a company must disclose useful lives. The method for determining fair value, as well as reconciliation between beginning and ending carrying amounts of investment property, is a required disclosure when the fair value model is used.

39. C is correct. Expensing rather than capitalizing an investment in long-term assets will result in higher expenses and lower net income and net profit margin in the current year. Future years' incomes will not include depreciation expense related to these expenditures. Consequently, year-to-year growth in profitability will be higher. If the expenses had been capitalized, the carrying amount of the assets would have been higher, and the 2009 total asset turnover would have been lower.

40. C is correct. In 2010, switching to an accelerated depreciation method would increase depreciation expense and decrease income before taxes, taxes payable, and net income. Cash flow from operating activities would increase because of the resulting tax savings.

41. B is correct. 2009 net income and net profit margin are lower because of the impairment loss. Consequently, net profit margins in subsequent years are likely to be higher. An impairment loss suggests that insufficient depreciation expense was recognized in prior years, and net income was overstated in prior years. The impairment loss is a non-cash item and will not affect operating cash flows.

42. A is correct. The estimated average remaining useful life is 20.75 years.

Estimate of remaining useful life = Net plant and equipment ÷ Annual depreciation expense

Net plant and equipment = Gross P & E − Accumulated depreciation

$$= €6000 − €1850 = €4150$$

Estimate of remaining useful life = Net P & E ÷ Depreciation expense

$$= €4150 ÷ €200 = 20.75$$

43. C is correct. The decision to capitalize the costs of the new computer system results in higher cash flow from operating activities; the expenditure is reported as an outflow of investing activities. The company allocates the capitalized amount over the asset's useful life as depreciation or amortisation expense rather than expensing it in the year of expenditure. Net income and total assets are higher in the current fiscal year.

44. B is correct. Alpha's fixed asset turnover will be lower because the capitalized interest will appear on the balance sheet as part of the asset being constructed. Therefore, fixed assets will be higher, and the fixed asset turnover ratio (total revenue/average net fixed assets) will be lower than if it had expensed these costs. Capitalized interest appears on the balance sheet as part of the asset being constructed instead of being reported as interest expense in the period incurred. However, the interest coverage ratio should be based on interest payments, not interest expense (earnings before interest and taxes/interest payments), and should be unchanged. To provide a true picture of a company's interest coverage, the entire amount of interest expenditure, both the capitalized portion and the expensed portion, should be used in calculating interest coverage ratios.

45. A is correct. Accelerated depreciation will result in an improving, not declining, net profit margin over time, because the amount of depreciation expense declines each year. Under straight-line depreciation, the amount of depreciation expense will remain the same each year. Under the units-of-production method, the amount of depreciation expense reported each year varies with the number of units produced.

46. B is correct. The estimated average total useful life of a company's assets is calculated by adding the estimates of the average remaining useful life and the average age of the assets. The average age of the assets is estimated by dividing accumulated depreciation by depreciation expense. The average remaining useful life of the asset base is estimated by dividing net property, plant, and equipment by annual depreciation expense.

47. C is correct. The impairment loss is a non-cash charge and will not affect cash flow from operating activities. The debt to total assets and fixed asset turnover ratios will increase, because the impairment loss will reduce the carrying amount of fixed assets and therefore total assets.

48. A is correct. In an asset revaluation, the carrying amount of the assets increases. The increase in the asset's carrying amount bypasses the income statement and is reported as other comprehensive income and appears in equity under the heading of revaluation surplus. Therefore, shareholders' equity will increase, but net income will not be affected, so return on equity will decline. Return on assets and debt to capital ratios will also decrease.

CHAPTER 9

INCOME TAXES

SOLUTIONS

1. C is correct. Because the differences between tax and financial accounting will correct over time, the resulting deferred tax liability, for which the expense was charged to the income statement but the tax authority has not yet been paid, will be a temporary difference. A valuation allowance would only arise if there was doubt over the company's ability to earn sufficient income in the future to require paying the tax.

2. A is correct. The taxes a company must pay in the immediate future are taxes payable.

3. C is correct. Higher reported tax expense relative to taxes paid will increase the deferred tax liability, whereas lower reported tax expense relative to taxes paid increases the deferred tax asset.

4. B is correct. If the liability is expected to reverse (and thus require a cash tax payment), the deferred tax represents a future liability.

5. A is correct. If the liability will not reverse, there will be no required tax payment in the future, and the "liability" should be treated as equity.

6. C is correct. The deferred tax liability should be excluded from both debt and equity when both the amounts and timing of tax payments resulting from the reversals of temporary differences are uncertain.

7. C is correct. Accounting items that are not deductible for tax purposes will not be reversed and thus result in permanent differences.

8. C is correct. Tax credits that directly reduce taxes are a permanent difference, and permanent differences do not give rise to deferred tax.

9. A is correct. The capitalization will result in an asset with a positive tax base and zero carrying value. The amortization means the difference is temporary. Because there is a temporary difference on an asset resulting in a higher tax base than carrying value, a deferred tax asset is created.

10. B is correct. The difference is temporary, and the tax base will be lower (because of more rapid amortization) than the carrying value of the asset. The result will be a deferred tax liability.

11. A is correct. The advances represent a liability for the company. The carrying value of the liability exceeds the tax base (which is now zero). A deferred tax asset arises when the carrying value of a liability exceeds its tax base.

12. B is correct. The income tax provision in Year 3 was $54,144, consisting of $58,772 in current income taxes, of which $4,628 were deferred.

13. B is correct. The effective tax rate of 30.1 percent ($56,860/$189,167) was higher than the effective rates in Year 2 and Year 3.

14. A is correct. In Year 3 the effective tax rate on foreign operations was 24.2 percent [($28,140 + $124)/$116,704], and the effective US tax rate was [($30,632 − $4,752)/$88,157] = 29.4 percent. In Year 2 the effective tax rate on foreign operations was 26.2 percent, and the US rate was 35.9 percent. In Year 1 the foreign rate was 24.1 percent, and the US rate was 35.5 percent.

15. B is correct. The valuation allowance is taken against deferred tax assets to represent uncertainty that future taxable income will be sufficient to fully utilize the assets. By decreasing the allowance, Zimt is signaling greater likelihood that future earnings will be offset by the deferred tax asset.

16. C is correct. The valuation allowance is taken when the company will "more likely than not" fail to earn sufficient income to offset the deferred tax asset. Because the valuation allowance equals the asset, by extension the company expects *no* taxable income prior to the expiration of the deferred tax assets.

17. A is correct. A lower tax rate would increase net income on the income statement, and because the company has a net deferred tax liability, the net liability position on the balance sheet would also improve (be smaller).

18. C is correct. The reduction in the valuation allowance resulted in a corresponding reduction in the income tax provision.

19. B is correct. The net deferred tax liability was smaller in Year 3 than it was in Year 2, indicating that in addition to meeting the tax payments provided for in Year 3 the company also paid taxes that had been deferred in prior periods.

20. C is correct. The income tax provision at the statutory rate of 34 percent is a benefit of $112,000, suggesting that the pre-tax income was a loss of $112,000/0.34 = ($329,412). The income tax provision was $227,000: ($329,412) − $227,000 = ($556,412).

21. C is correct. Accounting expenses that are not deductible for tax purposes result in a permanent difference, and thus do not give rise to deferred taxes.

22. B is correct. Over the three-year period, changes in the valuation allowance reduced cumulative income taxes by $1,670,000. The reductions to the valuation allowance were a result of the company being "more likely than not" to earn sufficient taxable income to offset the deferred tax assets.

CHAPTER 10

NON-CURRENT
(LONG-TERM) LIABILITIES

SOLUTIONS

1. B is correct. The company receives €1 million in cash from investors at the time the bonds are issued, which is recorded as a financing activity.
2. B is correct. The effective interest rate is greater than the coupon rate, and the bonds will be issued at a discount.
3. A is correct. Under US GAAP, expenses incurred when issuing bonds are generally recorded as an asset and amortized to the related expense (legal, etc.) over the life of the bonds. Under IFRS, they are included in the measurement of the liability. The related cash flows are financing activities.
4. C is correct. The bonds will be issued at a premium because the coupon rate is higher than the market interest rate. The future cash outflows, the present value of the cash outflows, and the total present value are as follows:

Date	Interest Payment ($)	Present Value at Market Rate 5% ($)		Present Value at Market Rate 5% ($)	Total Present Value ($)
December 31, 2015	60,000.00	57,142.86			
December 31, 2016	60,000.00	54,421.77			
December 31, 2017	60,000.00	51,830.26			
December 31, 2018	60,000.00	49,362.15			
December 31, 2019	60,000.00	47,011.57			
December 31, 2020	60,000.00	44,772.92			
December 31, 2021	60,000.00	42,640.88			
December 31, 2022	60,000.00	40,610.36			
December 31, 2023	60,000.00	38,676.53			
December 31, 2024	60,000.00	36,834.80	1,000,000.00	613,913.25	
		463,304.10		613,913.25	1,077,217.35
					Sales Proceeds

The following illustrates the keystrokes for many financial calculators to calculate sales proceeds of $1,077,217.35:

Calculator Notation	Numerical Value for This Problem
N	10
% i or I/Y	5
FV	$1,000,000.00
PMT	$60,000.00
PV compute	X

Thus, the sales proceeds are reported on the balance sheet as an increase in long-term liability, bonds payable of $1,077,217.

5. A is correct. The bonds payable reported at issue is equal to the sales proceeds. The interest payments and future value of the bond must be discounted at the market interest rate of 3% to determine the sales proceeds.

Date	Interest Payment	Present Value at Market Rate (3%)	Face Value Payment	Present Value at Market Rate (3%)	Total Present Value
December 31, 2015	$125,000.00	$121,359.22			
December 31, 2016	$125,000.00	$117,824.49			
December 31, 2017	$125,000.00	$114,392.71	$5,000,000.00	$4,575,708.30	
Total		$353,576.42		$4,575,708.30	$4,929,284.72

The following illustrates the keystrokes for many financial calculators to calculate sales proceeds of $4,929,284.72:

Calculator Notation	Numerical Value for This Problem
N	3
% i or I/Y	3.0
FV	$5,000,000.00
PMT	$125,000.00
PV compute	X

6. B is correct. The market interest rate at the time of issuance is the effective interest rate that the company incurs on the debt. The effective interest rate is the discount rate that equates the present value of the coupon payments and face value to their selling price. Consequently, the effective interest rate is 5.50%.

7. B is correct. The bonds will be issued at a discount because the market interest rate is higher than the stated rate. Discounting the future payments to their present value indicates that at the time of issue, the company will record £978,938 as both a liability and a cash inflow from financing activities. Interest expense in 2010 is £58,736 (£978,938 times 6.0 percent). During the year, the company will pay cash of £55,000 related to the interest payment, but interest expense on the income statement will also reflect £3,736 related to amortization of the initial discount (£58,736 interest expense less the £55,000 interest payment). Thus, the value of the liability at December 31, 2010 will reflect the

initial value (£978,938) plus the amortized discount (£3,736), for a total of £982,674. The cash outflow of £55,000 may be presented as either an operating or financing activity under IFRS.

8. A is correct. The coupon rate on the bonds is higher than the market rate, which indicates that the bonds will be issued at a premium. Taking the present value of each payment indicates an issue date value of €10,210,618. The interest expense is determined by multiplying the carrying amount at the beginning of the period (€10,210,618) by the market interest rate at the time of issue (6.0 percent) for an interest expense of €612,637. The value after one year will equal the beginning value less the amount of the premium amortized to date, which is the difference between the amount paid (€650,000) and the expense accrued (€612,637) or €37,363. €10,210,618 − €37,363 = €10,173,255 or €10.17 million.

9. A is correct. The future cash outflows, the present value of the cash outflows, and the total present value are as follows:

Date	Interest Payment (€)	Present Value at Market Rate 6% (€)		Present Value at Market Rate 6% (€)	Total Present Value (€)
December 31, 2015	700,000.00	660,377.36			
December 31, 2016	700,000.00	622,997.51			
December 31, 2017	700,000.00	587,733.50			
December 31, 2018	700,000.00	554,465.56			
December 31, 2019	700,000.00	523,080.72			
December 31, 2020	700,000.00	493,472.38			
December 31, 2021	700,000.00	465,539.98			
December 31, 2022	700,000.00	439,188.66			
December 31, 2023	700,000.00	414,328.92			
December 31, 2024	700,000.00	390,876.34	10,000,000.00	5,583,947.77	
		5,152,060.94		5,583,947.77	10,736,008.71
					Sales Proceeds

The following illustrates the keystrokes for many financial calculators to calculate sales proceeds of €10,736,008.71:

Calculator Notation	Numerical Value for This Problem
N	10
% *i* or I/Y	6
FV	$10,000,000.00
PMT	$700,000.00
PV compute	X

The interest expense is calculated by multiplying the carrying amount at the beginning of the year by the effective interest rate at issuance. As a result, the interest expense at December 31, 2015 is €644,161 (€10,736,008.71 × 6%).

10. C is correct. The future cash outflows, the present value of the cash outflows, and the total present value are as follows:

Date	Interest Payment ($)	Present Value at Market Rate 5% ($)		Present Value at Market Rate 5% ($)	Total Present Value ($)
December 31, 2015	1,200,000	1,142,857.14			
December 31, 2016	1,200,000	1,088,435.37			
December 31, 2017	1,200,000	1,036,605.12			
December 31, 2018	1,200,000	987,242.97			
December 31, 2019	1,200,000	940,231.40	30,000,000	23,505,785.00	
		5,195,372.00		23,505,785.00	28,701,157.00
					Sales Proceeds

The following illustrates the keystrokes for many financial calculators to calculate sales proceeds of $28,701,157.00:

Calculator Notation	Numerical Value for This Problem
N	5
% i or I/Y	5
FV	$30,000,000.00
PMT	$1,200,000.00
PV compute	X

The following table illustrates interest expense, premium amortization, and carrying amount (amortized cost) for 2015.

Year	Carrying Amount (beginning of year)	Interest Expense (at effective interest rate of 5%)	Interest Payment (at coupon rate of 4%)	Amortization of Discount	Carrying Amount (end of year)
2015	$28,701,157.00	$1,435,057.85	$1,200,000.00	$235,057.85	$28,936,214.85

The carrying amount at the end of the year is found by adding the amortization of the discount to the carrying amount at the beginning of the year. As a result, the carrying amount on December 31, 2015 is $28,936,215.

Alternatively, the following illustrates the keystrokes for many financial calculators to calculate the carrying value at the end of first year of $28,936, 215:

Calculator Notation	Numerical Value for This Problem
N	4
% i or I/Y	5
FV	$30,000,000.00
PMT	$1,200,000.00
PV compute	X

11. B is correct. The interest expense for a given year is equal to the carrying amount at the beginning of the year times the effective interest of 4%. Under the effective interest rate method, the difference between the interest expense and the interest payment (based on the coupon rate and face value) is the discount amortized in the period, which increases the carrying amount annually. For 2017, the interest expense is the beginning carrying amount ($1,944,499) times the effective interest of 4%.

Year	Carrying Amount (beginning)	Interest Expense (at effective interest of 4%)	Interest Payment (at coupon rate of 3%)	Amortization of Discount	Carrying Amount (end of year)
2015	$1,910,964	$76,439	$60,000.00	$16,439	$1,927,403
2016	$1,927,403	$77,096	$60,000.00	$17,096	$1,944,499
2017	$1,944,499	$77,780	$60,000.00	$17,780	$1,962,279

12. B is correct. The amortization of the premium equals the interest payment minus the interest expense. The interest payment is constant, and the interest expense decreases as the carrying amount decreases. As a result, the amortization of the premium increases each year.

13. B is correct. Under the straight-line method, the bond premium is amortized equally over the life of the bond. The annual interest payment is $165,000 ($3,000,000 × 5.5%), and annual amortization of the premium under the straight-line method is $13,616 [($3,040,849 − $3,000,000)/3)]. The interest expense is the interest payment less the amortization of the premium ($165,000 − $13,616 = $151,384).

14. C is correct. A gain of €3.3 million (carrying amount less amount paid) will be reported on the income statement.

15. B is correct. If a company decides to redeem a bond before maturity, bonds payable is reduced by the carrying amount of the debt. The difference between the cash required to redeem the bonds and the carrying amount of the bonds is a gain or loss on the extinguishment of debt. Because the call price is 104 and the face value is $1,000,000, the redemption cost is 104% of $1,000,000 or $1,040,000. The company's loss on redemption would be $50,000 ($990,000 carrying amount of debt minus $1,040,000 cash paid to redeem the callable bonds).

16. A is correct. The value of the liability for zero-coupon bonds increases as the discount is amortized over time. Furthermore, the amortized interest will reduce earnings at an increasing rate over time as the value of the liability increases. Higher relative debt and lower relative equity (through retained earnings) will cause the debt-to-equity ratio to increase as the zero-coupon bonds approach maturity.

17. A is correct. When interest rates rise, bonds decline in value. Thus, the carrying amount of the bonds being carried on the balance sheet is higher than the market value. The company could repurchase the bonds for less than the carrying amount, so the economic liabilities are overestimated. Because the bonds are issued at a fixed rate, there is no effect on interest coverage.

18. C is correct. Affirmative covenants require certain actions of the borrower. Requiring the company to perform regular maintenance on equipment pledged as collateral is an example of an affirmative covenant because it requires the company to do something. Negative covenants require that the borrower not take certain actions. Prohibiting the borrower

from entering into mergers and preventing the borrower from issuing excessive additional debt are examples of negative covenants.

19. C is correct. Covenants protect debtholders from excessive risk taking, typically by limiting the issuer's ability to use cash or by limiting the overall levels of debt relative to income and equity. Issuing additional equity would increase the company's ability to meet its obligations, so debtholders would not restrict that ability.

20. C is correct. The non-current liabilities section of the balance sheet usually includes a single line item of the total amount of a company's long-term debt due after 1 year, and the current liabilities section shows the portion of a company's long-term debt due in the next 12 months. Notes to the financial statements generally present the stated and effective interest rates and maturity dates for a company's debt obligations

21. B is correct. An operating lease is not recorded on the balance sheet (debt is lower), and lease payments are entirely categorized as rent (interest expense is lower.) Because the rent expense is an operating outflow but principal repayments are financing cash flows, the operating lease will result in lower cash flow from operating activity.

22. B is correct. The lessee will disclose the future obligation by maturity of its operating leases. The future obligations by maturity, leased assets, and lease liabilities will all be shown for finance leases.

23. B is correct. When a lease is classified as an operating lease, the underlying asset remains on the lessor's balance sheet. The lessor will record a depreciation expense that reduces the asset's value over time.

24. A is correct. A sales-type lease treats the lease as a sale of the asset, and revenue is recorded at the time of sale equal to the present value of future lease payments. Under a direct financing lease, only interest income is reported as earned. Under an operating lease, revenue from rent is reported when collected.

25. A is correct. A portion of the payments for capital leases, either direct financing or sales-type, is reported as interest income. With an operating lease, all revenue is recorded as rental revenue.

26. A is correct. An operating lease is an agreement that allows the lessee to use an asset for a period of time. Thus, an operating lease is similar to renting an asset, whereas a finance lease is equivalent to the purchase of an asset by the lessee that is directly financed by the lessor.

27. C is correct. If the present value of the lease payments is greater than 90% of the fair value of the asset, the lease is considered a capital lease. A lease with a term that is 75% or more of the useful life of the asset is deemed to be a capital lease. The option to purchase the asset must be deemed to be cheap (bargain purchase option), not just to include the option to purchase the asset.

28. A is correct. A finance lease is similar to borrowing money and buying an asset; a company that enters into a finance lease as the lessee reports an asset (leased asset) and related debt (lease payable) on its balance sheet. A company that enters into a finance lease as the lessee will report interest expense and depreciation expense on its income statement. A company that enters into an operating lease will report the lease payment on its income statement. For a finance lease, only the portion of the lease payment relating to interest expense reduces operating cash flow; the portion of the lease payment that reduces the lease liability appears as a cash outflow in the financing section. A company that enters into an operating lease as the lessee will report the full lease payment as an operating cash outflow.

29. A is correct. A company that enters into a finance lease reports the value of both the leased asset and lease payable as the lower of the present value of future lease payments and the fair value of the leased asset. The present value of the future lease payments, €47,250,188, is lower than the fair market value of the leased asset, €49,000,000. The company will record a lease payable on the balance sheet of €47,250,188.

30. B is correct. An operating lease is economically similar to renting an asset. A company that enters into an operating lease as a lessee reports a lease expense on its income statement during the period it uses the asset and reports no asset or liability on its balance sheet. The operating lease is disclosed in notes to the financial statements.

31. C is correct. The current debt-to-total-capital ratio is $840/($840 + $520) = 0.62. To adjust for the lease commitments, an analyst should add $100 to both the numerator and denominator: $940/($940 + $520) = 0.64.

32. C is correct. The financial leverage ratio is calculated as follows:

$$\frac{\text{Average total assets}}{\text{Average shareholder's equity}} = \frac{\$45,981 \text{ million}}{\$18,752 \text{ million}} = \$2.452 \text{ million}$$

33. B is correct. Company B has the lowest debt-to-equity ratio, indicating the lowest financial leverage, and the highest interest coverage ratio, indicating the greatest number of times that EBIT covers interest payments.

34. A is correct because the debt-to-assets (total debt)/(total assets) ratio is $(1,258 + 321)/(8,750) = 1,579/8,750 = 0.18$

35. B is correct. The company will report a net pension obligation of €1 million equal to the pension obligation (€10 million) less the plan assets (€9 million).

36. A is correct. A company that offers a defined benefit plan makes payments into a pension fund, and the retirees are paid from the fund. The payments that a company makes into the fund are invested until they are needed to pay retirees. If the fair value of the fund's assets is higher than the present value of the estimated pension obligation, the plan has a surplus, and the company's balance sheet will reflect a net pension asset. Because the fair value of the fund's assets are $1,500,000,000 and the present value of estimated pension obligations is $1,200,000,000, the company will present a net pension asset of $300,000,000 on its balance sheet.

CHAPTER 11

FINANCIAL REPORTING QUALITY

SOLUTIONS

1. B is correct. Financial reporting quality pertains to the quality of information in financial reports. High-quality financial reporting provides decision-useful information, which is relevant and faithfully represents the economic reality of the company's activities. Earnings of high quality are sustainable and provide an adequate level of return. Highest-quality financial reports reflect both high financial reporting quality and high earnings quality.

2. C is correct. Financial reporting quality pertains to the quality of the information contained in financial reports. High-quality financial reports provide decision-useful information that faithfully represents the economic reality of the company. Low-quality financial reports impede assessment of earnings quality. Financial reporting quality is distinguishable from earnings quality, which pertains to the earnings and cash generated by the company's actual economic activities and the resulting financial condition. Low-quality earnings are not sustainable and decrease company value.

3. B is correct. Financial reporting quality pertains to the quality of the information contained in financial reports. If financial reporting quality is low, the information provided is of little use in assessing the company's performance. Financial reporting quality is distinguishable from earnings quality, which pertains to the earnings and cash generated by the company's actual economic activities and the resulting financial condition.

4. B is correct. Earnings quality pertains to the earnings and cash generated by the company's actual economic activities and the resulting financial condition. Low-quality earnings are likely not sustainable over time because the company does not expect to generate the same level of earnings in the future or because earnings will not generate sufficient return on investment to sustain the company. Earnings that are not sustainable decrease company value. Earnings quality is distinguishable from financial reporting quality, which pertains to the quality of the information contained in financial reports.

5. A is correct. Earnings that result from non-recurring activities are unsustainable. Unsustainable earnings are an example of lower-quality earnings. Recognizing earnings that

result from non-recurring activities is neither a biased accounting choice nor indicative of lower quality financial reporting because it faithfully represents economic events.

6. B is correct. At the top of the quality spectrum of financial reports are reports that conform to GAAP, are decision useful, and have earnings that are sustainable and offer adequate returns. In other words, these reports have both high financial reporting quality and high earnings quality.

7. A is correct. Financial reports span a quality continuum from high to low based on decision-usefulness and earnings quality (see Exhibit 2 of the chapter). The lowest-quality reports portray fictitious events, which may misrepresent the company's performance and/or obscure fraudulent misappropriation of the company's assets.

8. B is correct. Deferring research and development (R&D) investments into the next reporting period is an example of earnings management by taking a *real* action.

9. B is correct. High-quality financial reports offer useful information, meaning information that is relevant and faithfully represents actual performance. Although low earnings quality may not be desirable, if the reported earnings are representative of actual performance, they are consistent with high-quality financial reporting. Highest-quality financial reports reflect both high financial reporting quality and high earnings quality.

10. B is correct. Aggressive accounting choices aim to enhance the company's reported performance by inflating the amount of revenues, earnings, and/or operating cash flow reported in the period. Consequently, the financial performance for that period would most likely exhibit an upward bias.

11. C is correct. Accounting choices are considered conservative if they decrease the company's reported performance and financial position in the period under review. Conservative choices may increase the amount of debt reported on the balance sheet. They may decrease the revenues, earnings, and/or operating cash flow reported for the period and increase those amounts in later periods.

12. A is correct. Conservatism reduces the possibility of litigation and, by extension, litigation costs. Rarely, if ever, is a company sued because it understated good news or overstated bad news. Accounting conservatism is a type of bias in financial reporting that decreases a company's reported performance. Conservatism directly conflicts with the characteristic of neutrality.

13. A is correct. Managers often have incentives to meet or beat market expectations, particularly if management compensation is linked to increases in stock prices or to reported earnings.

14. B is correct. Managers may be motivated to understate earnings in the reporting period and increase the probability of meeting or exceeding the next period's earnings target.

15. C is correct. Typically, conditions of opportunity, motivation, and rationalization exist when individuals issue low-quality financial reports. Rationalization occurs when an individual is concerned about a choice and needs to be able to justify it to herself or himself. If the manager is concerned about a choice in a financial report, she or he may ask for other opinions to convince herself or himself that it is okay.

16. C is correct. In a period of strong financial performance, managers may pursue accounting choices that increase the probability of exceeding earnings forecasts for the next period. By accelerating expense recognition or delaying revenue recognition, managers may inflate earnings in the next period and increase the likelihood of exceeding targets.

17. B is correct. Motivation can result from pressure to meet some criteria for personal reasons, such as a bonus, or corporate reasons, such as concern about future financing. Poor internal controls and an inattentive board of directors offer opportunities to issue low-quality financial reports.

18. A is correct. The possibility of bond covenant violations may motivate managers to inflate earnings in the reporting period. In so doing, the company may be able to avoid the consequences associated with violating bond covenants.

19. A is correct. Opportunities to issue low-quality financial reports include internal conditions, such as an ineffective board of directors, and external conditions, such as accounting standards that provide scope for divergent choices. Pressure to achieve a certain level of performance and corporate concerns about future financing are examples of motivations to issue low-quality financial reports. Typically, three conditions exist when low-quality financial reports are issued: opportunity, motivation, and rationalization.

20. C is correct. An audit is intended to provide assurance that the company's financial reports are presented fairly, thus providing discipline regarding financial reporting quality. Regulatory agencies usually require that the financial statements of publicly traded companies be audited by an independent auditor to provide assurance that the financial statements conform to accounting standards. Privately held companies may also choose to obtain audit opinions either voluntarily or because an outside party requires it. An audit is not typically intended to detect fraud. An audit is based on sampling, and it is possible that the sample might not reveal misstatements.

21. B is correct. If a company uses a non-GAAP financial measure in an SEC filing, it is required to provide the most directly comparable GAAP measure with equivalent prominence in the filing. In addition, the company is required to provide a reconciliation between the non-GAAP measure and the equivalent GAAP measure. Similarly, IFRS require that any non-IFRS measures included in financial reports must be defined and their potential relevance explained. The non-IFRS measures must be reconciled with IFRS measures.

22. B is correct. If a company wants to increase reported earnings, the company's managers may reduce the allowance for uncollected accounts and the related expense reported for the period. Decreasing the useful life of depreciable assets would increase depreciation expense and decrease earnings in the reporting period. Classifying a purchase as an expense, rather than capital expenditure, would decrease earnings in the reporting period. The use of accrual accounting may result in estimates in financial reports, because all facts associated with events may not be known at the time of recognition. These estimates can be grounded in reality or managed by the company to present a desired financial picture.

23. B is correct. Bias in revenue recognition can lead to manipulation of information presented in financial reports. Addressing the question as to whether revenue is higher or lower than the previous period is not sufficient to determine if there is bias in revenue recognition. Additional analytical procedures must be performed to identify warning signals of accounting malfeasance. Barter transactions are difficult to value properly and may result in bias in revenue recognition. Policies that make it easier to prematurely recognize revenue, such as before goods are shipped to customers, may be a warning sign of accounting malfeasance.

24. A is correct. Managers can temporarily show a higher cash flow from operations by stretching the accounts payable credit period. In other words, the managers delay payments until the next accounting period. Applying all non-cash discount amortization against interest capitalized causes reported interest expenses and operating cash outflow to be higher, resulting in a lower cash flow provided by operations. Shifting the classification of interest paid from financing to operating cash flows lowers the cash flow provided by operations.

25. C is correct. If a company's days sales outstanding (DSO) is increasing relative to competitors, this may be a signal that revenues are being recorded prematurely or are even

fictitious. There are numerous analytical procedures that can be performed to provide evidence of manipulation of information in financial reporting. These warning signs are often linked to bias associated with revenue recognition and expense recognition policies.

26. B is correct. If the ratio of cash flow to net income for a company is consistently below 1 or has declined repeatedly over time, this may be a signal of manipulation of information in financial reports through aggressive accrual accounting policies. When net income is consistently higher than cash provided by operations, one possible explanation is that the company may be using aggressive accrual accounting policies to shift current expenses to later periods.

27. C is correct. To extrapolate historical earnings trends, an analyst should consider making pro forma analytical adjustments of prior years' earnings to reflect in those prior years a reasonable share of the current period's restructuring and impairment charges.

CHAPTER 12

APPLICATIONS OF FINANCIAL STATEMENT ANALYSIS

SOLUTIONS

1. C is correct. For a large, diversified company, margin changes in different business segments may offset each other. Furthermore, margins are most likely to be stable in mature industries.

2. C is correct. Accounts receivable turnover is equal to 365/19 (collection period in days) = 19.2 for 2003 and needs to equal 365/15 = 24.3 in 2004 for Galambos to meet its goal. Sales/turnover equals the accounts receivable balance. For 2003, $300,000,000/19.2 = $15,625,000, and for 2004, $400,000,000/24.3 = $16,460,905. The difference of $835,905 is the increase in receivables needed for Galambos to achieve its goal.

3. C is correct. Credit analysts consider both business risk and financial risk.

4. A is correct. Requiring that net income be positive would eliminate companies that report a positive return on equity only because both net income and shareholders' equity are negative.

5. B is correct. A lower value of debt/total assets indicates greater financial strength. Requiring that a company's debt/total assets be below a certain cutoff point would allow the analyst to screen out highly leveraged and, therefore, potentially financially weak companies.

6. C is correct. Survivorship bias exists when companies that merge or go bankrupt are dropped from the database and only surviving companies remain. Look-ahead bias involves using updated financial information in back-testing that would not have been available at the time the decision was made. Back-testing involves testing models in prior periods and is not, itself, a bias.

7. C is correct. Financial statements should be adjusted for differences in accounting standards (as well as accounting and operating choices). These adjustments should be made prior to common-size and ratio analysis.

8. A is correct. LIFO is not permitted under IFRS.

9. C is correct. To convert LIFO inventory to FIFO inventory, the entire LIFO reserve must be added back: $600,000 + $70,000 = $670,000.

10. C is correct. The company made no additions to or deletions from the fixed asset account during the year, so depreciation expense is equal to the difference in accumulated depreciation at the beginning of the year and the end of the year, or $0.4 million. Average age is equal to accumulated depreciation/depreciation expense, or $1.6/$0.4 = 4 years. Average depreciable life is equal to ending gross investment/depreciation expense = $2.8/$0.4 = 7 years.

11. C is correct. Tangible book value removes all intangible assets, including goodwill, from the balance sheet.

12. B is correct. Operating leases can be used as an off-balance-sheet financing technique because neither the asset nor liability appears on the balance sheet. Inventory and capital leases are reported on the balance sheet.

13. C is correct. The present value of future operating lease payments would be added to total assets and total liabilities.

CHAPTER **13**

INTERCORPORATE INVESTMENTS

SOLUTIONS

1. B is correct. If Cinnamon is deemed to have control over Cambridge, it would use the acquisition method to account for Cambridge and prepare consolidated financial statements. Proportionate consolidation is used for joint ventures; the equity method is used for some joint ventures and when there is significant influence but not control.

2. A is correct. If Cinnamon is deemed to have control over Cambridge, consolidated financial statements would be prepared, and Cinnamon's total shareholders' equity would increase and include the amount of the noncontrolling interest. If Cinnamon is deemed to have significant influence, the equity method would be used, and there would be no change in the total shareholders' equity of Cinnamon.

3. C is correct. If Cinnamon is deemed to have significant influence, it would report half of Cambridge's net income as a line item on its income statement, but no additional revenue is shown. Its profit margin is thus higher than if it consolidated Cambridge's results, which would impact revenue and income, or if it only reported 19 percent of Cambridge's dividends (no change in ownership).

4. C is correct. The full and partial goodwill method will have the same amount of debt; however, shareholders' equity will be higher under full goodwill (and the debt to equity ratio will be lower). Therefore, the debt to equity will be higher under partial goodwill. If control is assumed, Cinnamon cannot use the equity method.

5. A is correct. Cambridge has a lower operating margin (88/1,100 = 8.0%) than Cinnamon (142/1,575 = 9.0%). If Cambridge's results are consolidated with Cinnamon's, the consolidated operating margin will reflect that of the combined company, or 230/2,675 = 8.6%.

6. A is correct. When a company is deemed to have control of another entity, it records all of the other entity's assets on its own consolidated balance sheet.

7. B is correct. If Zimt is deemed to have significant influence, it would use the equity method to record its ownership. Under the equity method, Zimt's share of Oxbow's net income would be recorded as a single line item. Net income of Zimt = 75 + 0.5(68) = 109.

213

8. B is correct. Under the proportionate consolidation method, Zimt's balance sheet would show its own total liabilities of €1,421 − 735 = €686 plus half of Oxbow's liabilities of €1,283 − 706 = €577. €686 + (0.5 × 577) = €974.5.

9. C is correct. Under the assumption of control, Zimt would record its own sales plus 100 percent of Oxbow's. €1,700 + 1,350 = €3,050.

10. C is correct. Net income is not affected by the accounting method used to account for active investments in other companies. "One-line consolidation" and consolidation result in the same impact on net income; it is the disclosure that differs.

11. B is correct. Under IFRS 9, FVPL and FVOCI securities are carried at market value, whereas amortized cost securities are carried at historical cost. €28,000 + 37,000 + 50,000 = €115,000.

12. C is correct. If Dumas had been classified as a FVPL security, its carrying value would have been the €55,000 fair value rather than the €50,000 historical cost.

13. B is correct. The coupon payment is recorded as interest income whether securities are amortized cost or FVPL. No adjustment is required for amortization since the bonds were bought at par.

14. C is correct. Unrealized gains and losses are included in income when securities are classified as FVPL. During 2018 there was an unrealized gain of €1,000.

15. B is correct. The difference between historical cost and par value must be amortized under the effective interest method. If the par value is less than the initial cost (stated interest rate is greater than the effective rate), the interest income would be lower than the interest received because of amortization of the premium.

16. B is correct. Under IFRS, SPEs must be consolidated if they are conducted for the benefit of the sponsoring entity. Further, under IFRS, SPEs cannot be classified as qualifying. Under US GAAP, qualifying SPEs (a classification that has been eliminated) do not have to be consolidated.

17. B is correct. Statewide Medical was accounted for under the pooling of interest method, which causes all of Statewide's assets and liabilities to be reported at historical book value. The excess of assets over liabilities generally is lower using the historical book value method than using the fair value method (this latter method must be used under currently required acquisition accounting). It would have no effect on revenue.

18. A is correct. Under the equity method, BetterCare would record its interest in the joint venture's net profit as a single line item, but would show no line-by-line contribution to revenues or expenses.

19. C is correct. Net income will be the same under the equity method and proportional consolidation. However, sales, cost of sales, and expenses are different because under the equity method the net effect of sales, cost of sales, and expenses is reflected in a single line.

20. B is correct. Under the proportionate consolidation method, Supreme Healthcare's consolidated financial statements will include its 50 percent share of the joint venture's total assets.

21. C is correct. The choice of equity method or proportionate consolidation does not affect reported shareholders' equity.

22. C is correct. Although Supreme Healthcare has no voting interest in the SPE, it is expected to absorb any losses that the SPE incurs. Therefore, Supreme Healthcare "in substance" controls the SPE and would consolidate it. On the consolidated balance sheet, the accounts receivable balance will be the same since the sale to the SPE will be reversed upon consolidation.

23. A is correct. The current ratio using the equity method of accounting is Current assets/ Current liabilities = £250/£110 = 2.27. Using consolidation (either full or partial goodwill), the current ratio = £390/£200 = 1.95. Therefore, the current ratio is highest using the equity method.

24. A is correct. Using the equity method, long-term debt to equity = £600/£1,430 = 0.42. Using the consolidation method, long-term debt to equity = long-term debt/equity = £1,000/£1,750 = 0.57. Equity includes the £320 noncontrolling interest under either consolidation. It does not matter if the full or partial goodwill method is used since there is no goodwill.

25. C is correct. The projected depreciation and amortization expense will include Nin-Mount's reported depreciation and amortization (£102), Boswell's reported depreciation and amortization (£92), and amortization of Boswell's licenses (£10 million). The licenses have a fair value of £60 million. £320 purchase price indicates a fair value of £640 for the net assets of Boswell. The net book (fair) value of the recorded assets is £580. The previously unrecorded licenses have a fair value of £60 million. The licenses have a remaining life of six years; the amortization adjustment for 2018 will be £10 million. Therefore, Projected depreciation and amortization = £102 + £92 + £10 = £204 million.

26. A is correct. Net income is the same using any of the methods but under the equity method, net sales are only £950; Boswell's sales are not included in the net sales figure. Therefore, net profit margin is highest using the equity method.

27. A is correct. Net income is the same using any of the choices. Beginning equity under the equity method is £1,430. Under either of the consolidations, beginning equity is £1,750 since it includes the £320 noncontrolling interest. Return on beginning equity is highest under the equity method.

28. A is correct. Using the equity method, Total asset turnover = Net sales/Beginning total assets = £950/£2,140 = 0.444. Total asset turnover on beginning assets using consolidation = £1,460/£2,950 = 0.495. Under consolidation, Assets = £2,140 − 320 + 1,070 + 60 = £2,950. Therefore, total asset turnover is lowest using the equity method.

29. A is correct. Because the investment is designated as amortized cost, it is reported at the end of Year 1 using the effective interest method, whereby the amortization is calculated as the difference between the amount received and the interest income.
    The amount received each period ($500,000) is based on the par value of $10,000,000 and the stated 5% coupon rate. The interest income of $440,000 is calculated by multiplying the 4.0% market rate by the initial fair value or amortized cost at the beginning of the period of $11,000,000. The difference between the $500,000 received and the interest income of $440,000 is the amortization amount, which is equal to $60,000.
    The initial fair value of $11,000,000 is reduced by amortization, resulting in an amortized cost at the end of Year 1 of $10,940,000. This amount represents the carrying value reported on the balance sheet if the security is classified as amortized cost.

30. B is correct. The SPE balance sheet will show accounts receivable of $50,000,000, long-term debt of $40,000,000, and equity of $10,000,000. When the balance sheets are consolidated, Blanca's cash will increase by $40,000,000 resulting from the sale of the receivables to the SPE (net of its $10,000,000 cash investment in the SPE). Long-term debt will also increase by $40,000,000. The consolidated balance sheet will show total assets of $140,000,000 and look exactly the same as if Blanca borrowed directly against the receivables.

SPE Balance Sheet

		Long-term debt	$40,000,000
Accounts receivable	$50,000,000	Equity	$10,000,000
Total assets	**$50,000,000**	**Total liabilities and equity**	**$50,000,000**

Blanca Co. Consolidated Balance Sheet

Cash	$60,000,000	Current liabilities	$25,000,000
Accounts receivable	$50,000,000	Noncurrent liabilities	$70,000,000
Other assets	$30,000,000	Shareholder's equity	$45,000,000
Total assets	**$140,000,000**	**Total liabilities and equity**	**$140,000,000**

31. A is correct. Topmaker's representation on the Rainer board of directors and participation in Rainer's policymaking process indicate significant influence. Significant influence is generally assumed when the percentage of ownership interest is between 20% and 50%. Topmaker's representation on the board of directors and participation in the policymaking process, however, demonstrate significant influence despite its 15% equity interest.

32. B is correct. The goodwill in Topmaker's $300 million purchase of Rainer's common shares using the equity method is $60 million and is calculated as follows:

	$ Millions
Purchase price	$300
Less: acquired equity in book value of Rainer's net assets (15% of $1,340 million)	201
Excess purchase price	99
Less: attributable to difference between fair and book value of net identifiable assets	39
(plant and equipment) (15% of $260 million)	
Goodwill	$60

33. B is correct. The carrying value of Topmaker's investment in Rainer using the equity method is $317 million and is calculated as follows:

	$ Millions
Purchase price	$300
Plus: Topmaker's share of Rainer's net income (15% of $360 million)	54
Less: Dividends received (15% of $220 million)	33
Less: Amortization of excess purchase price attributable to plant and equipment	3.9
(15% of $260 million) divided by 10 years	
Investment in associate (Rainer) at the end of 2018	$317.1

34. B is correct. The inventory sale between Rainer (associate) and Topmaker (parent) is an upstream transaction. Under the equity method, the deferral process for unrealized profits is identical under upstream and downstream inventory transfers. The investor company's (Topmaker's) share of unrealized profits is deferred by reducing the recorded amount of equity income on the investor's income statement. In later periods, when the inventory is sold to third parties, the deferred profits are added to equity income.

35. B is correct. The goodwill impairment loss under IFRS is $300 million and is calculated as the difference between the recoverable amount of a cash-generating unit and the carrying value of the cash-generating unit. Topmaker's recoverable amount of the cash-generating

unit is $14,900 million, which is less than the carrying value of the cash-generating unit ($15,200 million). The result is an impairment loss of $300 million ($14,900 – $15,200).

A is incorrect because $120 million results from incorrectly calculating the impairment loss under US GAAP rather than under IFRS. Under US GAAP, the impairment loss is calculated using the following two-step approach:

Step 1:   *Determination of Impairment Loss*
Because the fair value of $14,800 million is below the carrying value of $15,200 million, a potential impairment loss has been identified.

Step 2:   *Measurement of the Impairment Loss*

	$ Millions
Fair value of reporting unit	$14,800
Less: identifiable net assets	$14,400
Implied goodwill	$400
Current carrying value of goodwill	$520
Less: implied goodwill	$400
Impairment loss	$120

36. A is correct. According to IFRS, under the partial goodwill method, the value of the minority interest is equal to the non-controlling interest's proportionate share of the subsidiary's identifiable net assets. Rainer's proportionate share is 20%, and the value of its identifiable assets on the acquisition date is $1.5 billion. The value of the minority interest is $300 million (20% × $1.5 billion).

CHAPTER 14

EMPLOYEE COMPENSATION: POST-EMPLOYMENT AND SHARE-BASED

SOLUTIONS

1. B is correct. The £28,879 million year-end benefit obligation represents the defined benefit obligation.

2. C is correct. The net interest expense of £273 million represents the interest cost on the beginning net pension obligation (beginning funded status) using the discount rate that the company uses in estimating the present value of its pension obligations. This is calculated as −£4,984 million times 5.48 percent = −£273 million; this represents an interest expense on the amount that the company essentially owes the pension plan.

3. C is correct. The remeasurement component of periodic pension cost includes both actuarial gains and losses on the pension obligation and net return on plan assets. Because Kensington does not have any actuarial gains and losses on the pension obligation, the remeasurement component includes only net return on plan assets. In practice, actuarial gains and losses are rarely equal to zero. The net return on plan assets is equal to actual returns minus beginning plan assets times the discount rate, or £1,302 million − (£23,432 million × 0.0548) = £18 million.

4. A is correct. The actual return on plan assets was 1,302/23,432 = 0.0556, or 5.56 percent. The rate of return included in the interest income/expense is the discount rate, which is given in this example as 5.48 percent.

   The rate of 1.17 percent, calculated as the net interest income divided by beginning plan assets, is not used in pension cost calculations.

5. C is correct. Under IFRS, the component of periodic pension cost that is shown in OCI rather than P&L is remeasurments.

6. A is correct. The relation between the periodic pension cost and the plan's funded status can be expressed as Periodic pension cost = Ending funded status − Employer contributions − Beginning funded status.

7. B is correct. Kensington's periodic pension cost was £483. The company's contributions to the plan were £693. The £210 difference between these two numbers can be viewed as a reduction of the overall pension obligation. To adjust the statement of cash flows to reflect this view, an analyst would reclassify the £210 million (excluding income tax effects) as an outflow related to financing activities rather than operating activities.

8. B is correct. The total periodic pension cost is the change in the net pension liability adjusted for the employer's contribution into the plan. The net pension liability increased from 3,000 to 3,020, and the employer's contribution was 1,000. The total periodic pension cost is 1,020. This will be allocated between P&L and OCI.

9. B is correct. Under IFRS, the components of periodic pension cost that would be reported in P&L are the service cost (composed of current service and past service costs) and the net interest expense or income, calculated by multiplying the net pension liability or net pension asset by the discount rate used to measure the pension liability. Here, the service costs are 320 (= 200 + 120), and the net interest expense is 210 [= (42,000 − 39,000) × 7%]. Thus, the total periodic pension cost is equal to 530.

10. A is correct. Under US GAAP—assuming the company chooses not to immediately recognise the actuarial loss and assuming there is no amortization of past service costs or actuarial gains and losses—the components of periodic pension cost that would be reported in P&L include the current service cost of 200, the interest expense on the pension obligation at the beginning of the period of 2,940 (= 7.0% × 42,000), and the expected return on plan assets, which is a reduction of the cost of 3,120 (= 8.0% × 39,000). Summing these three components gives 20.

11. B is correct. The component of periodic pension cost that would be reported in OCI is the remeasurements component. It consists of actuarial gains and losses on the pension obligation and net return on plan assets. Here, the actuarial loss was 460. In addition, the actual return on plan assets was 2,700, which was 30 lower than the return of 2,730 (= 39,000 × 0.07) incorporated in the net interest income/expense. Therefore, the total remeasurements are 490.

12. A is correct. In 2009, XYZ used a lower volatility assumption than it did in 2008. Lower volatility reduces the fair value of an option and thus the reported expense. Using the 2008 volatility estimate would have resulted in higher expense and thus lower net income.

13. C is correct. The assumed long-term rate of return on plan assets is not a component that is used in calculating the pension obligation, so there would be no change.

14. B is correct. A higher discount rate (5.38 percent instead of 4.85 percent) will reduce the present value of the pension obligation (liability). In most cases, a higher discount rate will decrease the interest cost component of the net periodic cost because the decrease in the obligation will more than offset the increase in the discount rate (except if the pension obligation is of short duration). Therefore, periodic pension cost would have been lower and reported net income higher. Cash flow from operating activities should not be affected by the change.

15. B is correct. In 2009, the three relevant assumptions were lower than in 2008. Lower expected salary increases reduce the service cost component of the periodic pension cost. A lower discount rate will increase the defined benefit obligation and increase the interest cost component of the periodic pension cost (the increase in the obligation will, in most cases, more than offset the decrease in the discount rate). Reducing the expected return on plan assets typically increases the periodic pension cost.

16. A is correct. The company's inflation estimate rose from 2008 to 2009. However, it lowered its estimate of future salary increases. Normally, salary increases will be positively related to inflation.

17. B is correct. A higher volatility assumption increases the value of the stock option and thus the compensation expense, which, in turn, reduces net income. There is no associated liability for stock options.

18. C is correct. A higher dividend yield reduces the value of the option and thus option expense. The lower expense results in higher earnings. Higher risk-free rates and expected lives result in higher call option values.

19. B is correct. Plan B is a defined contribution (DC) pension plan because the amount of future benefit is not defined and SKI has an obligation to make only agreed-upon contributions. The actual future benefits depend on the investment performance of the individual's plan assets, and the employee bears the investment risk.

    A is incorrect because Plan A is a defined benefit (DB) pension plan. In a DB plan, the amount of future benefit is defined based on the plan's formula (i.e., 1% of the employee's final salary for each year of service). With a DB pension plan, SKI bears the investment risk.

    C is incorrect because Plan C is a health care plan and is classified as a DB plan. Under IFRS and US GAAP, all plans for pensions and other post-employment benefits (OPB) other than those explicitly structured as DC plans are classified as DB plans. The amount of future benefit depends on plan specifications and type of benefit, and it represents a promise by the firm to pay benefits in the future. SKI, not the employee, is responsible for estimating future increases in costs, such as health care, over a long time horizon.

20. B is correct. Plan B is a DC pension plan. SKI's financial obligation is defined in each period, and the employer makes its agreed-upon contribution to the plan on behalf of the employee in the same period during which the employee provides the service. SKI is current on this obligation and has no additional financial obligation for the current period.

21. B is correct. SKI's DB pension plan is overfunded by €1.18 billion, the amount by which the fair value of the pension plan assets exceeds the defined benefit obligation (€5.98 billion − €4.80 billion). When a company has a surplus in a DB pension plan, the amount of assets that can be reported is the lower of the surplus or the asset ceiling (the present value of future economic benefits, such as refunds from the plan or reductions in future contributions). In this case, the asset ceiling is given as €1.50 billion, so the amount of SKI's reported net pension asset is the amount of the surplus, because this amount is lower than the asset ceiling.

22. A is correct. A higher percentage of employees is expected to leave before the full 10-year vesting period, which would decrease the present value of the DB obligation. If the employee leaves the company before meeting the 10-year vesting requirement, she may be entitled to none or a portion of the benefits earned up until that point. In measuring the DB obligation, the company considers the probability that some employees may not satisfy the vesting requirements (i.e., may leave before the vesting period) and use this probability to calculate the current service cost and the present value of the obligation.

23. B is correct. Operating income is adjusted to include only the current service costs, the interest cost component is reclassified as interest expense, and the actual return on plan assets is added as investment income. Profit before taxation adjusted for actual rather than expected return on plan assets will decrease by €94 million (205 − 299).

	Total (€ millions)
Current service costs	− €40
Interest costs	− €263
Expected return on plan assets	+ €299
Total of pension and OPB expenses	− €4 million
Actual return (loss) on plan assets	€205 million

Because the actual return on plan assets is less than the expected return on plan assets, operating income will be adjusted downward by 299 − 205 = 94. Alternatively, the adjustments to the individual pension cost components are as follows:

Line Items to Adjust	Adjustments (€ millions)
Revenue	—
Net operating expenses	+4 − 40 = −36
Operating profit	—
Interest expense	−263
Interest and investment income	+205
Share of post-tax results of associates	—
Adjustment to profit before taxation	−€94 million

24. B is correct. The final year's estimated earnings at the end of Year 1 for the average participant would decrease by approximately €35,747.71.

	Current Assumptions	Case Study Assumptions
Current salary	€100,000	€100,000
Years until retirement	17	17
Years of service (includes prior 10)	27	27
Retirement life expectancy	20	20
Annual compensation increases	6%	5%
Discount rate	4%	4%
Final year's estimated earnings	€254,035.17	€218,287.46
Estimated annual payment for each of the 20 years	€68,589.50	€58,937.61
Value at the end of year 17 (retirement date) of the estimated future payments	€932,153.69	€800,981.35
Annual unit credit	€34,524.21	€29,665.98

Because there are now 17 years until retirement, there are 16 years until retirement from the end of Year 1. The final year's estimated earnings, estimated at the end of Year 1, are as follows:

Current year's salary × [(1 + Annual compensation increase)$^{\text{Years until retirement}}$]

Annual compensation increase of 6%: €100,000 × [(1.06)^{16}] = €254,035.17

Annual compensation increase of 5%: €100,000 × [(1.05)^{16}] = €218,287.46

The estimated annual payment for each of the 20 years (retirement life expectancy) is

(Estimated final salary × Benefit formula) × Years of service

Annual compensation increase of 6%: (€254,035.17 × 0.01) × (10 + 17) = €68,589.50

Annual compensation increase of 5%: (€218,287.46 × 0.01) × (10 + 17) = €58,937.61

The value at the end of Year 17 (retirement date) of the estimated future payments is the PV of the estimated annual payment for each of the 20 years at the discount rate of 4%:

Annual compensation increase of 6%: PV of €68,589.50 for 20 years at 4% = €932,153.69

Annual compensation increase of 5%: PV of €58,937.61 for 20 years at 4% = €800,981.35

The annual unit credit = Value at retirement/Years of service:

Annual compensation increase of 6%: €932,153.69/27 = €34,524.21

Annual compensation increase of 5%: €800,981.35/27 = €29,665.98

The annual unit credit for the average participant would decrease by €34,524.21 − €29,665.98 = €4,858.23.

25. B is correct. An increase in the retirement life expectancy (from 20 to 28 years) will increase the DB pension obligation, because Plan A pays annual payments for life.
26. A is correct. Current service cost is the present value of annual unit credit earned in the current period.

Annual unit credit (benefit) per service year = Value at retirement/Years of service

Years of service = 15 (vested years of past service) + 7 (expected years until retirement) = 22

Annual unit credit = $393,949/22 = $17,906.77.

Current service cost (for 1 year) = Annual unit credit/[(1 + Discount rate)$^{\text{(Years until retirement at the end of Year 1)}}$

= $17,906.77/(1+0.04)^{6} = $14,151.98.

27. A is correct. To estimate the PVDBO, the company must make a number of assumptions, such as future compensation increases, discount rates, and expected vesting. If changes in assumptions increase the obligation, the increase is referred to as an actuarial loss.
B is incorrect because the PVDBO does not include the value of plan assets in the calculation.

C is incorrect because the expected long-term rate of return on plan assets is not used to calculate the PVDBO. The interest rate used to calculate the PVDBO is based on current rates of return on high-quality corporate bonds (or government bonds, in the absence of a deep market in corporate bonds) with currency and durations consistent with the currency and durations of the benefits.

28. B is correct. The funded status of a pension plan is calculated as follows:

> Funded status = Fair value of the plan assets − PVDBO

> Based on the information provided in Exhibit 1, the PVDBO is calculated as follows:

$$PVDBO = \text{Funded status (Net pension liability)} + \text{Plan assets}$$

$$\$525 + \$3,108 = \$3,633 \text{ million}$$

29. A is correct. A decrease in the assumed future compensation growth rate will decrease a company's pension obligation when the pension formula is based on the final year's salary. Lowering the assumed future compensation growth rate decreases the service and interest components of periodic pension costs because of a decreased annual unit credit.

30. B is correct. A change in the assumed future compensation growth rate is a change in the plan's actuarial assumptions. The remeasurement cost component includes actuarial gains and losses resulting from changes in the future compensation growth rate.

31. A is correct. Rickards' task is to adjust the balance sheet and cash flow statement information to better reflect the economic nature of certain items related to the pension plan. When a company's periodic contribution to a plan is lower than the total pension cost of the period, it can be viewed as a source of financing. To reflect this event, the deficit amount is adjusted by the effective tax rate and should be reclassified from an operating cash flow to a financing cash flow. The company's contribution to the pension plan was $66 million, which is $30 million less than the pension cost of $96 million. The $30 million difference is $21 million on an after-tax basis, using the effective tax rate of 30%. Therefore, $21 million should be classified as an operating cash outflow (negative value) and a financing cash inflow (positive value).

32. C is correct. To calculate the debt-to-equity ratio, both liabilities and total equity need to be adjusted for the estimated impact of a 100-bp increase in health care costs. The proposed increase in health care costs will increase total liabilities and decrease equity by the same amount. Consequently, the debt-to-equity ratio changes as follows:

$$\text{Sensitivity of benefit obligation to 100-bp increase} = \$93$$

$$\text{Adjusted liabilities} = \$17,560 + \$93 = \$17,653$$

$$\text{Adjusted equity} = \$6,570 - \$93 = \$6,477$$

$$\text{Adjusted debt-to-equity ratio} = \$17,653/\$6,477 = 2.7255 \approx 2.73$$

Consequently, a 100-bp increase in health care costs increases the debt-to-equity ratio to approximately 2.73.

CHAPTER 15

MULTINATIONAL OPERATIONS

SOLUTIONS

1. B is correct. IAS 21 requires that the financial statements of the foreign entity first be restated for local inflation using the procedures outlined in IAS 29, "Financial Reporting in Hyperinflationary Economies." Then, the inflation-restated foreign currency financial statements are translated into the parent's presentation currency using the current exchange rate. Under US GAAP, the temporal method would be used with no restatement.

2. B is correct. Ruiz expects the EUR to appreciate against the UAH and expects some inflation in the Ukraine. In an inflationary environment, FIFO will generate a higher gross profit than weighted-average cost. For either inventory choice, the current rate method will give higher gross profit to the parent company if the subsidiary's currency is depreciating. Thus, using FIFO and translating using the current rate method will generate a higher gross profit for the parent company, Eurexim SA, than any other combination of choices.

3. B is correct. If the parent's currency is chosen as the functional currency, the temporal method must be used. Under the temporal method, fixed assets are translated using the rate in effect at the time the assets were acquired.

4. C is correct. Monetary assets and liabilities such as accounts receivable are translated at current (end-of-period) rates regardless of whether the temporal or current rate method is used.

5. B is correct. When the foreign currency is chosen as the functional currency, the current rate method is used. All assets and liabilities are translated at the current (end-of-period) rate.

6. C is correct. When the foreign currency is chosen as the functional currency, the current rate method must be used, and all gains or losses from translation are reported as a cumulative translation adjustment to shareholder equity. When the foreign currency decreases in value (weakens), the current rate method results in a negative translation adjustment in stockholders' equity.

7. B is correct. When the parent company's currency is used as the functional currency, the temporal method must be used to translate the subsidiary's accounts. Under the temporal

method, monetary assets and liabilities (e.g., debt) are translated at the current (year-end) rate, non-monetary assets and liabilities measured at historical cost (e.g., inventory) are translated at historical exchange rates, and non-monetary assets and liabilities measured at current value are translated at the exchange rate at the date when the current value was determined. Because beginning inventory was sold first and sales and purchases were evenly acquired, the average rate is most appropriate for translating inventory, and C$77 million × 0.92 = $71 million. Long-term debt is translated at the year-end rate of 0.95. C$175 million × 0.95 = $166 million.

8. B is correct. Translating the 20X2 balance sheet using the temporal method, as is required in this instance, results in assets of US$369 million. The translated liabilities and common stock are equal to US$325 million, meaning that the value for 20X2 retained earnings is US$369 million − US$325 million = US$44 million.

Temporal Method (20X2)			
Account	C$	Rate	US$
Cash	135	0.95	128
Accounts receivable	98	0.95	93
Inventory	77	0.92	71
Fixed assets	100	0.86	86
Accumulated depreciation	(10)	0.86	(9)
Total assets	400		369
Accounts payable	77	0.95	73
Long-term debt	175	0.95	166
Common stock	100	0.86	86
Retained earnings	48	to balance	44
Total liabilities and shareholders' equity	400		369

9. C is correct. The Canadian dollar would be the appropriate reporting currency when substantially all operating, financing, and investing decisions are based on the local currency. The parent country's inflation rate is never relevant. Earnings manipulation is not justified, and at any rate changing the functional currency would take the gains off of the income statement.

10. C is correct. If the functional currency were changed from the parent currency (US dollar) to the local currency (Canadian dollar), the current rate method would replace the temporal method. The temporal method ignores unrealized gains and losses on non-monetary assets and liabilities, but the current rate method does not.

11. B is correct. If the Canadian dollar is chosen as the functional currency, the current rate method will be used, and the current exchange rate will be the rate used to translate all assets and liabilities. Currently, only monetary assets and liabilities are translated at the current rate. Sales are translated at the average rate during the year under either method. Fixed assets are translated using the historical rate under the temporal method but would switch to current rates under the current rate method. Therefore, there will most likely be an effect on sales/fixed assets. Because the cash ratio involves only monetary assets and liabilities, it is unaffected by the translation method. Receivables turnover pairs a monetary asset with sales and is thus also unaffected.

12. B is correct. If the functional currency were changed, then Consol-Can would use the current rate method, and the balance sheet exposure would be equal to net assets (total assets − total liabilities). In this case, $400 - 77 - 175 = 148$.

13. B is correct. Julius is using the current rate method, which is most appropriate when it is operating with a high degree of autonomy.

14. A is correct. If the current rate method is being used (as it is for Julius), the local currency (euro) is the functional currency. When the temporal method is being used (as it is for Augustus), the parent company's currency (US dollar) is the functional currency.

15. C is correct. When the current rate method is being used, all currency gains and losses are recorded as a cumulative translation adjustment to shareholder equity.

16. C is correct. Under the current rate method, all assets are translated using the year-end 20X2 (current) rate of $1.61/€1.00. €2,300 × 1.61 = $3,703.

17. A is correct. Under the current rate method, both sales and cost of goods sold would be translated at the 20X2 average exchange rate. The ratio would be the same as reported under the euro. €2,300 − €1,400 = €900, €900/€2,300 = 39.1%. Or, $3,542 − $2,156 = $1,386, $1,386/$3,542 = 39.1%.

18. C is correct. Augustus is using the temporal method in conjunction with FIFO inventory accounting. If FIFO is used, ending inventory is assumed to be composed of the most recently acquired items, and thus inventory will be translated at relatively recent exchange rates. To the extent that the average weight used to translate sales differs from the historical rate used to translate inventories, the gross margin will be distorted when translated into US dollars.

19. C is correct. If the US dollar is the functional currency, the temporal method must be used. Revenues and receivables (monetary asset) would be the same under either accounting method. Inventory and fixed assets were purchased when the US dollar was stronger, so at historical rates (temporal method), translated they would be lower. Identical revenues/ lower fixed assets would result in higher fixed-asset turnover.

20. A is correct. If the US dollar is the functional currency, the temporal method must be used, and the balance sheet exposure will be the net monetary assets of $125 + 230 - 185 - 200 = -30$, or a net monetary liability of SGD30 million. This net monetary liability would be eliminated if fixed assets (non-monetary) were sold to increase cash. Issuing debt, either short-term or long-term, would increase the net monetary liability.

21. A is correct. Because the US dollar has been consistently weakening against the Singapore dollar, cost of sales will be lower and gross profit higher when an earlier exchange rate is used to translate inventory, compared with using current exchange rates. If the Singapore dollar is the functional currency, current rates would be used. Therefore, the combination of the US dollar (temporal method) and FIFO will result in the highest gross profit margin.

22. A is correct. Under the current rate method, revenue is translated at the average rate for the year, SGD4,800 × 0.662 = USD3,178 million. Debt should be translated at the current rate, SGD200 × 0.671 = USD134 million. Under the current rate method, Acceletron would have a net asset balance sheet exposure. Because the Singapore dollar has been strengthening against the US dollar, the translation adjustment would be positive rather than negative.

23. B is correct. Under the temporal method, inventory and fixed assets would be translated using historical rates. Accounts receivable is a monetary asset and would be translated at year-end (current) rates. Fixed assets are found as $(1,000 \times 0.568) + (640 \times 0.606) = $ USD 956 million.

24. B is correct. USD0.671/SGD is the current exchange rate. That rate would be used regardless of whether Acceletron uses the current rate or temporal method. USD0.654 was the weighted-average rate when inventory was acquired. That rate would be used if the company translated its statements under the temporal method but not the current rate method. USD0.588/SGD was the exchange rate in effect when long-term debt was issued. As a monetary liability, long-term debt is always translated using current exchange rates. Consequently, that rate is not applicable regardless of how Acceletron translates its financial statements.

25. C is correct. In Transaction 3, the payment for the inventory is due in Bindiar francs, a different currency from the Norvoltian krone, which is Ambleu's presentation currency. Because the import purchase (account payable) is under 45-day credit terms, Ambleu has foreign currency transaction exposure. The payment is subject to fluctuations in the FB/NVK exchange rate during the 45-day period between the sale and payment dates. Thus, Ambleu is exposed to potential foreign currency gains if the Bindiar franc weakens against the Norvoltian krone or foreign currency losses if the Bindiar franc strengthens against the Norvoltian krone.

26. C is correct. The currency of Ngcorp as the borrowing foreign subsidiary, relative to that of Ambleu, determines Ambleu's choice of translation method for Transaction 2. Because Ngcorp's functional currency is the Bindiar franc and Ambleu's presentation currency is the Norvoltian krone, the current rate method rather than the temporal method should be used. Regardless of the currency in which the loan is denominated, the loan is first recorded in Ngcorp's financial statements. Then, Ngcorp's financial statements, which include the bank loan, are translated into Ambleu's consolidated financial statements.

27. A is correct. On Ambleu's balance sheet, the cost included in the inventory account is the translation of FB27,000/ton into Norvoltian krone on the purchase date. Ambleu could have paid this amount on the purchase date but chose to wait 45 days to settle the account. The inventory cost is determined using the FB/NVK exchange rate of 4.1779 on the purchase date of June 1, 2016. FB27,000/FB4.1779/NVK = NVK6,462.58/ton.

The cash outflow is the amount exchanged from the Norvoltian krone to the Bindiar franc to pay the FB27,000/ton owed for the inventory 45 days after the transaction date. This payment uses the FB/NVK exchange rate of 4.1790 on the settlement date of 15 July 2016.

$$\text{FB } 27{,}000/\text{FB}4.1790 \text{ per NVK} = \text{NVK}6{,}460.88/\text{ton}$$

$$\text{Foreign exchange gain} = \text{Inventory cost} - \text{Cash payment}$$

$$= \text{NVK}6{,}462.58 - \text{NVK}6{,}460.88$$

$$= \text{NVK}1.70/\text{ton}$$

Thus, Ambleu's cash outflow is less than the cost included in the inventory account, and NVK1.70/ton is the realized foreign exchange gain relating to this transaction. By deferring payment for 45 days, and because the Bindiar franc decreased in value during this period, Ambleu pays NVK1.70/ton less than the inventory cost on the purchase date of 1 June 2016. Thus, Ambleu will report a foreign exchange gain in its 2016 net income.

28. A is correct. Net sales growth equals organic sales growth plus or minus the effects of acquisitions, divestitures, and foreign exchange. A foreign currency translation loss would reduce net sales growth. Thus the answer to Question 1 is yes.

29. C is correct. IFRS requires that Ambleu disclose "the amount of exchange differences recognized in profit or loss" when determining net income for the period. Because companies may present foreign currency transaction gains and losses in various places on the income statement, it is useful for companies to disclose both the amount of transaction gain or loss that is included in income as well as the presentation alternative used.

30. A is correct. Crenland experienced hyperinflation from December 31, 2015 to December 31, 2017, as shown by the General Price Index, with cumulative inflation of 128.2% during this period. According to IFRS, Cendaró's financial statements must be restated for local inflation, then translated into Norvoltian kroner using the current exchange rate. The 2017 revenue from Cendaró that should be included in Ambleu's income statement is calculated as follows:

$$\text{Revenue in CRG} \times (\text{GPI December 31, 2017/GPI average 2017}) = \text{Inflation-adjusted revenue in CRG}$$

$$\text{CRG125.23 million} \times (228.2/186.2) = \text{CRG153.48 million}$$

$$\text{Inflation-adjusted revenue in CRG/December 31, 2017 exchange rate (CRG/NVK)} = \text{Revenue in Norvoltian kroner}$$

$$\text{CRG153.48 million}/14.4810 = \text{NVK10.60 million}$$

31. B is correct. The consolidated income tax rate is calculated as income tax expense divided by profit before tax. Note 2 shows that Ambleu's consolidated income tax rate decreases by 2.29%, from 34.94% (=94/269) in 2016 to 32.65% (=96/294) in 2017. The largest component of the decrease stems from the 1.42% change in the effect of tax rates in non-domestic jurisdictions, which lowers Ambleu's consolidated income tax rate in 2016 by 3.34% (=9/269) and in 2017 by 4.76% (=14/294). The decrease in 2017 could indicate that Ambleu's business mix shifted to countries with lower marginal tax rates, resulting in a lower consolidated income tax rate and more profit. (The change could also indicate that the marginal tax rates decreased in the countries in which Ambleu earns profits.)

32. B is correct. IAS 29 indicates that a cumulative inflation rate approaching or exceeding 100% over three years would be an indicator of hyperinflation. Because the cumulative inflation rate for 2016 and 2017 in Crenland was 128.2%, Cendaró's accounts must first be restated for local inflation. Then, the inflation-restated Crenland guinea financial statements can be translated into Ambleu's presentation currency, the Norvoltian krone, using the current exchange rate.

Using this approach, the cumulative translation loss on December 31, 2017 for the CRG85.17 million patent purchase is −NVK1.58 million, as shown in the following table.

Date	Inflation Rate (%)	Restated Carrying Value (CRG/ MM)	Current Exchange Rate (CRG/NVK)	Translated Amount (NVK MM)	Annual Translation Gain/Loss (NVK MM)	Cumulative Translation Gain/Loss (NVK MM)
Jan 1, 2016	—	85.17	5.6780	15.00	N/A	N/A
Dec 31, 2016	40.6	119.75	8.6702	13.81	−1.19	−1.19
Dec 31, 2017	62.3	194.35	14.4810	13.42	−0.39	−1.58

33. B is correct. Because Ngcorp has a functional currency that is different from Ambleu's presentation currency, the intangible assets are translated into Norvoltian kroner using the current rate method. The current FB/NVK exchange rate is 4.2374 as of December 31, 2016. Thus, the intangible assets on Ngcorp's 2016 balance sheet are NVK3 million × FB4.2374/NVK = FB12.71 million.

34. B is correct. Using the temporal method, monetary assets (i.e., cash) are translated using the current exchange rate (as of December 31, 2016) of BRD1.20/NER (or NER0.8333/ BRD), and non-monetary assets are translated using the historical exchange rate when acquired. Inventory is translated at its 2016 weighted-average rate of BRD1.19/NER (or NER0.8403/BRD). Therefore, the total assets for Triofind-B translated into Norvolt euros (Triofind's presentation currency) as of December 31, 2016 are calculated as follows:

Assets	December 31, 2016 (BRD)	Applicable Exchange Rate (NER/BRD)	Rate Used	NER
Cash	900,000	0.8333	Current	750,000
Inventory	750,000	0.8403	Average	630,252
Total	1,650,000			1,380,252

35. A is correct. The monetary balance sheet items for Triofind-B are translated at the current exchange rate, which reflects that the Borland dollar weakened during the period relative to the Norvolt euro. The rate as of June 30, 2016 was BRD1.15/NER (or NER0.8696/ BRD) and as of December 31, 2016 was BRD1.20/NER (or NER0.8333/BRD). Therefore, notes payable translates to NER416,667 (BRD500,000 × NER/BRD0.8333) as of December 31, 2016, compared with NER434,783 (BRD500,000 × NER/BRD0.8696) as of June 30, 2016. Thus, the translation adjustment for liabilities is negative.

36. A is correct. Triofind uses the temporal method to translate the financial statements of Triofind-B. The temporal method uses the current exchange rate for translating monetary assets and liabilities and the historical exchange rate (based on the date when the assets were acquired) for non-monetary assets and liabilities. Monetary assets and liabilities are translated using the current exchange rate (as of June 30, 2017) of NER1 = BRD1.17 (or NER0.8547/BRD), and non-monetary assets and liabilities are translated using the historical exchange rate (as of June 30, 2016) of NER1 = BRD1.15 (or NER0.8696/ BRD). Inventory is translated at the 2017 weighted average rate of NER1 = BRD1.18 (or NER0.8475/BRD). The difference required to maintain equality between (a) total assets and (b) total liabilities and shareholder's equity is then recorded as retained earnings. The retained earnings for Triofind-B translated into Norvolt euros (Triofind's presentation currency) as of June 30, 2017 is calculated as follows:

Assets	June 30, 2017 (BRD)	Exchange Rate (NER/BRD)	Rate Used	June 30, 2017 (NER)
Cash	1,350,000	0.8547	C	1,153,846
Inventory	500,000	0.8475	H	423,729
	1,850,000			1,577,575

Liabilities and Stockholders' Equity	June 30, 2017 (BRD)	Exchange Rate (NER/BRD)	Rate Used	June 30, 2017 (NER)
Notes Payable	500,000	0.8547	C	427,350
Common Stock	1,150,000	0.8696	H	1,000,000
Retained Earnings	200,000			**150,225**
Total	1,850,000			1,577,575

37. C is correct. The functional currency is the currency of the primary economic environment in which an entity operates. Abuelio is Triofind-A's primary economic environment, and its currency is the Abuelio peso (ABP). Another important factor used to determine the functional currency is the currency that mainly influences sales prices for goods and services. The fact that Triofind-A prices its goods in Abuelio pesos supports the case for the ABP to be the functional currency.

38. B is correct. Triofind complies with IFRS, and Abuelio can be considered a highly inflationary economy because its cumulative inflation rate exceeded 100% from 2015 to 2017. Thus, Triofind-A's financials must be restated to include local inflation rates and then translated using the current exchange rate into Norvolt euros, which is Triofind's presentation currency. This approach reflects both the likely change in the local currency value of the warehouse as well as the actual change in the exchange rate. The original purchase price is ABP1,008,065 (NER50,000/ABP0.0496). The value of the new warehouse in Abuelio as of July 31, 2017 is NER47,964, calculated as follows:

Date	Abuelio Monthly Inflation Rate (%)	Restated Warehouse Value (ABP)	NER/ABP	Warehouse Value (NER)
May 31, 2017		1,008,065	0.0496	50,000
June 30, 2017	25	1,260,081	0.0388	48,891
July 31, 2017	22	1,537,298	0.0312	47,964

39. A is correct. Norvolt exempts the non-domestic income of multinationals from taxation. Because Norvolt has a corporate tax rate of 34%, the 0% tax rate in Borliand and the fact that 25% of Triofind's net income comes from Borliand should result in a lower effective tax rate on Triofind's consolidated financial statements compared with Triofind's domestic tax rate. Abuelio's tax rate of 35% is very close to that of Norvolt, and it constitutes only 15% of Triofind's net income, so its effect is unlikely to be significant.

40. B is correct. Although Borliand shows the highest growth in Norvolt euro terms, this result is partially because of currency fluctuations, which cannot be controlled. Abuelio had the highest change in sales resulting from price and volume at 13% (excluding foreign currency exchange). This growth is more sustainable than net sales growth, which includes currency fluctuations, because Triofind's management has more control over growth in sales resulting from greater volume or higher prices.

CHAPTER 16

ANALYSIS OF FINANCIAL INSTITUTIONS

SOLUTIONS

1. A is correct. Banks are more likely to be systemically important than non-financial companies because, as intermediaries, they create financial linkages across all types of entities, including households, banks, corporates, and governments. The network of linkages across entities means that the failure of one bank will negatively affect other financial and non-financial entities (a phenomenon known as financial contagion). The larger the bank and the more widespread its network of linkages, the greater its potential impact on the entire financial system. The assets of banks are predominantly financial assets, such as loans and securities (not deposits, which represent most of a bank's liabilities). Compared to the tangible assets of non-financial companies, financial assets create direct exposure to a different set of risks, including credit risks, liquidity risks, market risks, and interest rate risks.

2. A is correct. Basel III specifies the minimum percentage of its risk-weighted assets that a bank must fund with equity capital. This minimum funding requirement prevents a bank from assuming so much financial leverage that it is unable to withstand loan losses or asset write-downs.

3. C is correct. The approach used by Johansson to evaluate banks, the CAMELS approach, has six components: (1) capital adequacy, (2) asset quality, (3) management capabilities, (4) earnings sufficiency, (5) liquidity position, and (6) sensitivity to market risk. While the CAMELS approach to evaluating a bank is fairly comprehensive, some attributes of a bank are not addressed by this method. One such attribute is a bank's competitive environment. A bank's competitive position relative to its peers may affect how it allocates capital and assesses risks.

4. A is correct. The underwriting expense ratio is an indicator of the efficiency of money spent on obtaining new premiums. The underwriting loss ratio is an indicator of the quality of a company's underwriting activities—the degree of success an underwriter has achieved in estimating the risks insured. The combined ratio, a measure of the overall

underwriting profitability and efficiency of an underwriting operation, is the sum of these two ratios.

5. C is correct. The products of the two types of insurance companies, P&C and L&H, differ in contract duration and claim variability. P&C insurers' policies are usually short term, and the final cost will usually be known within a year of the occurrence of an insured event, while L&H insurers' policies are usually longer term. P&C insurers' claims are more variable and "lumpier" because they arise from accidents and other less predictable events, while L&H insurers' claims are more predictable because they correlate closely with relatively stable, actuarially based mortality rates applied to large populations. The relative predictability of L&H insurers' claims generally allows these companies to have lower capital requirements and to seek higher returns than P&C insurers.

6. C is correct. The combined ratio, which is the sum of the underwriting expense ratio and the loss and loss adjustment expense ratio, is a measure of the efficiency of an underwriting operation. A combined ratio of less than 100% is considered efficient; a combined ratio greater than 100% indicates an underwriting loss. Insurer C is the only insurer that has a combined ratio less than 100%.

7. C is correct. Over the past three years, there has been a downward trend in the two VaR measures—total trading VaR (all market risk factors) and total trading and credit portfolio VaR. This trend indicates an improvement in ABC Bank's sensitivity, or a reduction in its exposure, to market risk. The two liquidity measures—the liquidity coverage ratio and the net stable funding ratio—have increased over the past three years, indicating an improvement in ABC Bank's liquidity position. Trends in the three capital adequacy measures—common equity Tier 1 capital ratio, Tier 1 capital ratio, and total capital ratio—indicate a decline in ABC Bank's capital adequacy. While the total capital ratio has remained fairly constant over the past three years, the common equity Tier 1 capital ratio and the Tier 1 capital ratio have declined. This trend suggests that ABC Bank has moved toward using more Tier 2 capital and less Tier 1 capital, indicating an overall decline in capital adequacy.

8. A is correct. Claims associated with life and health insurance companies (Cobalt) are more predicable than those for property and casualty insurance companies (Vermillion). Property and casualty insurers' claims are more variable and "lumpier" because they arise from accidents and other unpredictable events, whereas life and health insurers' claims are more predictable because they correlate closely with relatively stable actuarially based mortality rates when applied to large populations.

9. B is correct. The loss and loss adjustment expense ratio decreased from 61.3% to 59.1% between 2016 and 2017. This ratio is calculated as follows: (Loss Expense + Loss Adjustment Expense)/Net Premiums Earned. The loss and loss adjustment expense ratio indicates the degree of success an underwriter has achieved in estimating the risks insured. A lower ratio indicates greater success in estimating insured risks.

10. B is correct. The quality of earnings is directly related to the level of sustainable sources of income. Trading income tends to be volatile and not necessarily sustainable. Higher-quality income would be net interest income and fee-based service income. Because N-bank's 2017 trading revenue contribution is the lowest relative to other banks, its quality of earnings would be considered the best of the three banks.

11. B is correct. Trading revenue per unit of risk can be represented by the ratio of annual trading revenue to average daily trading value at risk (VaR) and represents a measure of reward-to-risk. The trading revenue per unit of risk improved at N-bank (from 134× to 160×) between 2016 and 2017, and there was no change at T-bank (80×). VaR can be used for gauging trends in intra-company risk taking.

12. B is correct. Exhibit 4 indicates that exposure to free-standing credit derivatives dramatically declined from a peak during the global financial crisis in 2008. If a derivatives contract is classified as freestanding, changes in its fair value are reported as income or expense in the income statement at each reporting period. The immediate recognition of a gain or loss in earnings, instead of reporting it in other comprehensive income, can lead to unexpected volatility of earnings and missed earnings targets. As a result, earnings volatility from the use of credit derivatives most likely decreased.

13. A is correct. A bank's net interest margin represents the difference between interest earned on loans and other interest-bearing assets and the level of interest paid on deposits and other interest-bearing liabilities. Banks typically borrow money for shorter terms (retail deposits) and lend to customers for longer periods (mortgages and car loans). If the yield curve unexpectedly inverts, the short-term funding costs will increase, and the net interest margin will most likely decrease (not remain unchanged or increase).

14. C is correct. Reverse repurchase agreements represent collateralized loans between a bank and a borrower. A reverse repo with a 30-day maturity is a highly liquid asset and thus would directly affect the liquidity coverage ratio (LCR). LCR evaluates short-term liquidity and represents the percentage of a bank's expected cash outflows in relation to highly liquid assets.

15. C is correct. Industry C, representing global commercial banks, most likely has the highest level of global systemic risk because global commercial banks have the highest proportion of cross-border business. Unlike banks, the overall insurance market (of which Industry A is a subset) has a smaller proportion of cross-border business, and insurance companies' foreign branches are generally required to hold assets in a jurisdiction that are adequate to cover the related policy liabilities in that jurisdiction. As an international property and casualty (P&C) insurer, Company A provides protection against adverse events related to autos, homes, or commercial activities; many of these events have local, rather than international, impact. Industry B, credit unions, most likely has the lowest level of global systemic risk. Credit unions are depository institutions that function like banks and offer many of the same services, but they are owned by their members rather than being publicly traded as many banks are.

16. A is correct. Company XYZ's key capital adequacy ratios show mixed conditions. The ratios are calculated as follows:

$$\text{Common Equity Tier 1 Capital Ratio} = \frac{\text{Total Common Equity Tier 1 Capital}}{\text{Total Risk-Weighted Assets}}$$

$$2015 \text{ Common Equity Tier 1 Capital Ratio} = \frac{137,100}{1,242,500} = 11.0\%$$

$$2016 \text{ Common Equity Tier 1 Capital Ratio} = \frac{142,367}{1,282,849} = 11.1\%$$

$$2017 \text{ Common Equity Tier 1 Capital Ratio} = \frac{146,424}{1,298,688} = 11.3\%$$

$$\text{Tier 1 Ratio} = \frac{\text{Common Equity Tier 1 Capital} + \text{Additional Tier 1 Capital}}{\text{Total Risk-Weighted Assets}}$$

$$2015 \text{ Tier 1 Ratio} = \frac{137,100 + 17,600}{1,242,500} = 12.5\%$$

$$\text{2016 Tier 1 Ratio} = \frac{142,367 + 20,443}{1,282,849} = 12.7\%$$

$$\text{2017 Tier 1 Ratio} = \frac{146,424 + 22,639}{1,298,688} = 13.0\%$$

$$\text{Total Capital Ratio} = \frac{\text{Total Capital}}{\text{Total Risk-Weighted Assets}}$$

$$\text{2015 Total Capital Ratio} = \frac{192,900}{1,242,500} = 15.5\%$$

$$\text{2016 Total Capital Ratio} = \frac{190,374}{1,282,849} = 14.8\%$$

$$\text{2017 Total Capital Ratio} = \frac{191,519}{1,298,688} = 14.7\%$$

	2017	2016	2015
Common equity Tier 1 capital ratio	11.3%	11.1%	11.0%
Tier 1 capital ratio	13.0%	12.7%	12.5%
Total capital ratio	14.7%	14.8%	15.5%

The common equity Tier 1 capital ratio and the Tier 1 capital ratio both strengthened from 2015 to 2017, but the total capital ratio weakened during that same period, signaling mixed conditions.

17. A is correct. Company XYZ's liquid assets as a percentage of total assets declined each year since 2015, indicating declining liquidity.

	2017		2016		2015	
	$m	% of Total Assets	$m	% of Total Assets	$m	% of Total Assets
Total liquid assets	361,164	18.7%	354,056	19.7%	356,255	21.1%
Investments	434,256	22.5%	367,158	20.4%	332,461	19.7%
Loans						
Consumer loans	456,957		450,576		447,493	
Commercial loans	499,647		452,983		403,058	
Total loans	956,604	49.6%	903,559	50.3%	850,551	50.4%
Goodwill	26,693	1.4%	26,529	1.5%	25,705	1.5%
Other assets	151,737	7.9%	144,210	8.0%	121,780	7.2%
Total assets	1,930,454	100%	1,795,512	100%	1,686,752	100%

18. C is correct. Impairment allowances have increased proportionately to the increases in the amount of past due but not impaired assets, which may be in anticipation of these past due assets becoming impaired. Impaired assets have decreased each year while strong credit quality assets have increased each year, which suggests lowering impairment allowances as a result of improving credit quality of these financial instruments.

At December 31	2017	2016	2015
	$m	$m	$m
Strong credit quality	338,948	327,345	320,340
Good credit quality	52,649	54,515	54,050
Satisfactory credit quality	51,124	55,311	56,409
Substandard credit quality	23,696	24,893	27,525
Past due but not impaired	2,823	2,314	2,058
Impaired	8,804	9,345	10,235
Total gross amount	478,044	473,723	470,617
Impairment allowances	−5,500	−4,500	−4,000
Total	472,544	469,223	466,617
YoY change in impaired assets	−5.8%	−8.7%	
YoY change in strong credit quality assets	3.5%	2.2%	
YoY change in past due but not impaired assets	22.0%	12.4%	
YoY change in impairment allowances	22.2%	12.5%	

Note: YoY = year-over-year

$$\text{2015 to 2016 change in impaired assets: } \left(\frac{9,345}{10,235}\right)-1=-8.7\%$$

$$\text{2015 to 2016 change in strong credit quality assets: } \left(\frac{327,345}{320,340}\right)-1=2.2\%$$

$$\text{2015 to 2016 change in past due but not impaired assets: } \left(\frac{2,314}{2,058}\right)-1=12.4\%$$

$$\text{2015 to 2016 change in impairment allowances: } \left(\frac{-4,500}{-4,000}\right)-1=12.5\%$$

$$\text{2016 to 2017 change in impaired assets: } \left(\frac{8,804}{9,345}\right)-1=-5.8\%$$

$$\text{2016 to 2017 change in strong credit quality assets: } \left(\frac{338,948}{327,345}\right)-1=3.5\%$$

$$\text{2016 to 2017 change in past due but not impaired assets: } \left(\frac{2,823}{2.314}\right)-1=22.0\%$$

$$\text{2016 to 2017 change in impairment allowances: } \left(\frac{-5,500}{-4,500}\right)-1=22.2\%$$

19. C is correct. The allowance for loan losses to net commercial loan charge-offs has been declining during the last three years, which indicates that the cushion between the allowance and the net commercial loan charge-offs has deteriorated.

$$\text{2015 Consumer: } \frac{\text{Allowance for Loan Losses}}{\text{Net Loan Charge-Offs}} = \frac{13,000}{2,901} = 4.48$$

$$\text{2016 Consumer: } \frac{\text{Allowance for Loan Losses}}{\text{Net Loan Charge-Offs}} = \frac{11,500}{2,505} = 4.59$$

$$\text{2017 Consumer: } \frac{\text{Allowance for Loan Losses}}{\text{Net Loan Charge-Offs}} = \frac{11,000}{2,460} = 4.47$$

$$\text{2015 Commercial: } \frac{\text{Allowance for Loan Losses}}{\text{Net Loan Charge-Offs}} = \frac{169}{44} = 3.84$$

$$\text{2016 Commercial: } \frac{\text{Allowance for Loan Losses}}{\text{Net Loan Charge-Offs}} = \frac{1,012}{387} = 2.61$$

$$\text{2017 Commercial: } \frac{\text{Allowance for Loan Losses}}{\text{Net Loan Charge-Offs}} = \frac{1,540}{1,060} = 1.45$$

$$\text{2015 Consumer: } \frac{\text{Provision for Loan Losses}}{\text{Net Loan Charge-Offs}} = \frac{1,300}{2,901} = 0.45$$

$$\text{2016 Consumer: } \frac{\text{Provision for Loan Losses}}{\text{Net Loan Charge-Offs}} = \frac{2,000}{2,505} = 0.80$$

$$\text{2017 Consumer: } \frac{\text{Provision for Loan Losses}}{\text{Net Loan Charge-Offs}} = \frac{3,000}{2,460} = 1.22$$

$$\text{2015 Commercial: } \frac{\text{Provision for Loan Losses}}{\text{Net Loan Charge-Offs}} = \frac{95}{44} = 2.16$$

$$\text{2016 Commercial: } \frac{\text{Provision for Loan Losses}}{\text{Net Loan Charge-Offs}} = \frac{442}{387} = 1.14$$

$$\text{2017 Commercial: } \frac{\text{Provision for Loan Losses}}{\text{Net Loan Charge-Offs}} = \frac{1,100}{1,060} = 1.04$$

	2017	2016	2015
	$m	$m	$m
Consumer loans			
Allowance for loan losses	11,000	11,500	13,000
Provision for loan losses	3,000	2,000	1,300
Charge-offs	3,759	3,643	4,007
Recoveries	1,299	1,138	1,106
Net charge-offs	2,460	2,505	2,901

	2017	2016	2015
	$m	$m	$m
Commercial loans			
Allowance for loan losses	1,540	1,012	169
Provision for loan losses	1,100	442	95
Charge-offs	1,488	811	717
Recoveries	428	424	673
Net charge-offs	1,060	387	44
Allowance for loan losses to net loan charge-offs: consumer	4.47	4.59	4.48
Allowance for loan losses to net loan charge-offs: commercial	1.45	2.61	3.84
Provision for loan losses to net loan charge-offs: consumer	1.22	0.80	0.45
Provision for loan losses to net loan charge-offs: commercial	1.04	1.14	2.16

20. B is correct. The net benefit plan obligation has steadily decreased during the last three years, which indicates a lower degree of risk posed by the benefit plan.

CHAPTER 17

EVALUATING QUALITY OF FINANCIAL REPORTS

SOLUTIONS

1. B is correct. Stellar's financial statements are GAAP compliant (Conclusion 1) but cannot be relied upon to assess earnings quality. There is evidence of earnings management: understating and overstating earnings depending upon the results of the period (Conclusion 1), understated amortizable intangibles (Conclusion 2), and a high accruals component in the company's earnings (Conclusion 3).

2. C is correct. Martinez believes that Stellar most likely understated the value of amortizable intangibles when recording the acquisition of a rival company last year. Impairment charges have not been taken since the acquisition (Conclusion 2). Consequently, the company's earnings are likely to be overstated because amortization expense is understated. This understatement has not been offset by an impairment charge.

3. B is correct. Martinez concluded that the accruals component of Stellar's earnings was large relative to the cash component (Conclusion 3). Earnings with a larger component of accruals are typically less persistent and of lower quality. An important distinction is between accruals that arise from normal transactions in the period (called nondiscretionary) and accruals that result from transactions or accounting choices outside the normal (called discretionary accruals). The discretionary accruals are possibly made with the intent to distort reported earnings. Outlier discretionary accruals are an indicator of possibly manipulated—and thus low quality earnings. Thus, Martinez is primarily focused on discretionary accruals, particularly outlier discretionary accruals (referred to as abnormal accruals).

4. B is correct. Because accounts receivable will be lower than reported in the past, Stellar's DSO [Accounts receivable/(Revenues/365)] will decrease. Stellar's accounts receivable turnover (365/days' sales outstanding) will increase with the lower DSO, giving the false impression of a faster turnover. The company's current ratio will decrease (current assets will decrease with no change in current liabilities).

5. B is correct. Higher growth in revenue than that of industry peers is an accounting warning sign of potential overstatement or non-sustainability of operating income. Shortening the depreciable lives of capital assets is a conservative change and not a warning sign. An increase (not a decrease) in discounts and returns would be a warning sign.

6. C is correct. Net income being greater than cash flow from operations is a warning sign that the firm may be using aggressive accrual accounting policies that shift current expenses to future periods. Decreasing, not increasing, inventory turnover could suggest inventory obsolescence problems that should be recognized. Decreasing, not increasing, receivables turnover could suggest that some revenues are fictitious or recorded prematurely or that the allowance for doubtful accounts is insufficient.

7. B is correct. When earnings are decomposed into a cash component and an accruals component, research has shown that the cash component is more persistent. A beta coefficient (β_1) on the cash flow variable that is larger than the beta coefficient (β_2) on the accruals variable indicates that the cash flow component of earnings is more persistent than the accruals component. This result provides evidence of earnings persistence.

8. B is correct. Earnings manipulators have learned to test the detectability of earnings manipulation tactics by using the model to anticipate analysts' perceptions. They can reduce their likelihood of detection; therefore, Statement 5 is correct. As a result, the predictive power of the Beneish model can decline over time. An additional limitation of using quantitative models is that they cannot determine cause and effect between model variables. Quantitative models establish only associations between variables, and Statement 4 is incorrect.

   A is incorrect because quantitative models cannot determine cause and effect between model variables. They are capable only of establishing associations between variables. Therefore, Statement 4 is incorrect.

9. A is correct. The DSR (days' sales receivable index) variable in the Beneish model is related positively to the Beneish model M-score. Therefore, a year-over-year increase in DSR from 0.9 to 1.20 would lead to an increase in the M-score, which implies an increase in Miland's likelihood of manipulation.

   B is incorrect because the LEVI (leverage index) variable in the Beneish model is related negatively to the Beneish model M-score. Therefore, a year-over-year increase in LEVI from 0.75 to 0.95 would lead to a decrease in the M-score, which implies a decrease (not increase) in Miland's likelihood of manipulation.

   C is incorrect because the SGAI (sales, general, and administrative expenses index) variable in the Beneish model is related negatively to the Beneish model M-score. Therefore, a year-over-year increase in SGAI from 0.60 to 0.75 would lead to a decrease in the M-score, which implies a decrease (not increase) in Miland's likelihood of manipulation.

10. C is correct. Recurring or core pre-tax earnings would be $7.1 billion, which is the company's reported pre-tax income of $5.4 billion plus the $1.2 billion of non-recurring (i.e., one-time) acquisitions and divestiture expenses plus the $0.5 billion of non-recurring restructuring expenses.

11. B is correct. The correction of the revenue misstatement would result in lower revenue by EUR50 million, and the correction of the cost of revenue misstatement would result in higher cost of revenue by EUR100 million. The result is a reduction in pre-tax income of EUR150 million. Applying a tax rate of 25%, the reduction in net income would be $150 \times (1 - 0.25) = $ EUR112.5 million.

12. A is correct. Based on the principle of mean reversion, the high ROE for both firms should revert toward the mean. Globales has a higher cash flow component to its return than the peer firm, however, so its high return on common equity should persist longer

than that of the peer firm. The peer firm has a higher accruals component, so it is likely to revert more quickly.

13. B is correct. Only Note 2 provides a warning sign. The combination of increases in accounts payable with substantial decreases in accounts receivable and inventory are an accounting warning sign that management may be overstating cash flow from operations. Note 1 does not necessarily provide a warning sign. Operating income being greater than operating cash flow is a warning sign of a potential reporting problem. In this case, however, BIG Industrial's operating income is lower than its operating cash flow.

14. A is correct. Neither Note 4 nor Note 5 provides an accounting warning sign of potential overstatement or non-sustainability of operating income.

    Increases in operating margins can be a warning sign of potential overstatement or non-sustainability of operating and/or net income. In this case, however, operating margins for Construction Supply have been relatively constant during the last three years.

    A growth rate in receivables exceeding the growth rate in revenue is an accounting warning sign of potential overstatement or non-sustainability of operating income. In this case, however, Construction Supply's revenue growth exceeds the growth rate in receivables.

15. B is correct. High-quality OCF means the performance is of high reporting quality and also of high results quality. For established companies, high-quality operating cash flow would typically be positive; be derived from sustainable sources; be adequate to cover capital expenditures, dividends, and debt repayments; and have relatively low volatility compared with industry peers. Construction Supply reported positive OCF during each of the last three years. The OCF appears to be derived from sustainable sources, because it compares closely with reported net income. Finally, OCF was adequate to cover capital expenditures, dividends, and debt repayments. Although the OCF for BIG Industrial has been positive and just sufficient to cover capital expenditures, dividends, and debt repayments, the increases in accounts payable and substantial decreases in accounts receivable and inventory during the last three years are an accounting warning sign that management may be overstating cash flow from operations. For Dynamic Production, OCF has been more volatile than other industry participants, and it has fallen short of covering capital expenditures, dividends, and debt repayments for the last three years. Both of these conditions are warning signs for Dynamic Production.

16. A is correct. Higher *M*-scores indicate an increased probability of earnings manipulation. The company with the highest *M*-score in 2017 is BIG Industrial, with an *M*-score of -1.54. Construction Supply has the lowest *M*-score at -2.60, and Dynamic Production also has a lower *M*-score at -1.86. The *M*-score for BIG Industrial is above the relevant cutoff of -1.78.

17. A is correct. The items primarily affected by improper revenue recognition include net income, receivables, and inventories. When revenues are overstated, net income and receivables will be overstated and inventories will be understated.

18. C is correct. Webster is concerned that innovations have made some of BIG Industrial's inventory obsolete. This scenario suggests impairment charges for inventory may be understated and that the inventory balance does not reflect unbiased measurement.

19. A is correct. The use of unconsolidated joint ventures or equity-method investees may reflect an overstated return on sales ratio, because the parent company's consolidated financial statements include its share of the investee's profits but not its share of the investee's sales. An analyst can adjust the reported amounts to better reflect the combined amounts of sales. Reported net income divided by the combined amount of sales will result in a decrease in the net profit margin.

CHAPTER 18

INTEGRATION OF FINANCIAL STATEMENT ANALYSIS TECHNIQUES

SOLUTIONS

1. C is correct. The ROE has been trending higher. ROE can be calculated by multiplying (net profit margin) × (asset turnover) × (financial leverage). Net profit margin is net income/sales. In 2018 the net profit margin was 2,576/55,781 = 4.6% and the ROE = 4.6% × 0.68 × 3.43 = 10.8%. Using the same method, ROE was 12.9 percent in 2019 and 13.6 percent in 2020.

2. A is correct. The DuPont analysis shows that profit margins and asset turnover have both increased over the last three years, but leverage has declined. The reduction in leverage offsets a portion of the improvement in profitability and turnover. Thus, ROE would have been higher if leverage had not decreased.

3. B is correct. The Power and Industrial segment has the lowest EBIT margins but uses about 31 percent of the capital employed. Further, Power and Industrial's proportion of the capital expenditures has increased from 32 percent to 36 percent over the three years. Its capital intensity only looked to get worse, as the segment's percentage of total capital expenditures was higher than its percentage of total capital in each of the three years. If Abay is considering divesting segments that do not earn sufficient returns on capital employed, this segment is most suitable.

4. A is correct. The cash-flow-based accruals ratio = [NI − (CFO + CFI)]/(Average NOA) = [4,038 − (9,822 − 10,068)]/43,192 = 9.9%.

5. A is correct. The cash-flow-based accruals ratio falls from 11.0 percent in 2018 to 5.9 percent in 2019, and then rises to 9.9 percent in 2020. However, the change over the three-year period is a net modest decline, indicating a slight improvement in earnings quality.

6. B is correct. Net cash flow provided by (used in) operating activity has to be adjusted for interest and taxes, as necessary, in order to be comparable to operating income (EBIT).

Bickchip, reporting under IFRS, chose to classify interest expense as a financing cash flow so the only necessary adjustment is for taxes. The operating cash flow before interest and taxes = 9,822 + 1,930 = 11,752. Dividing this by EBIT of 6,270 yields 1.9.

7. A is correct. Operating cash flow before interest and taxes to operating income rises steadily (not erratically) from 1.2 to 1.3 to 1.9. The ratios over 1.0 and the trend indicate that earnings are supported by cash flow.

ABOUT THE
CFA PROGRAM

The Chartered Financial Analyst® designation (CFA®) is a globally recognized standard of excellence for measuring the competence and integrity of investment professionals. To earn the CFA charter, candidates must successfully pass through the CFA Program, a global graduate-level self-study program that combines a broad curriculum with professional conduct requirements as preparation for a wide range of investment specialties.

Anchored by a practice-based curriculum, the CFA Program is focused on the knowledge identified by professionals as essential to the investment decision-making process. This body of knowledge maintains current relevance through a regular, extensive survey of practicing CFA charterholders across the globe. The curriculum covers 10 general topic areas, ranging from equity and fixed-income analysis to portfolio management, all with a heavy emphasis on the application of ethics in professional practice. Known for its rigor and breadth, the CFA Program curriculum highlights principles common to every market so that professionals who earn the CFA designation have a thoroughly global investment perspective and a profound understanding of the global marketplace.

www.cfainstitute.org